$12.99 perback Original
on1230462179 ght © 2021 Keigo Maki
2021 Keigo Maki

Published in the United States by Kodansha Comics, an imprint of
Kodansha USA Publishing, LLC, New York.

Publication rights for this English edition arranged through
Kodansha Ltd., Tokyo.

First published in Japan in 2021 by Kodansha Ltd., Tokyo.

ISBN 978-1-64651-289-8

Printed in the United States of America.

www.kodansha.us

2nd Printing
Translation: Stephen Paul
Lettering: Mercedes McGarry
Editing: David Yoo
Kodansha Comics edition cover design by My Truong

Publisher: Kiichiro Sugawara

Director of publishing services: Ben Applegate
Associate director of operations: Stephen Pakula
Publishing services managing editors: Madison Salters, Alanna Ruse
Production manager: Emi Lotto, Angela Zurlo
Logo and character art ©Kodansha USA Publishing, LLC

The prestigious Dahlia Academy
educates the elite of society from
two countries; To the East is the
Nation of Touwa; across the sea
the other way, the Principality of
West. The nations, though, are
fierce rivals, and their students are
constantly feuding—which means
Romio Inuzuka, head of Touwa's
first-year students, has a problem.
He's fallen for his counterpart
from West, Juliet Persia, and
when he can't take it any more, he
confesses his feelings.

Now Romio has two problems:
A girlfriend, and a secret...

Boarding School *Juliet*

By Yousuke Kaneda

"A fine romantic comedy... The chemistry between
the two main characters is excellent and the humor
is great, backed up by a fun enough supporting cast
and a different twist on the genre." –AiPT

KC
KODANSHA
COMICS

◄ KAMOME ►
SHIRAHAMA

Witch Hat Atelier

A magical manga adventure for fans of Disney and Studio Ghibli!

Witch Hat Atelier © Kamome Shirahama/Kodansha Ltd.

The magical adventure that took Japan by storm is finally here, from acclaimed DC and Marvel cover artist Kamome Shirahama!

In a world where everyone takes wonders like magic spells and dragons for granted, Coco is a girl with a simple dream: She wants to be a witch. But everybody knows magicians are born, not made, and Coco was not born with a gift for magic. Resigned to her un-magical life, Coco is about to give up on her dream to become a witch...until the day she meets Qifrey, a mysterious, traveling magician. After secretly seeing Qifrey perform magic in a way she's never seen before, Coco soon learns what everybody "knows" might not be the truth, and discovers that her magical dream may not be as far away as it may seem...

KC
KODANSHA
COMICS

Magus of the Library

Mitsu Izumi

MITSU IZUMI'S STUNNING ARTWORK BRINGS A FANTASTICAL LITERARY ADVENTURE TO LUSH, THRILLING LIFE!

Young Theo adores books, but the prejudice and hatred of his village keeps them ever out of his reach. Then one day, he chances to meet Sedona, a traveling librarian who works for the great library of Aftzaak, City of Books, and his life changes forever...

KC/
KODANSHA
COMICS

LOVE IN FOCUS

Love in Focus © Yoko Nogiri/Kodansha Ltd.

CARDCAPTOR SAKURA
COLLECTOR'S EDITION
CLAMP

Ten-year-old Sakura Kinomoto lives a pretty normal life with her older brother, Tōya, and widowed father, Fujitaka—until the day she discovers a strange book in her father's library, and her life takes a magical turn...

- A deluxe large-format hardcover edition of CLAMP's shojo manga classic
- All-new foil-stamped cover art on each volume
- Comes with exclusive collectible art card

KC
KODANSHA
COMICS

KC
KODANSHA
COMICS

The boys are back, in 400-page hardcovers that are as pretty and badass as they are!

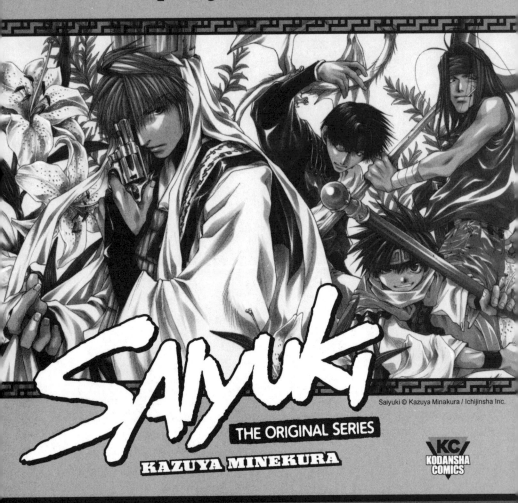

Saiyuki © Kazuya Minakura / Ichijinsha Inc.

SAIYUKI
THE ORIGINAL SERIES
KAZUYA MINEKURA

"AN EDGY COMIC LOOK AT AN ANCIENT CHINESE TALE." —YALSA

Genjo Sanzo is a Buddhist priest in the city of Togenkyo, which is being ravaged by yokai spirits that have fallen out of balance with the natural order. His superiors send him on a journey far to the west to discover why this is happening and how to stop it. His companions are three yokai with human souls. But this is no day trip — the four will encounter many discoveries and horrors on the way.

FEATURES NEW TRANSLATION, COLOR PAGES, AND BEAUTIFUL WRAPAROUND COVER ART!

CUTE ANIMALS AND LIFE LESSONS, PERFECT FOR ASPIRING PET VETS OF ALL AGES!

For an 11-year-old, Yuzu has a lot on her plate. When her mom gets sick and has to be hospitalized, Yuzu goes to live with her uncle who runs the local veterinary clinic. Yuzu's always been scared of animals, but she tries to help out. Through all the tough moments in her life, Yuzu realizes that she can help make things all right with a little help from her animal pals, peers, and kind grown-ups.

Every new patient is a furry friend in the making!

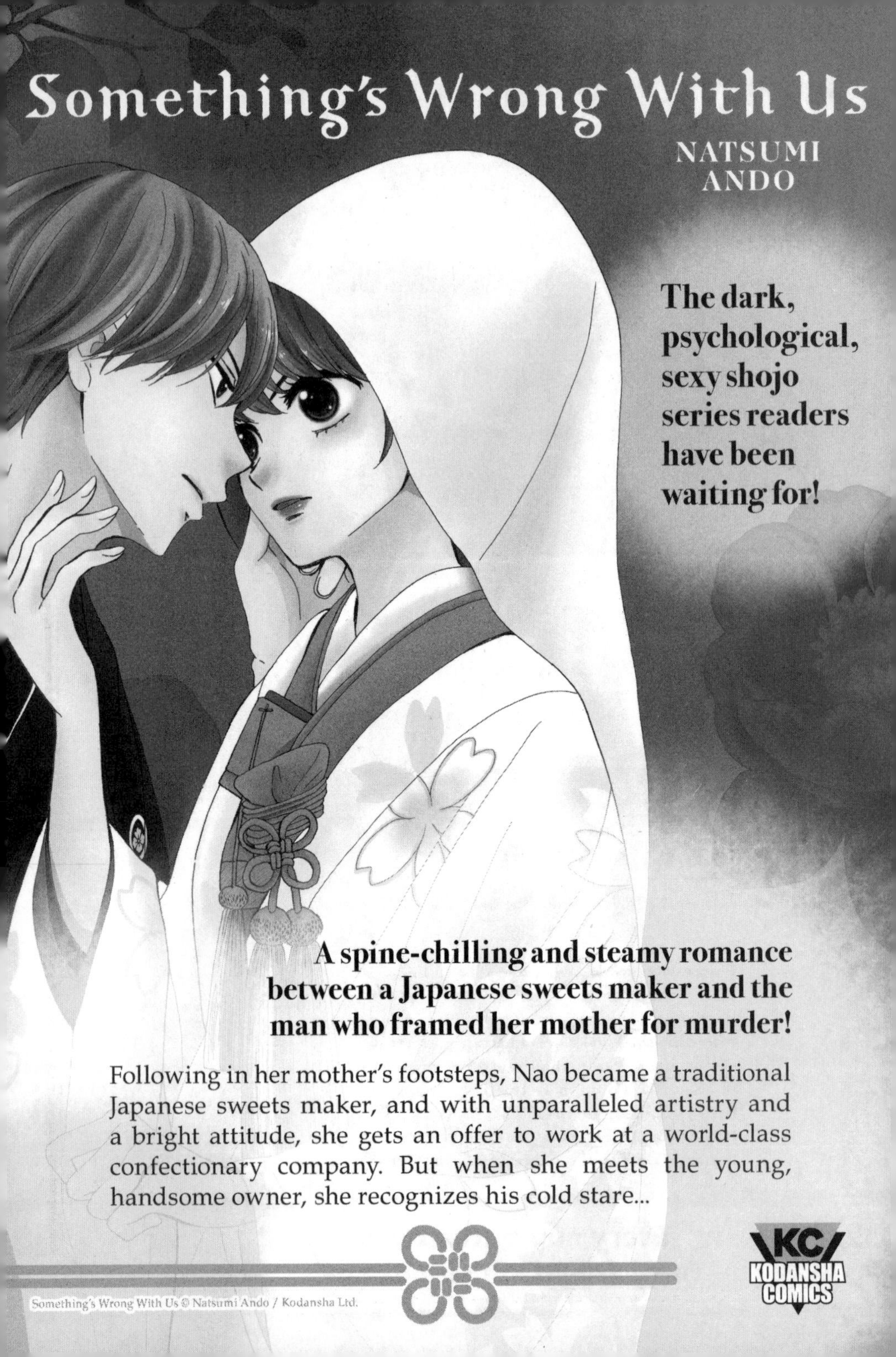
Something's Wrong With Us
NATSUMI ANDO
The dark, psychological, sexy shojo series readers have been waiting for!
A spine-chilling and steamy romance between a Japanese sweets maker and the man who framed her mother for murder!
Following in her mother's footsteps, Nao became a traditional Japanese sweets maker, and with unparalleled artistry and a bright attitude, she gets an offer to work at a world-class confectionary company. But when she meets the young, handsome owner, she recognizes his cold stare...
KC
KODANSHA COMICS
Something's Wrong With Us © Natsumi Ando / Kodansha Ltd.

Young characters and steampunk setting, like *Howl's Moving Castle* and *Battle Angel Alita*

A boy with a talent for machines and a mysterious girl whose wings he's fixed will take you beyond the clouds! In the tradition of the high-flying, resonant adventure stories of Studio Ghibli comes a gorgeous tale about the longing of young hearts for adventure and friendship!

Knight of the Ice ©Yayoi Ogawa/Kodansha Ltd.

SKATING THRILLS AND ICY CHILLS WITH THIS NEW TINGLY ROMANCE SERIES!

Yayoi Ogawa

A rom-com on ice, perfect for fans of *Princess Jellyfish* and *Wotakoi*. Kokoro is the talk of the figure-skating world, winning trophies and hearts. But little do they know... he's actually a huge nerd! From the beloved creator of *You're My Pet* (*Tramps Like Us*).

Chitose is a serious young woman, working for the health magazine *SASSO*. Or at least, she would be, if she wasn't constantly getting distracted by her childhood friend, international figure skating star Kokoro Kijinami! In the public eye and on the ice, Kokoro is a gallant, flawless knight, but behind his glittery costumes and breathtaking spins lies a secret: He's actually a hopelessly romantic otaku, who can only land his quad jumps when Chitose is on hand to recite a spell from his favorite magical girl anime!

SHIKIMORI'S
Not just a cutie

(7)

KEIGO MAKI

SHIKIMORI'S
Not just a cutie

volume.7

Contents

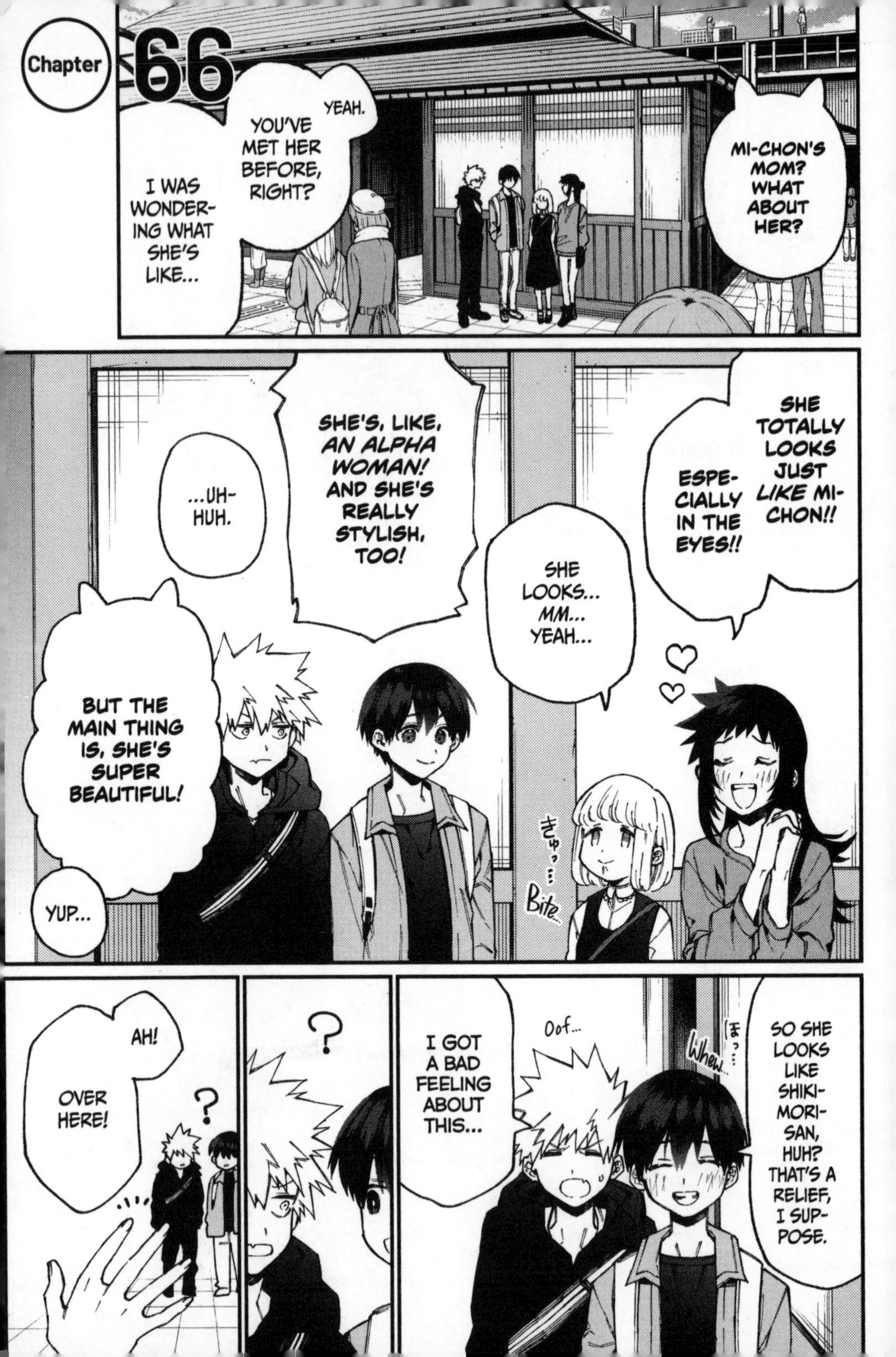
Chapter 66
MI-CHON'S MOM? WHAT ABOUT HER?
YEAH.
YOU'VE MET HER BEFORE, RIGHT?
I WAS WONDERING WHAT SHE'S LIKE...
SHE TOTALLY LOOKS JUST LIKE MI-CHON!!
ESPECIALLY IN THE EYES!!
SHE'S, LIKE, AN ALPHA WOMAN! AND SHE'S REALLY STYLISH, TOO!
...UH-HUH.
SHE LOOKS... MM... YEAH...
きゅっ... Bite...
BUT THE MAIN THING IS, SHE'S SUPER BEAUTIFUL!
YUP...
SO SHE LOOKS LIKE SHIKIMORI-SAN, HUH? THAT'S A RELIEF, I SUPPOSE.
ほっ... Whew...
Oof...
I GOT A BAD FEELING ABOUT THIS...
?
?
AH!
OVER HERE!

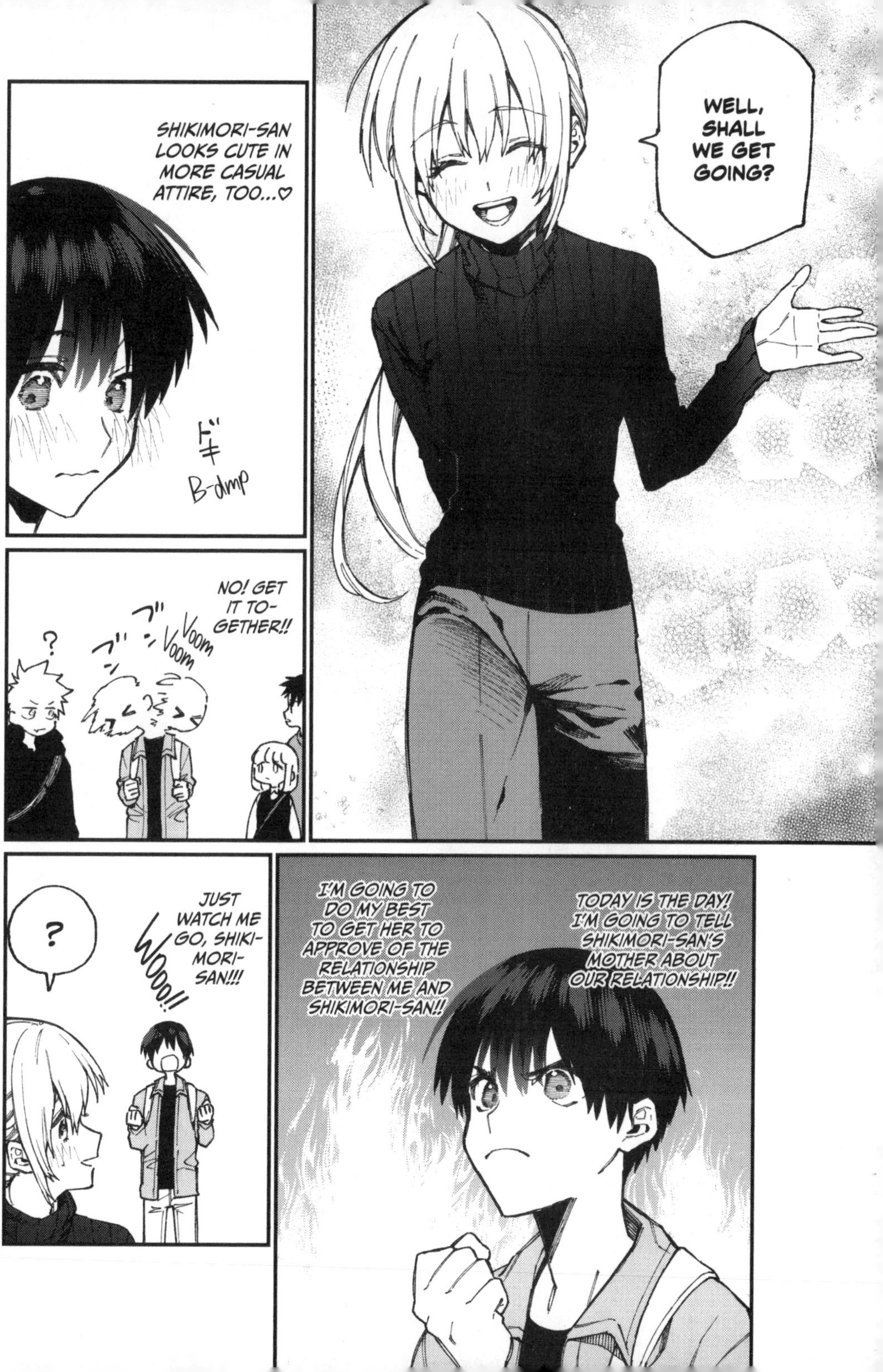
WELL, SHALL WE GET GOING?
SHIKIMORI-SAN LOOKS CUTE IN MORE CASUAL ATTIRE, TOO...♡
ドキ
B-dmp
NO! GET IT TO-GETHER!!
ブンブン
Voom Voom
?
TODAY IS THE DAY! I'M GOING TO TELL SHIKIMORI-SAN'S MOTHER ABOUT OUR RELATIONSHIP!!
I'M GOING TO DO MY BEST TO GET HER TO APPROVE OF THE RELATIONSHIP BETWEEN ME AND SHIKIMORI-SAN!!
JUST WATCH ME GO, SHIKI-MORI-SAN!!!
WOOO!!
?

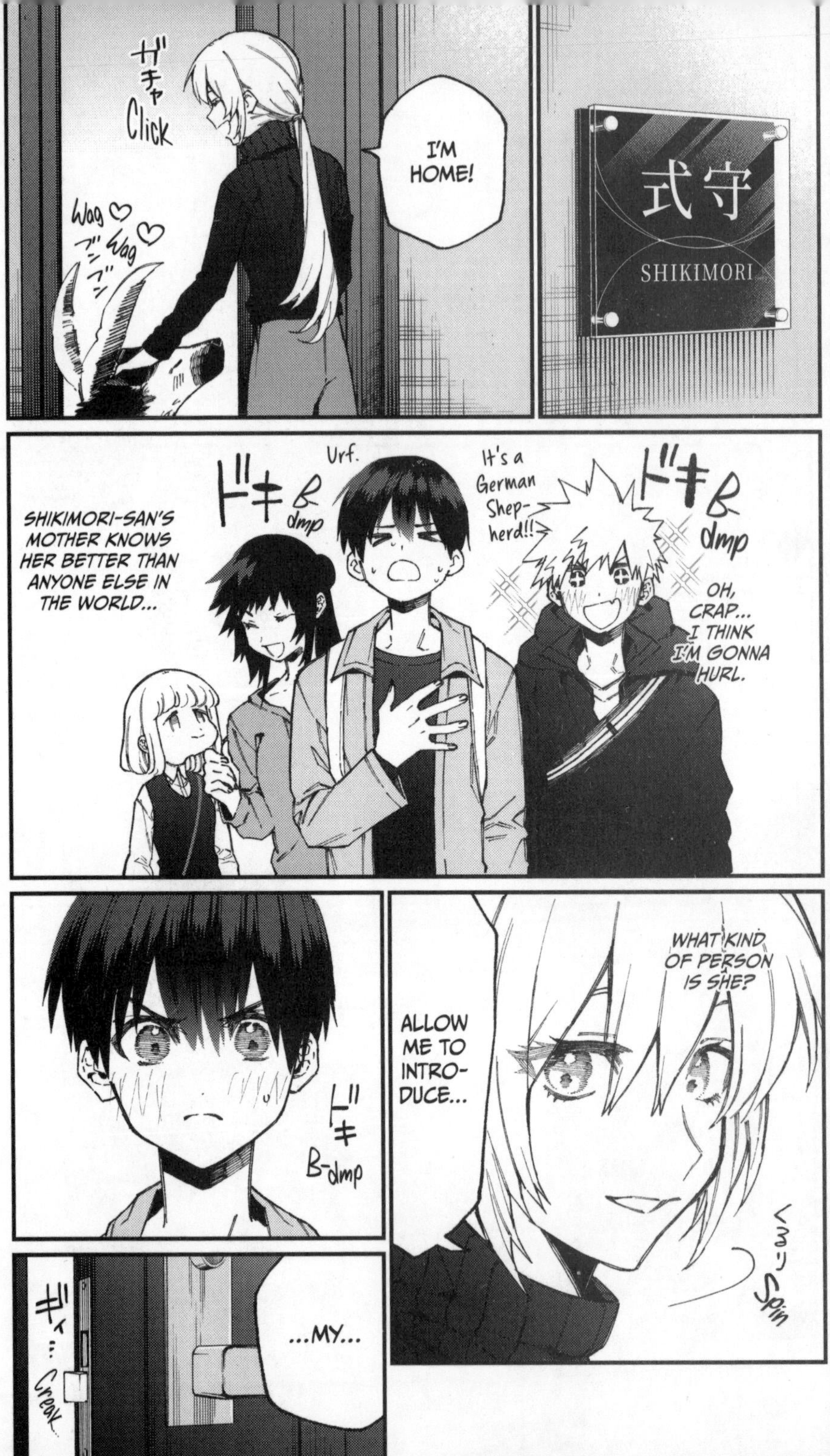
式守
SHIKIMORI
ガチャ
Click
I'M HOME!
Wag ♡
ブンブン
Wag ♡
ドキ
B-dmp
OH, CRAP... I THINK I'M GONNA HURL.
It's a German Shep-herd!!
Urf.
ドキ
B-dmp
SHIKIMORI-SAN'S MOTHER KNOWS HER BETTER THAN ANYONE ELSE IN THE WORLD...
WHAT KIND OF PERSON IS SHE?
ALLOW ME TO INTRO-DUCE...
くるり
Spin
ドキ
B-dmp
...MY...
ギィ...
Creak...

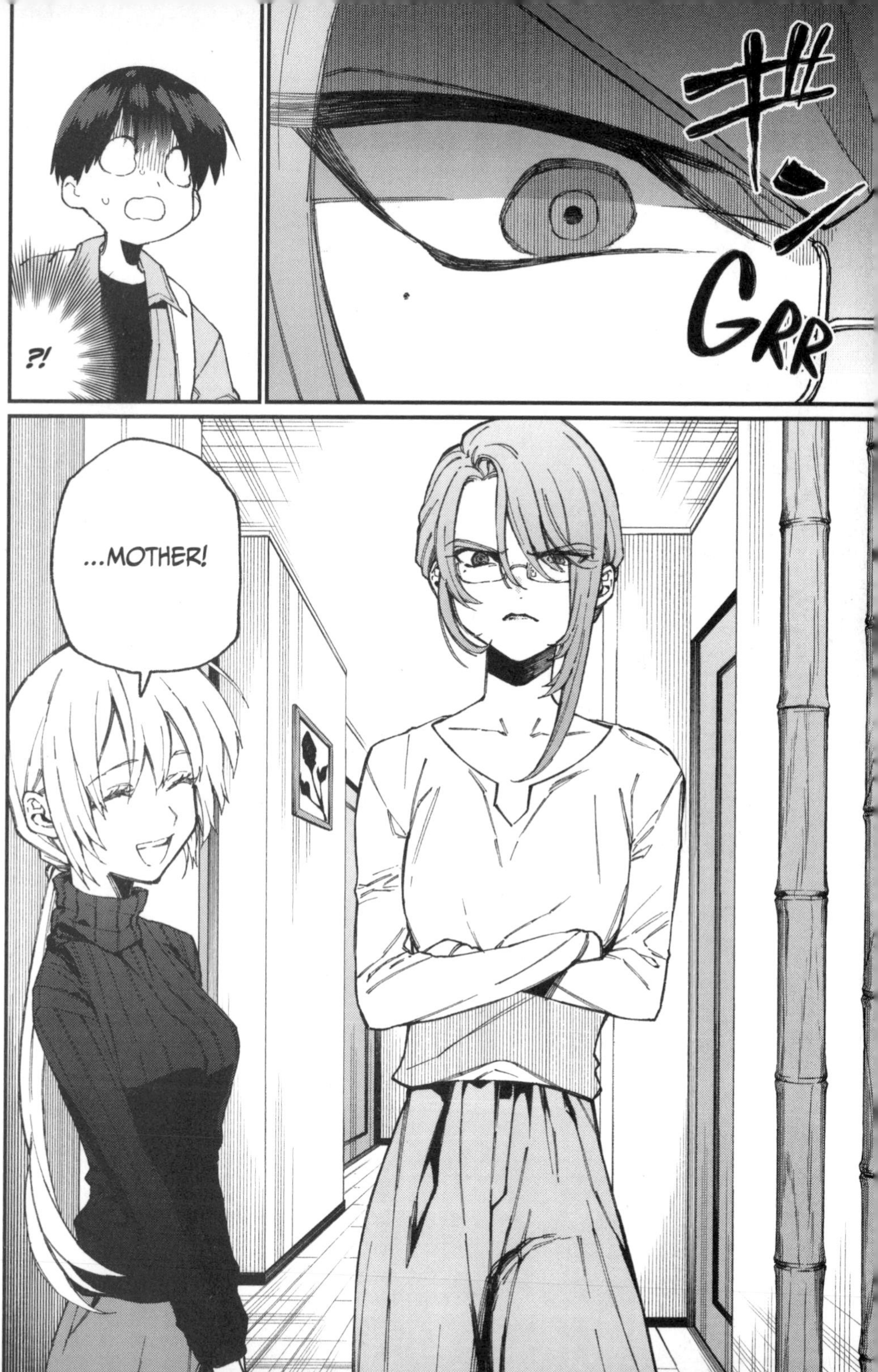
ギン
GRR
?!
...MOTHER!

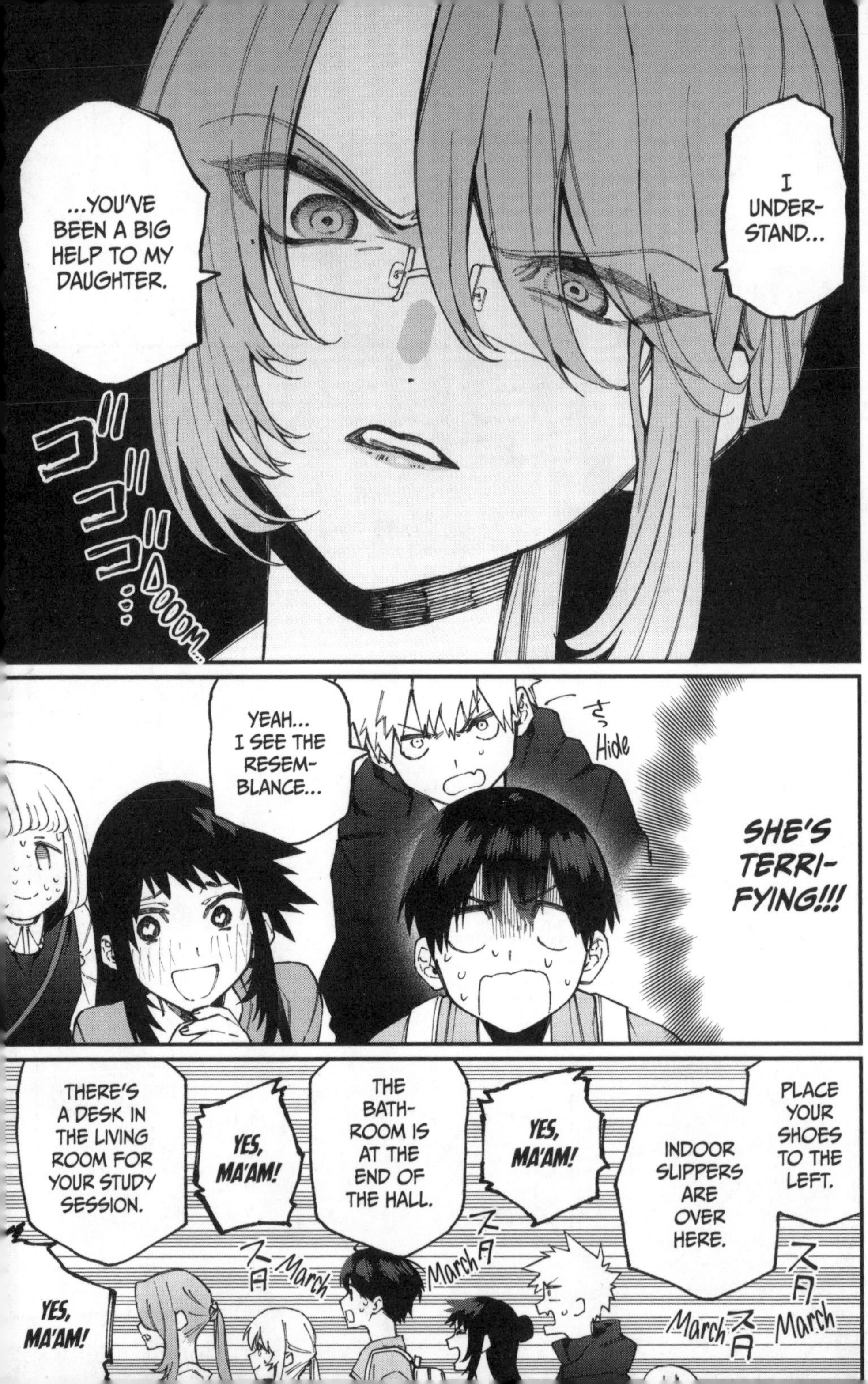
I UNDER-STAND...
...YOU'VE BEEN A BIG HELP TO MY DAUGHTER.
DOOOM...
SHE'S TERRI-FYING!!!
Hide
YEAH... I SEE THE RESEM-BLANCE...
PLACE YOUR SHOES TO THE LEFT.
INDOOR SLIPPERS ARE OVER HERE.
YES, MA'AM!
THE BATH-ROOM IS AT THE END OF THE HALL.
YES, MA'AM!
THERE'S A DESK IN THE LIVING ROOM FOR YOUR STUDY SESSION.
March
March
March
March
March
YES, MA'AM!

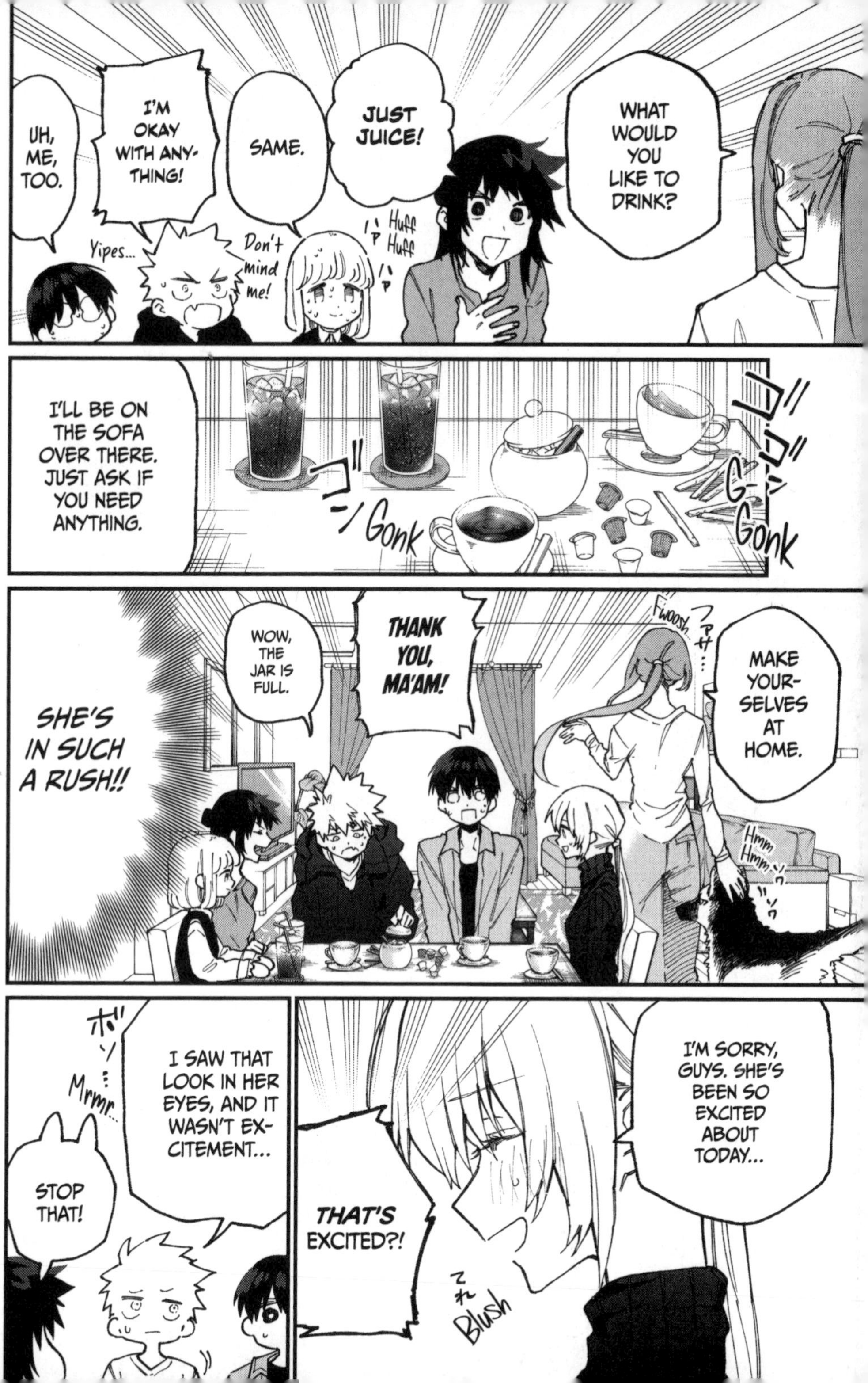
WHAT WOULD YOU LIKE TO DRINK?
Huff Huff
JUST JUICE!
SAME.
Don't mind me!
I'M OKAY WITH ANYTHING!
Yipes...
UH, ME, TOO.
Gonk
Gonk
I'LL BE ON THE SOFA OVER THERE. JUST ASK IF YOU NEED ANYTHING.
MAKE YOURSELVES AT HOME.
Fwoosh...
Hmm Hmm
THANK YOU, MA'AM!
WOW, THE JAR IS FULL.
SHE'S IN SUCH A RUSH!!
I'M SORRY, GUYS. SHE'S BEEN SO EXCITED ABOUT TODAY...
Blush
THAT'S EXCITED?!
I SAW THAT LOOK IN HER EYES, AND IT WASN'T EXCITEMENT...
Mrmr...
STOP THAT!

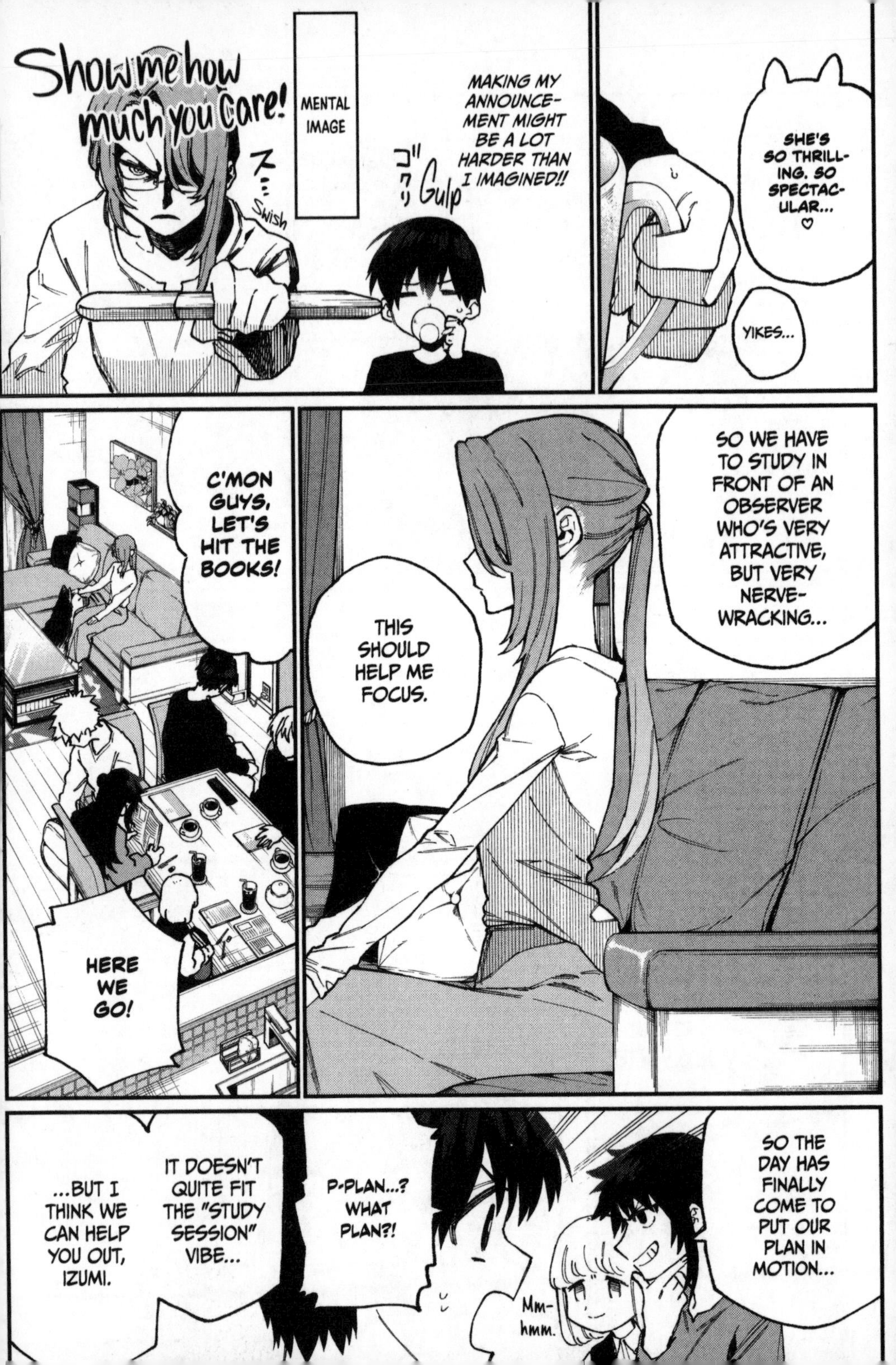
SHE'S SO THRILLING. SO SPECTACULAR... ♡
YIKES...
MAKING MY ANNOUNCEMENT MIGHT BE A LOT HARDER THAN I IMAGINED!!
ゴクリ
Gulp
MENTAL IMAGE
Show me how much you care!
ス…
Swish
SO WE HAVE TO STUDY IN FRONT OF AN OBSERVER WHO'S VERY ATTRACTIVE, BUT VERY NERVE-WRACKING...
THIS SHOULD HELP ME FOCUS.
C'MON GUYS, LET'S HIT THE BOOKS!
HERE WE GO!
SO THE DAY HAS FINALLY COME TO PUT OUR PLAN IN MOTION...
Mm-hmm.
P-PLAN...? WHAT PLAN?!
IT DOESN'T QUITE FIT THE "STUDY SESSION" VIBE...
...BUT I THINK WE CAN HELP YOU OUT, IZUMI.

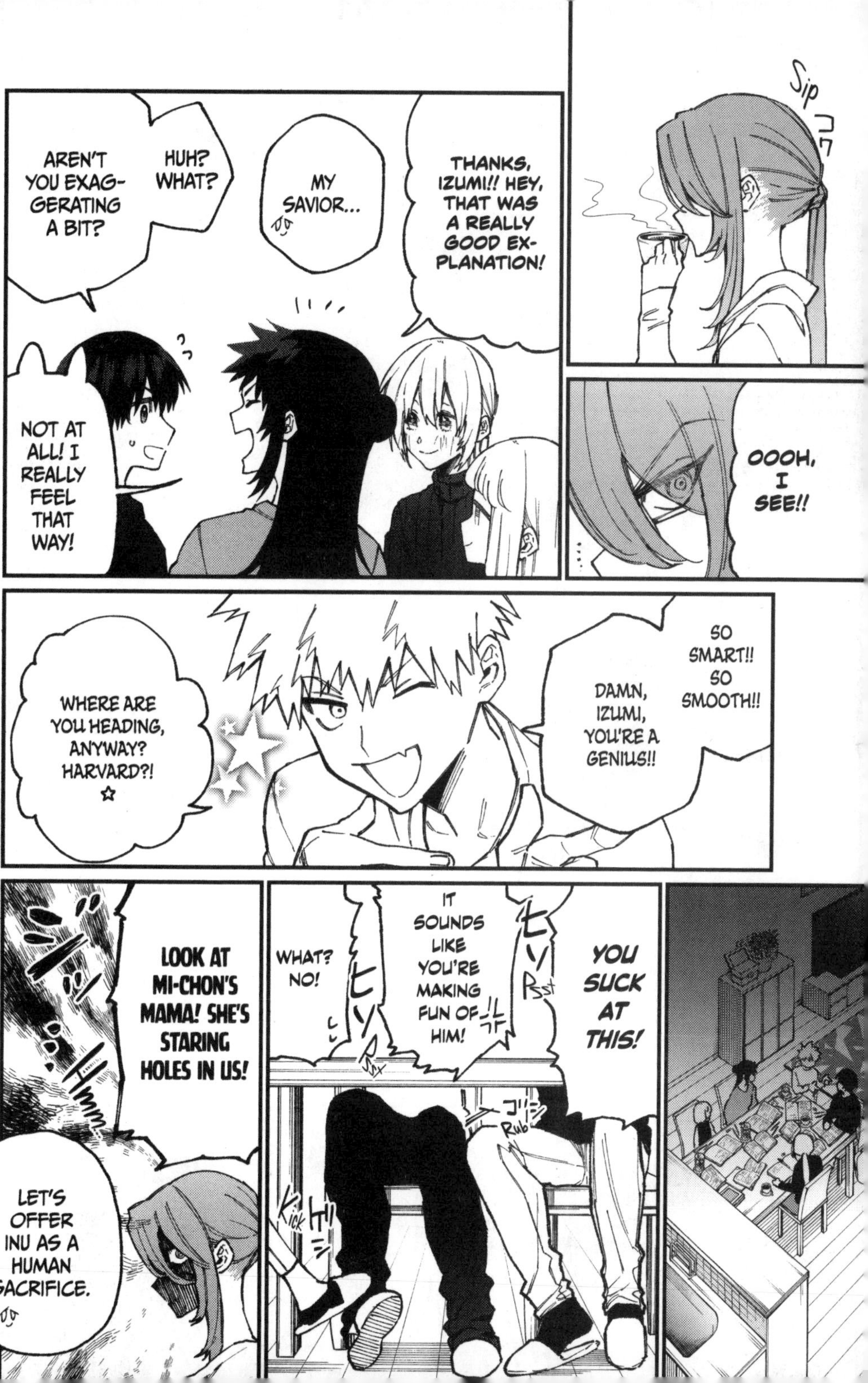
Sip
OOOH, I SEE!!
THANKS, IZUMI!! HEY, THAT WAS A REALLY GOOD EX-PLANATION!
MY SAVIOR...
HUH? WHAT?
AREN'T YOU EXAG-GERATING A BIT?
NOT AT ALL! I REALLY FEEL THAT WAY!
SO SMART!! SO SMOOTH!!
DAMN, IZUMI, YOU'RE A GENIUS!!
WHERE ARE YOU HEADING, ANYWAY? HARVARD?! ☆
YOU SUCK AT THIS!
Psst
IT SOUNDS LIKE YOU'RE MAKING FUN OF HIM!
WHAT? NO!
Psst
Rub
Kick
LOOK AT MI-CHON'S MAMA! SHE'S STARING HOLES IN US!
Hmm
LET'S OFFER INU AS A HUMAN SACRIFICE.

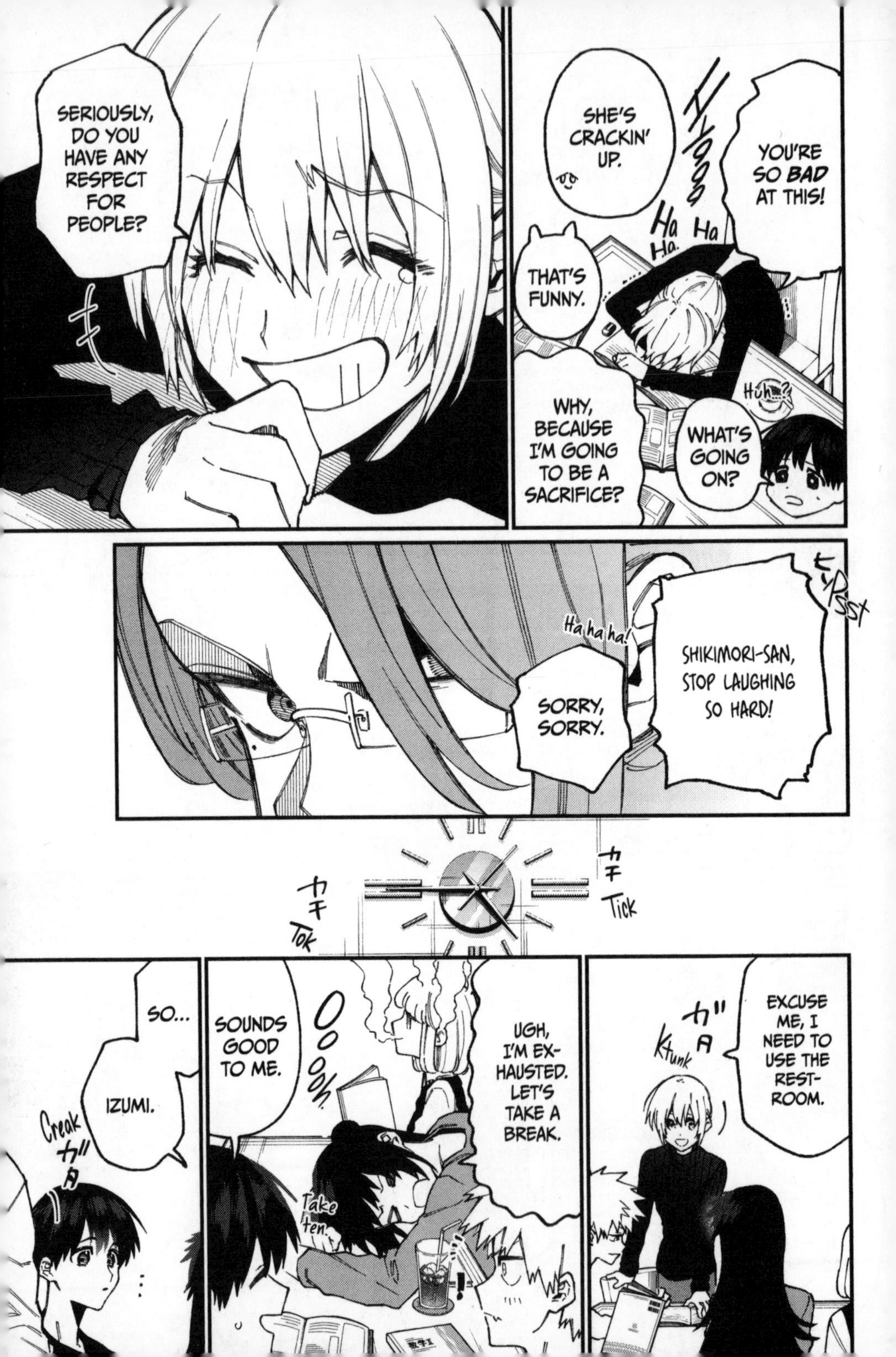
YOU'RE SO BAD AT THIS!
HYOOOO
SHE'S CRACKIN' UP.
Ha Ha Ha.
THAT'S FUNNY.
Huh...?
WHAT'S GOING ON?
WHY, BECAUSE I'M GOING TO BE A SACRIFICE?
SERIOUSLY, DO YOU HAVE ANY RESPECT FOR PEOPLE?
Pssst
SHIKIMORI-SAN, STOP LAUGHING SO HARD!
Ha ha ha!
SORRY, SORRY.
Tick
Tok
EXCUSE ME, I NEED TO USE THE REST-ROOM.
Ktunk
UGH, I'M EX-HAUSTED. LET'S TAKE A BREAK.
Ooooh
SOUNDS GOOD TO ME.
Take ten.
SO...
IZUMI.
Creak
...

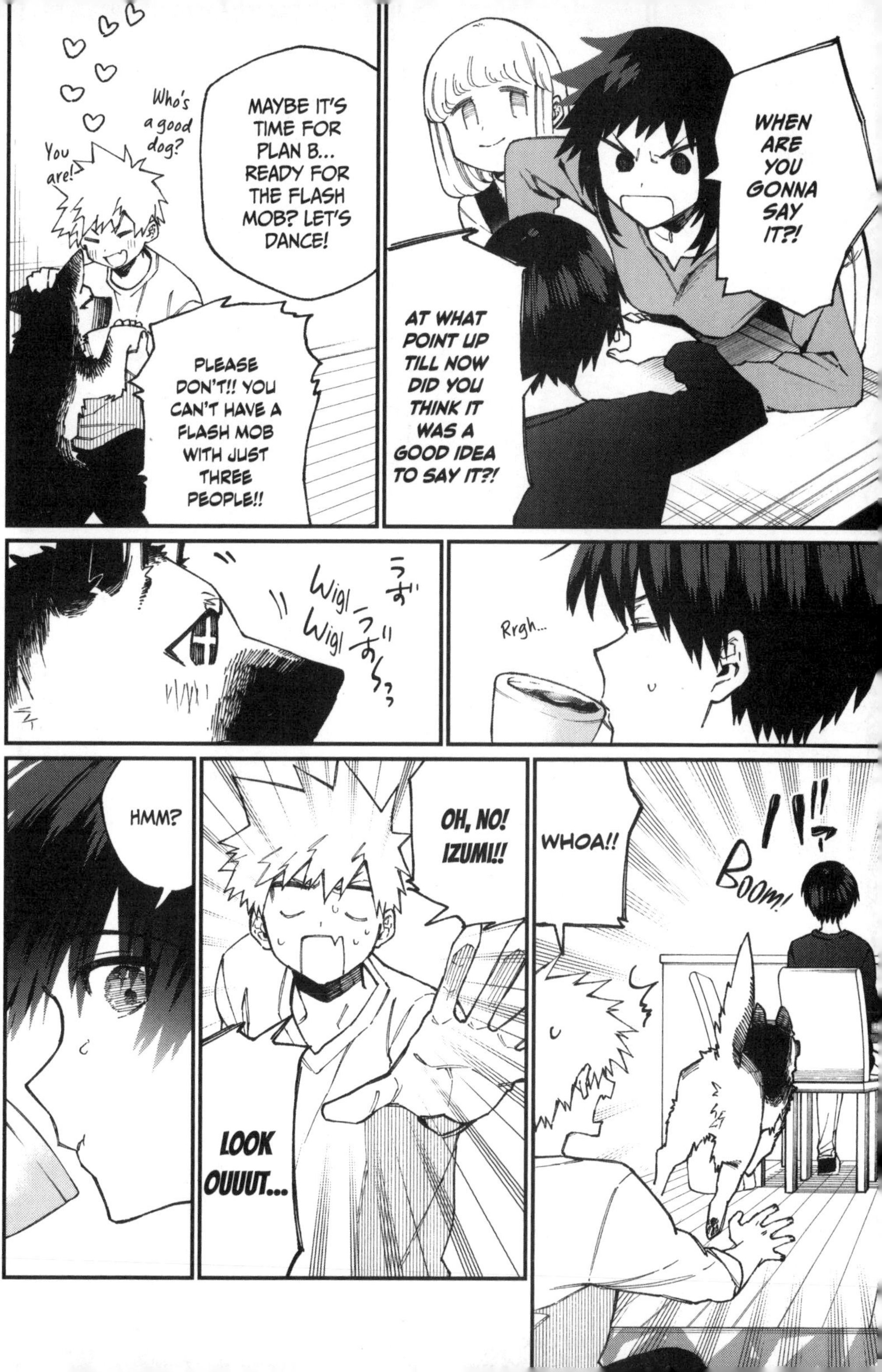
WHEN ARE YOU GONNA SAY IT?!
AT WHAT POINT UP TILL NOW DID YOU THINK IT WAS A GOOD IDEA TO SAY IT?!
MAYBE IT'S TIME FOR PLAN B... READY FOR THE FLASH MOB? LET'S DANCE!
Who's a good dog?
You are!
PLEASE DON'T!! YOU CAN'T HAVE A FLASH MOB WITH JUST THREE PEOPLE!!
Rrgh...
うず
Wigl Wigl
Boom!
WHOA!!
OH, NO! IZUMI!!
LOOK OUUUT...
HMM?

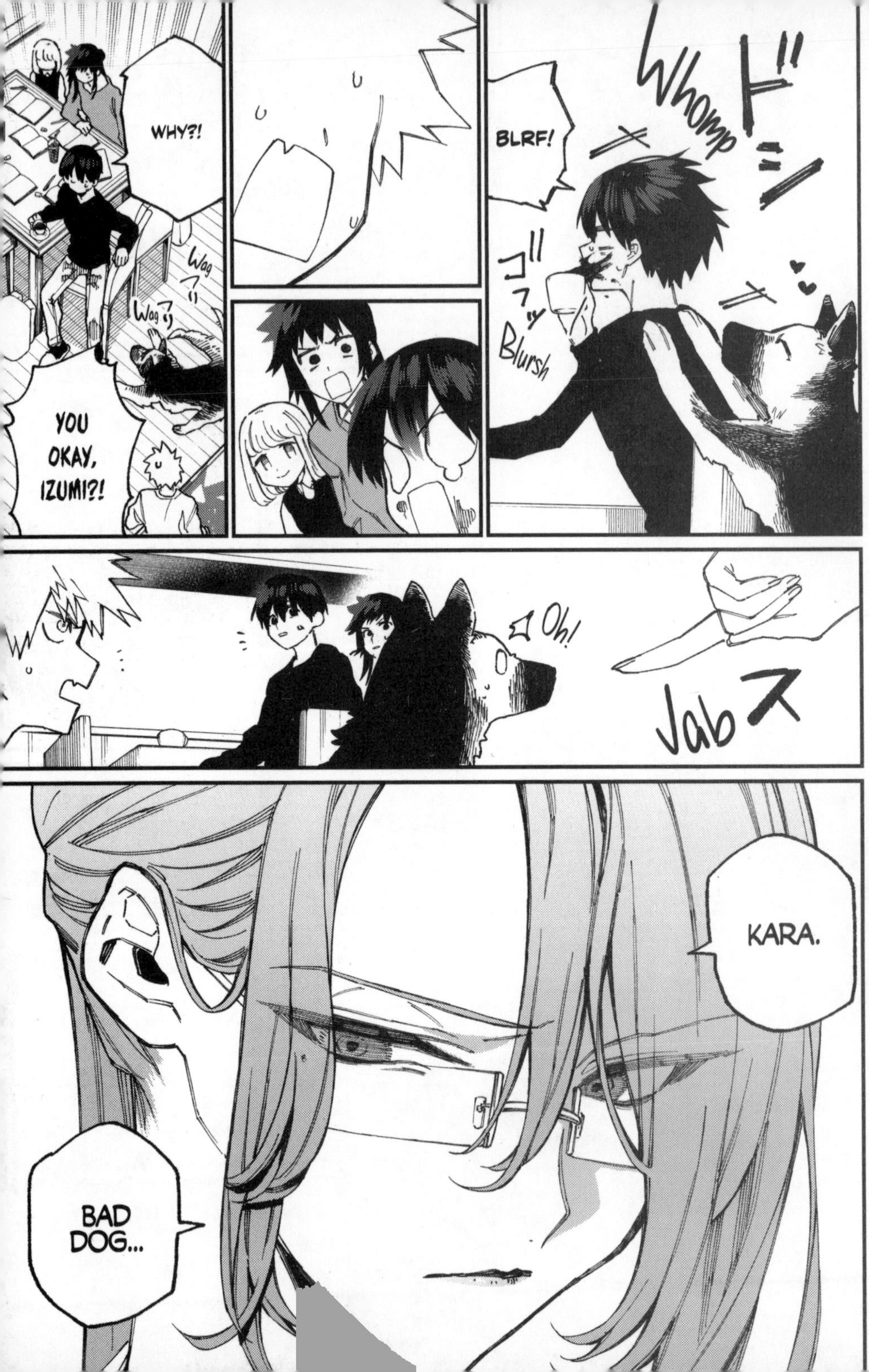
Whomp ド!!
BLRF!
ゴフッ
Blursh
WHY?!
Wag
Wag
YOU OKAY, IZUMI?!
Jab ス
Oh!
KARA.
BAD DOG...

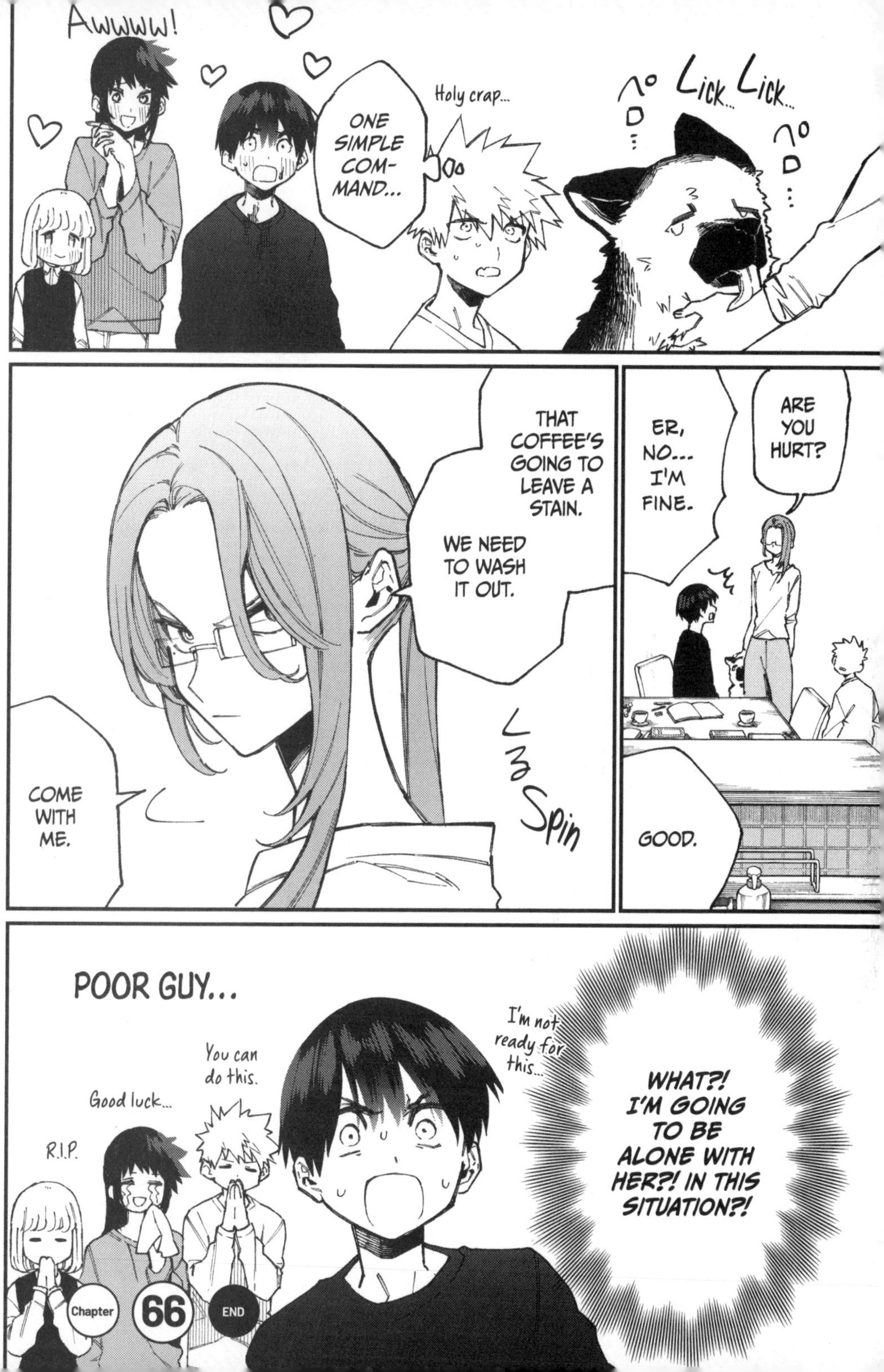

Lick... Lick...
ペロ...
ペロ...
Holy crap...
ONE SIMPLE COMMAND...
Awwww!
ARE YOU HURT?
ER, NO... I'M FINE.
GOOD.
THAT COFFEE'S GOING TO LEAVE A STAIN.
WE NEED TO WASH IT OUT.
くる
Spin
COME WITH ME.
WHAT?! I'M GOING TO BE ALONE WITH HER?! IN THIS SITUATION?!
I'm not ready for this...
You can do this.
Good luck...
R.I.P.
POOR GUY...
Chapter 66 END

CHARACTERS

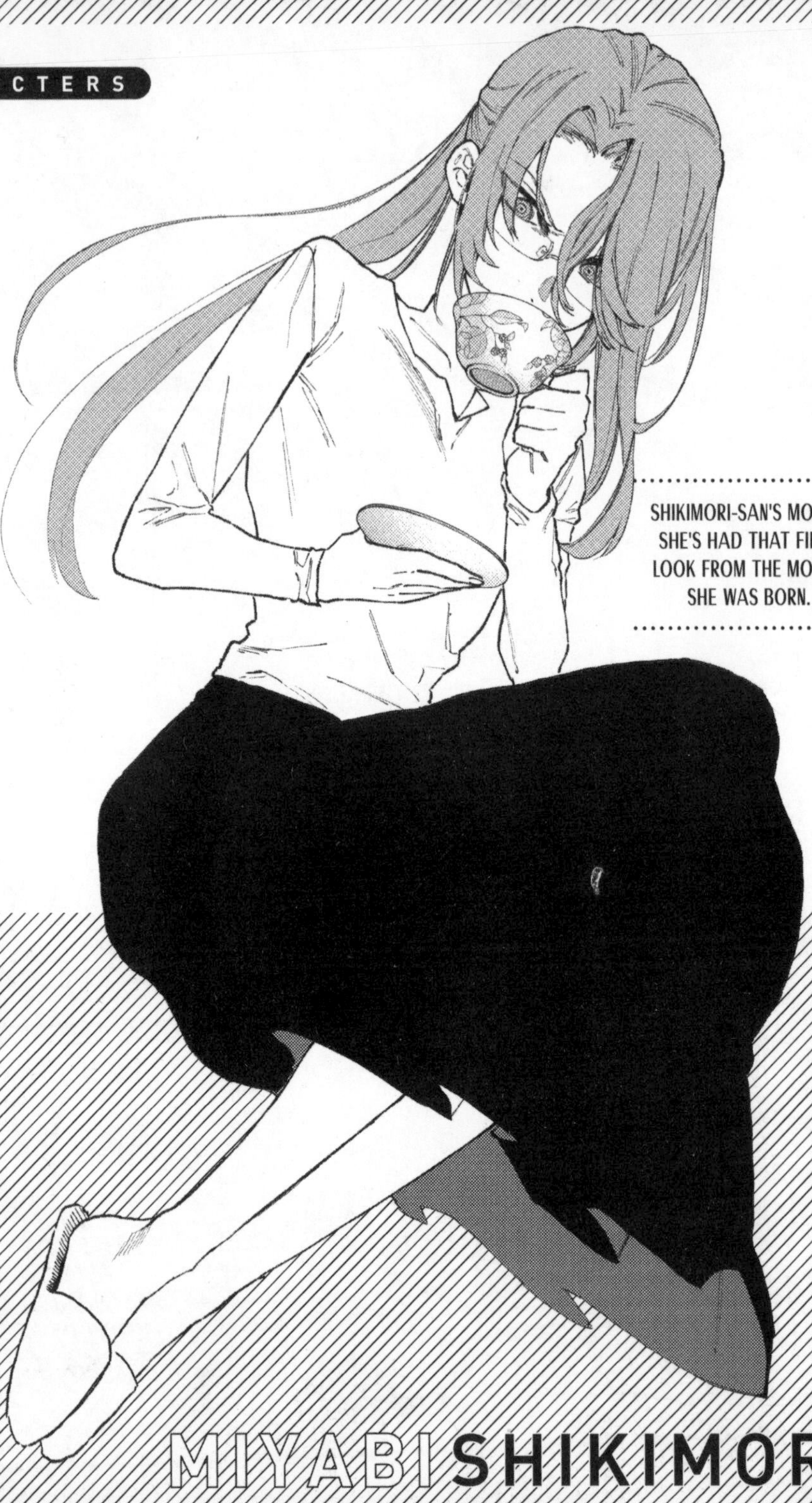

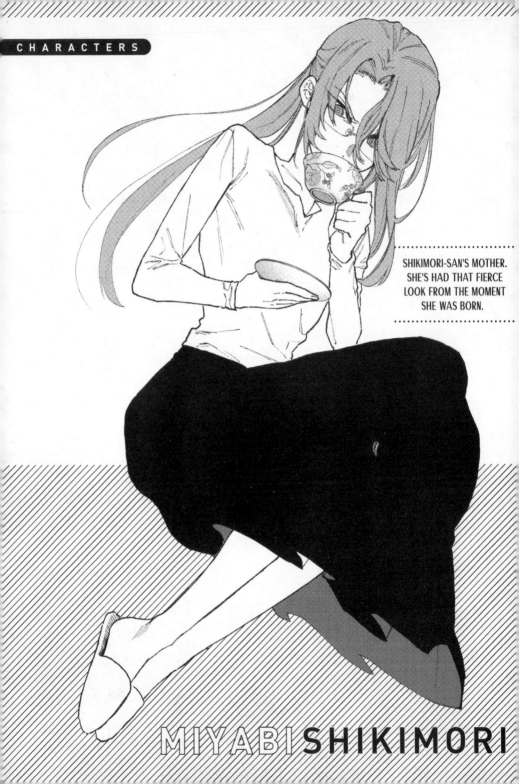

SHIKIMORI-SAN'S MOTHER.
SHE'S HAD THAT FIERCE
LOOK FROM THE MOMENT
SHE WAS BORN.

MIYABI SHIKIMORI

SHIKIMORI'S not just a cutie

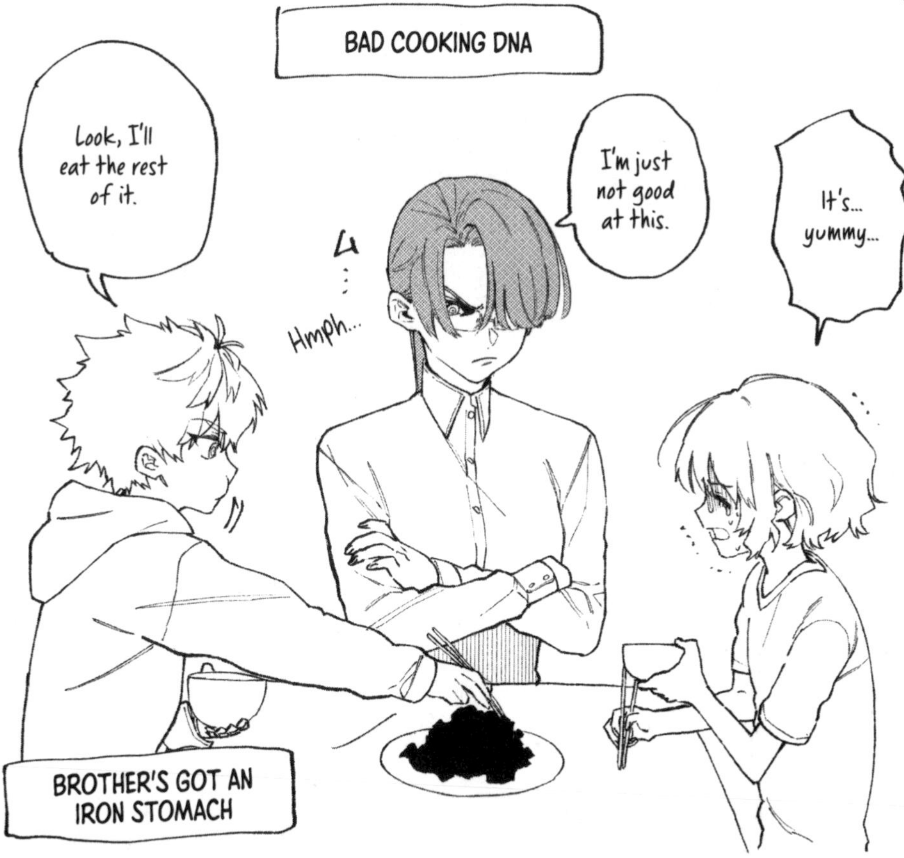
BAD COOKING DNA
It's... yummy...
I'm just not good at this.
Hmph...
Look, I'll eat the rest of it.
BROTHER'S GOT AN IRON STOMACH

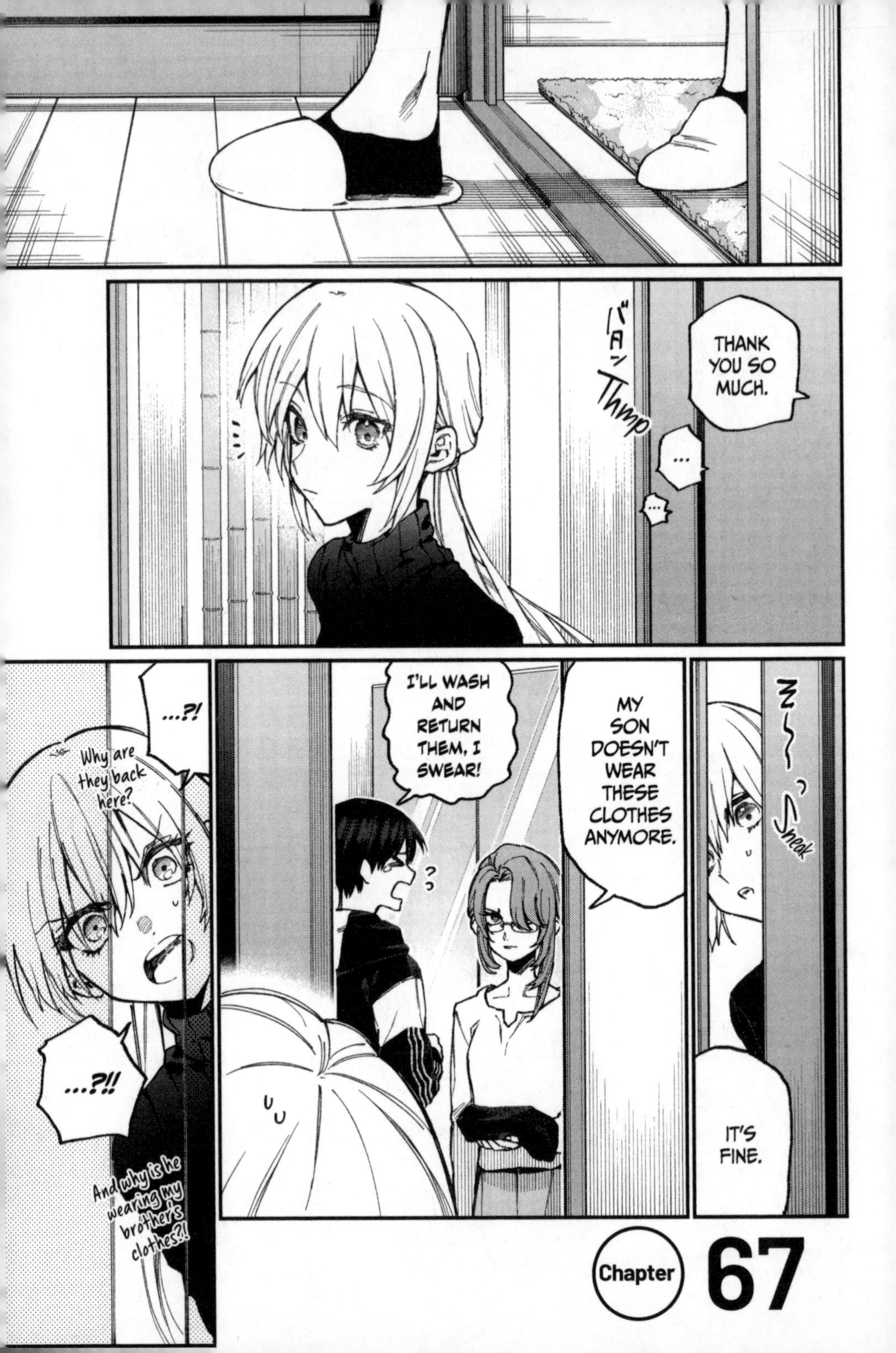
THANK YOU SO MUCH.
バタン
Thmp
...
...
Sneak
IT'S FINE.
MY SON DOESN'T WEAR THESE CLOTHES ANYMORE.
I'LL WASH AND RETURN THEM, I SWEAR!
...?!
Why are they back here?
...?!!
And why is he wearing my brother's clothes?!
Chapter 67

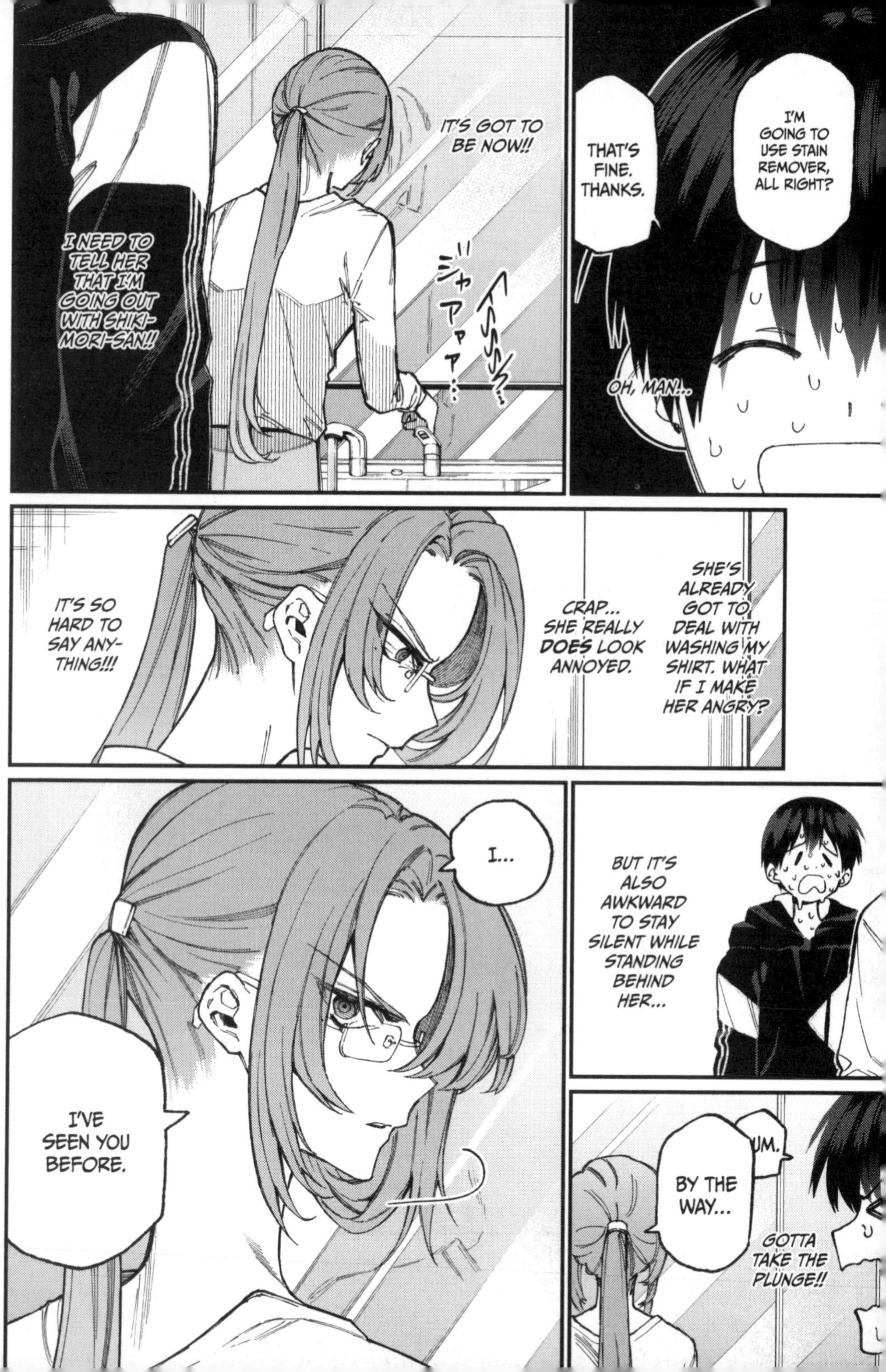
I'M GOING TO USE STAIN REMOVER, ALL RIGHT?
THAT'S FINE. THANKS.
OH, MAN...
IT'S GOT TO BE NOW!!
ジャァァ...
FSSSH...
I NEED TO TELL HER THAT I'M GOING OUT WITH SHIKI-MORI-SAN!!
SHE'S ALREADY GOT TO DEAL WITH WASHING MY SHIRT. WHAT IF I MAKE HER ANGRY?
CRAP... SHE REALLY DOES LOOK ANNOYED.
IT'S SO HARD TO SAY ANY-THING!!!
BUT IT'S ALSO AWKWARD TO STAY SILENT WHILE STANDING BEHIND HER...
UM.
BY THE WAY...
GOTTA TAKE THE PLUNGE!!
I...
I'VE SEEN YOU BEFORE.

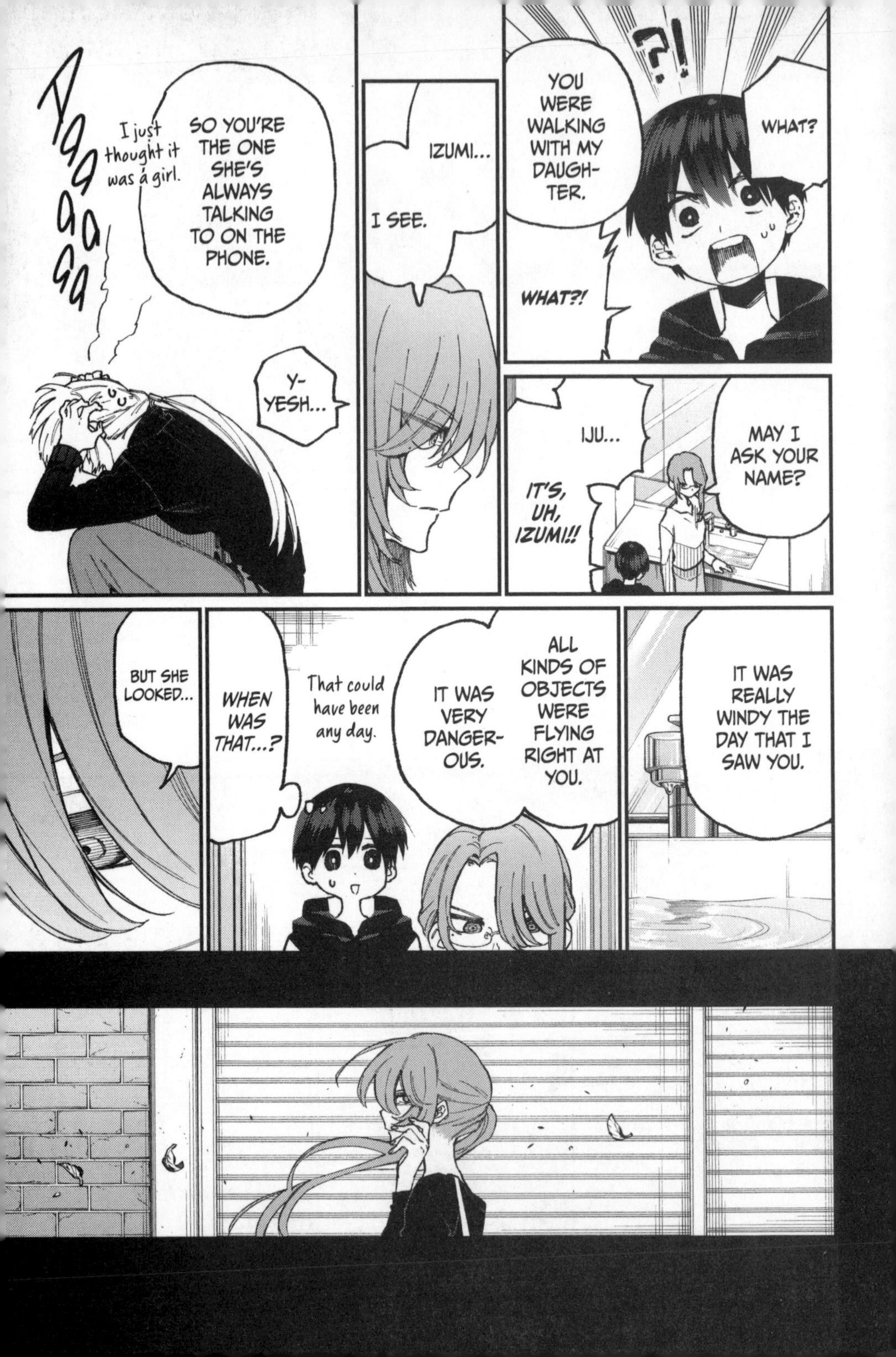
?!
WHAT?
YOU WERE WALKING WITH MY DAUGHTER.
WHAT?!
MAY I ASK YOUR NAME?
IJU...
IT'S, UH, IZUMI!!
IZUMI...
I SEE.
Y-YESH...
SO YOU'RE THE ONE SHE'S ALWAYS TALKING TO ON THE PHONE.
I just thought it was a girl.
Aaaaaaa
IT WAS REALLY WINDY THE DAY THAT I SAW YOU.
ALL KINDS OF OBJECTS WERE FLYING RIGHT AT YOU.
IT WAS VERY DANGEROUS.
That could have been any day.
WHEN WAS THAT...?
BUT SHE LOOKED...

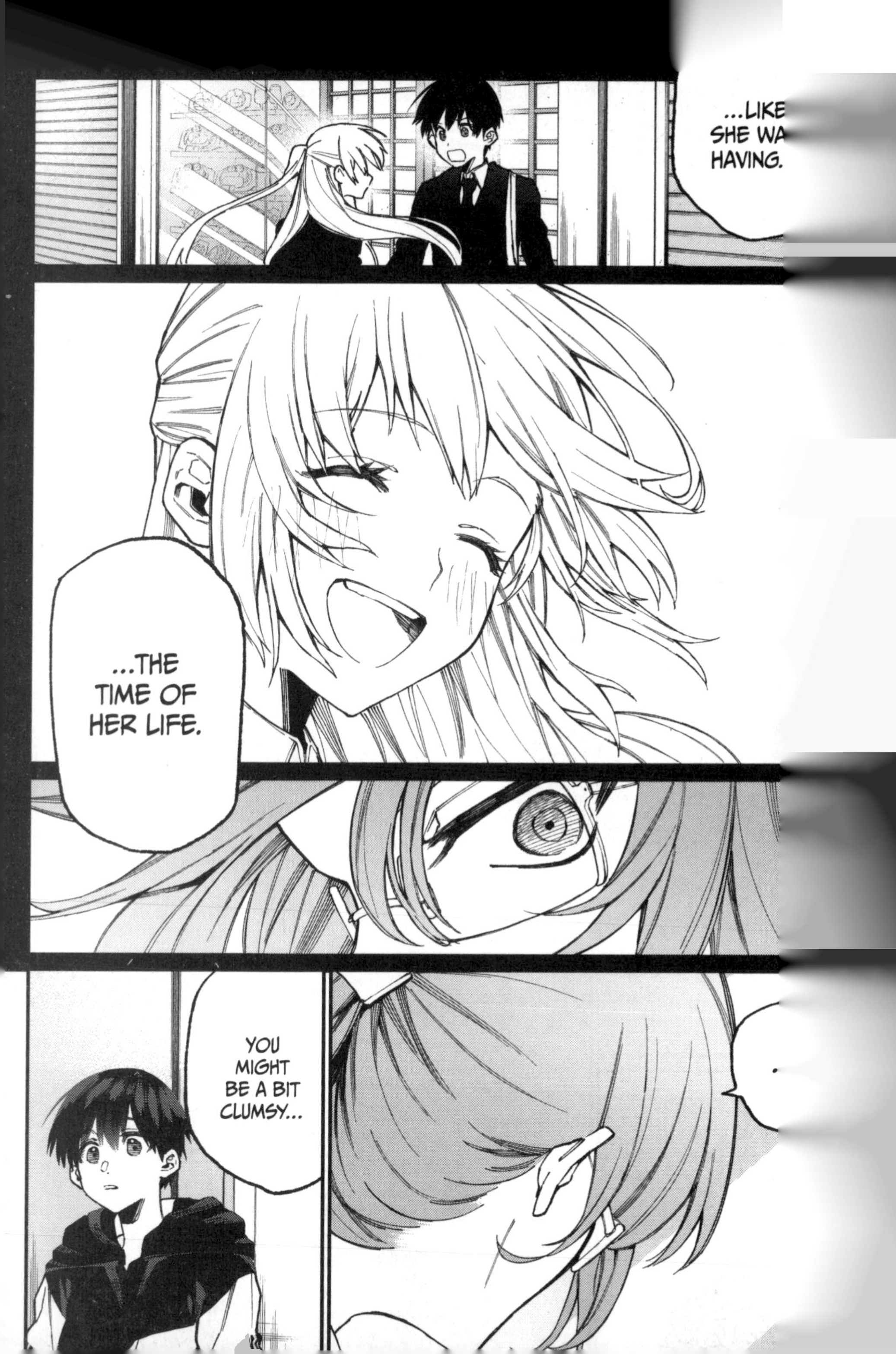

...LIKE SHE WA
HAVING.
...THE TIME OF HER LIFE.
YOU MIGHT BE A BIT CLUMSY...

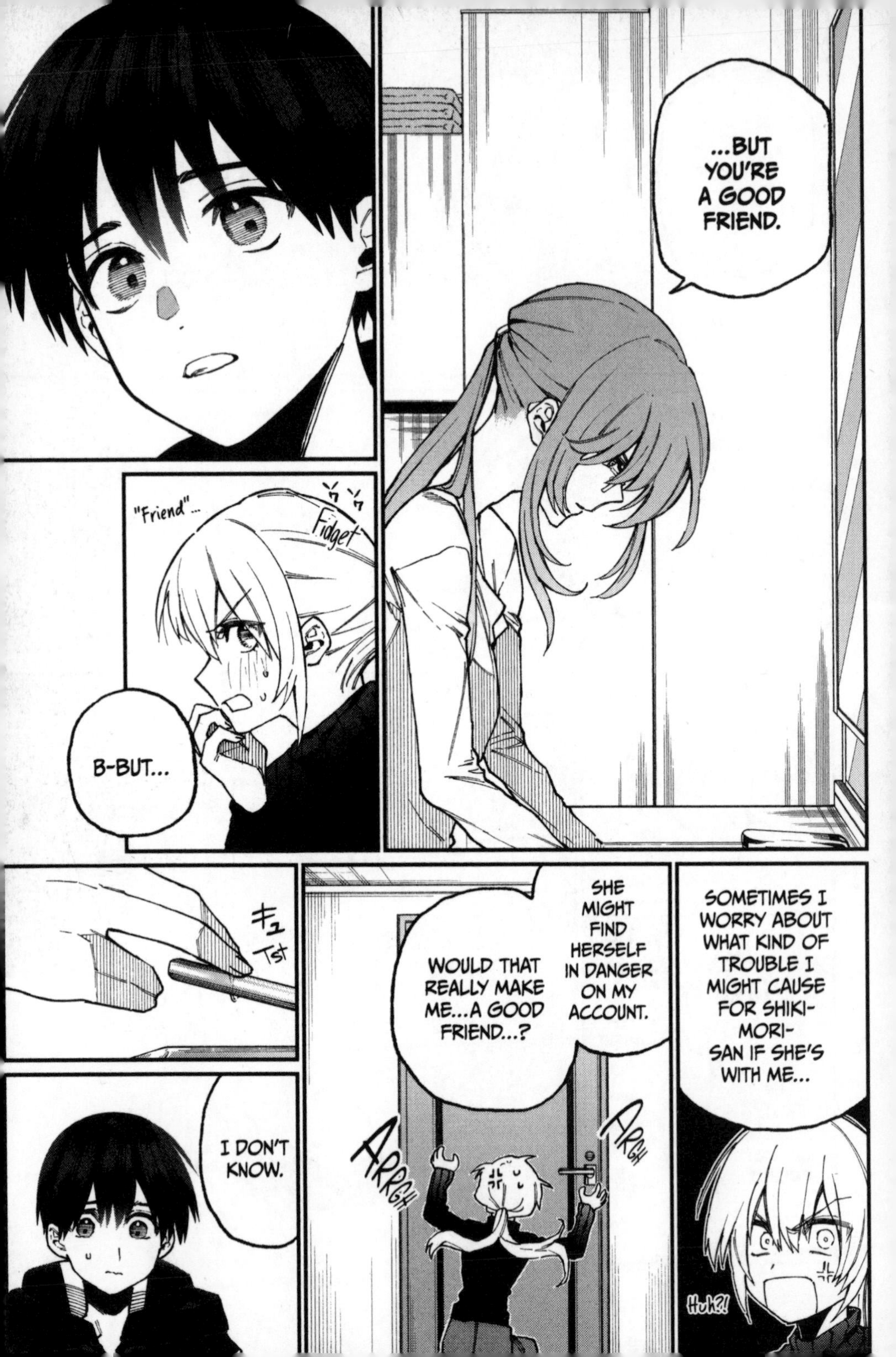
...BUT YOU'RE A GOOD FRIEND.
"Friend"...
ソワ ソワ
Fidget
B-BUT...
SOMETIMES I WORRY ABOUT WHAT KIND OF TROUBLE I MIGHT CAUSE FOR SHIKI-MORI-SAN IF SHE'S WITH ME...
Huh?!
SHE MIGHT FIND HERSELF IN DANGER ON MY ACCOUNT.
WOULD THAT REALLY MAKE ME...A GOOD FRIEND...?
ARGH
ARRGH
キュ
Tst
I DON'T KNOW.

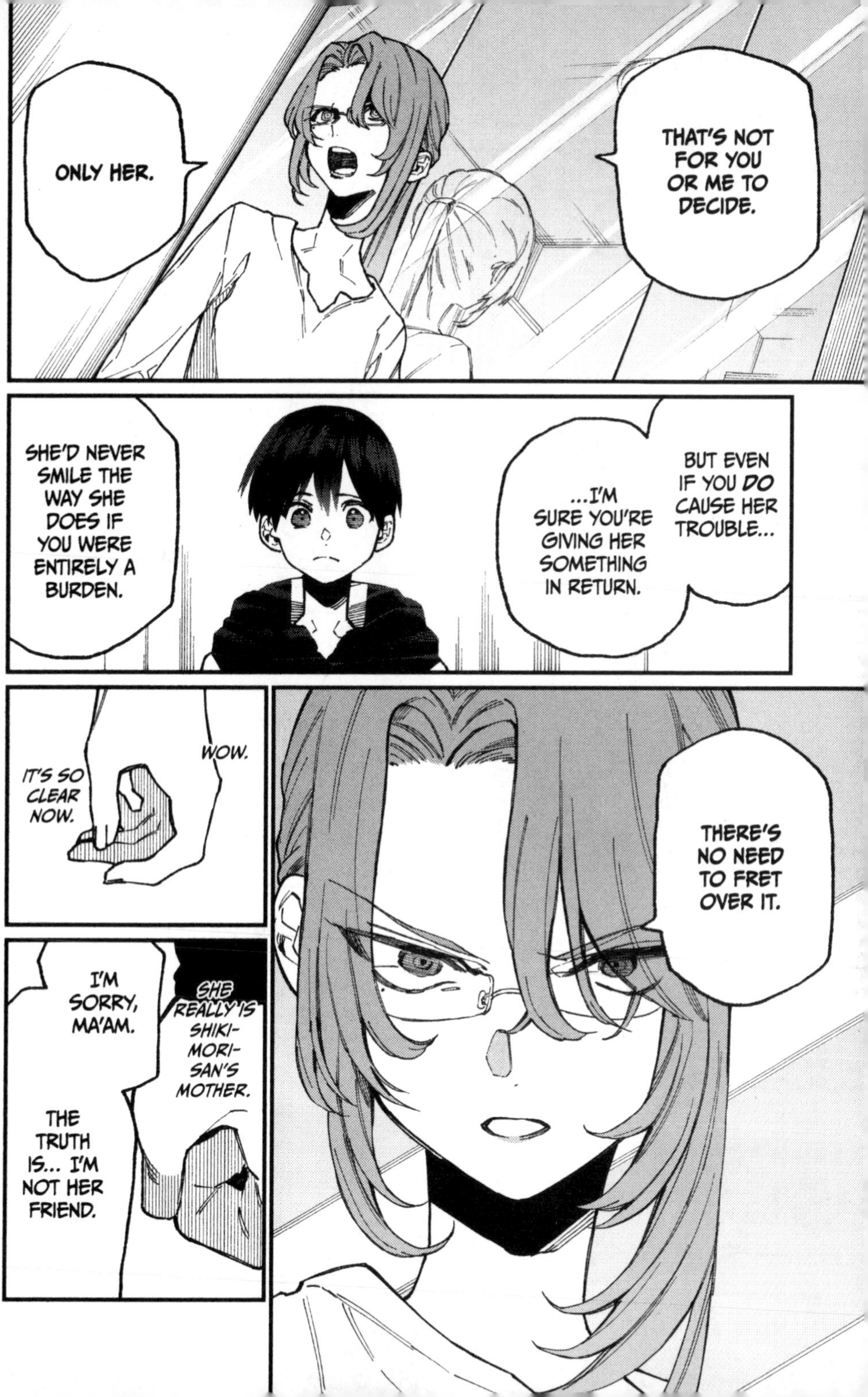
THAT'S NOT FOR YOU OR ME TO DECIDE.
ONLY HER.
BUT EVEN IF YOU *DO* CAUSE HER TROUBLE...
...I'M SURE YOU'RE GIVING HER SOMETHING IN RETURN.
SHE'D NEVER SMILE THE WAY SHE DOES IF YOU WERE ENTIRELY A BURDEN.
THERE'S NO NEED TO FRET OVER IT.
WOW.
IT'S SO CLEAR NOW.
SHE REALLY IS SHIKI-MORI-SAN'S MOTHER.
I'M SORRY, MA'AM.
THE TRUTH IS... I'M NOT HER FRIEND.

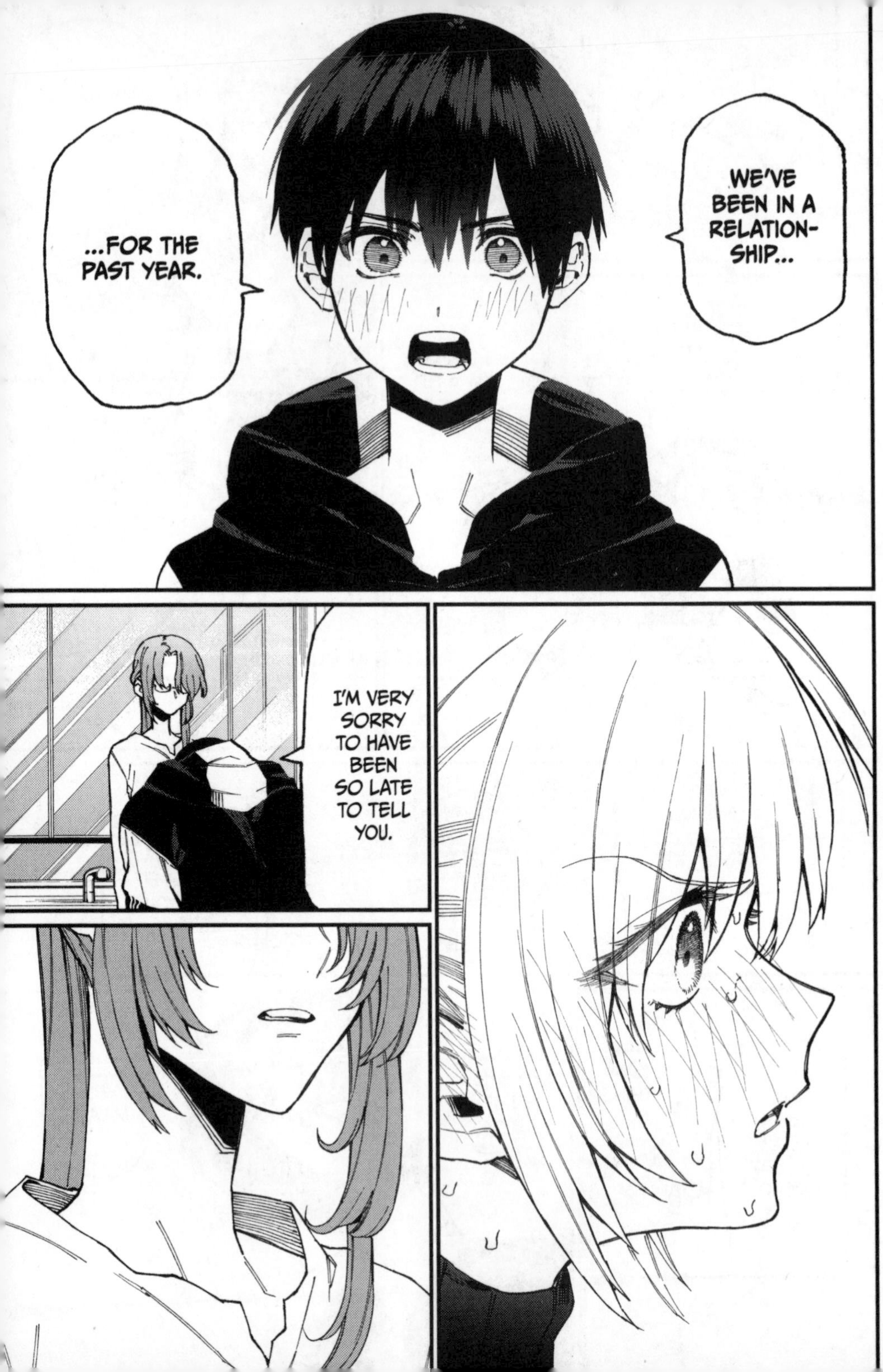
WE'VE BEEN IN A RELATIONSHIP...
...FOR THE PAST YEAR.
I'M VERY SORRY TO HAVE BEEN SO LATE TO TELL YOU.

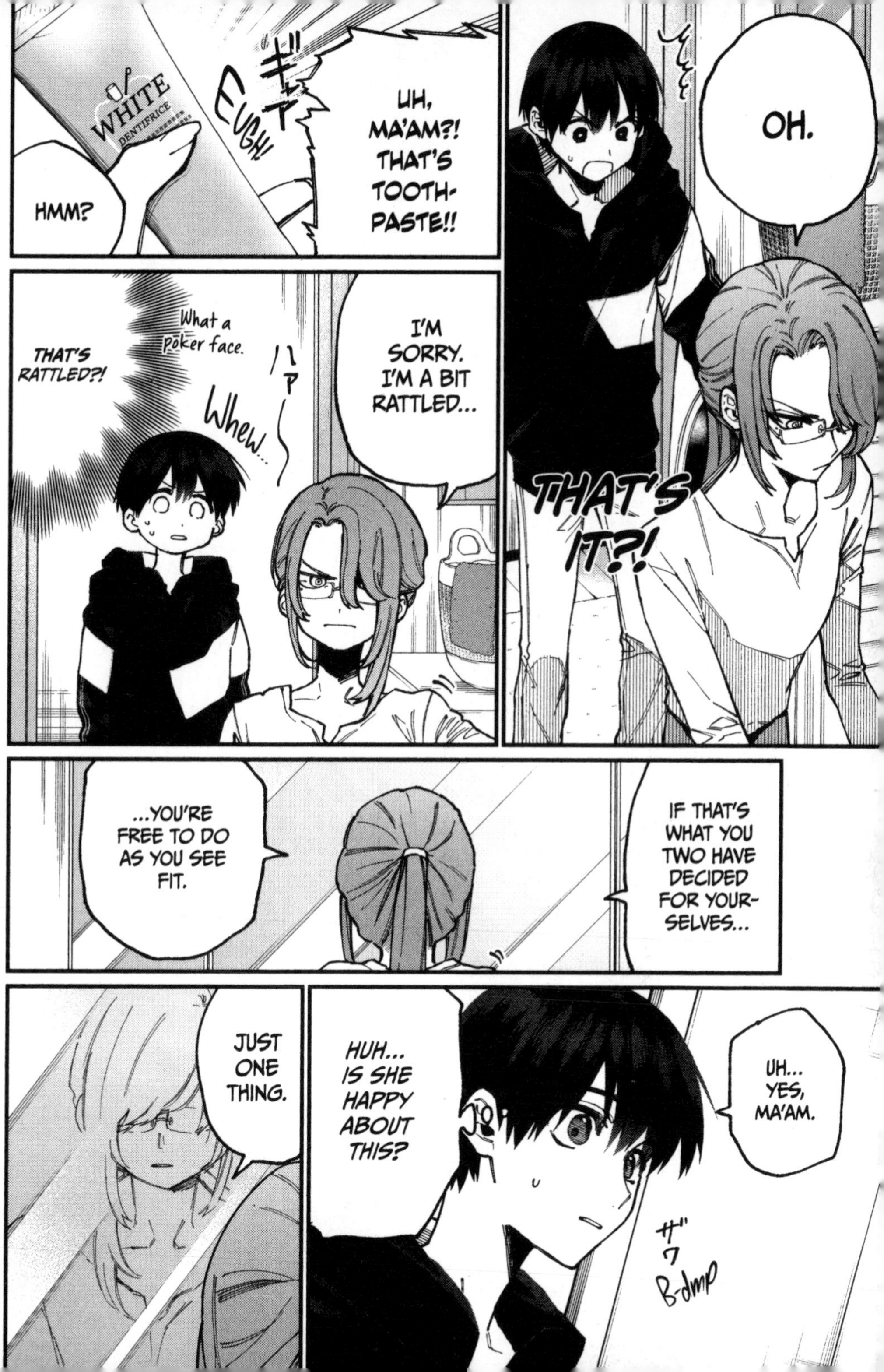
OH.
THAT'S IT?!
UH, MA'AM?! THAT'S TOOTH-PASTE!!
EUGH!
WHITE DENTIFRICE
HMM?
I'M SORRY. I'M A BIT RATTLED...
Whew...
What a poker face.
THAT'S RATTLED?!
IF THAT'S WHAT YOU TWO HAVE DECIDED FOR YOUR-SELVES...
...YOU'RE FREE TO DO AS YOU SEE FIT.
UH... YES, MA'AM.
B-dmp
HUH... IS SHE HAPPY ABOUT THIS?
JUST ONE THING.

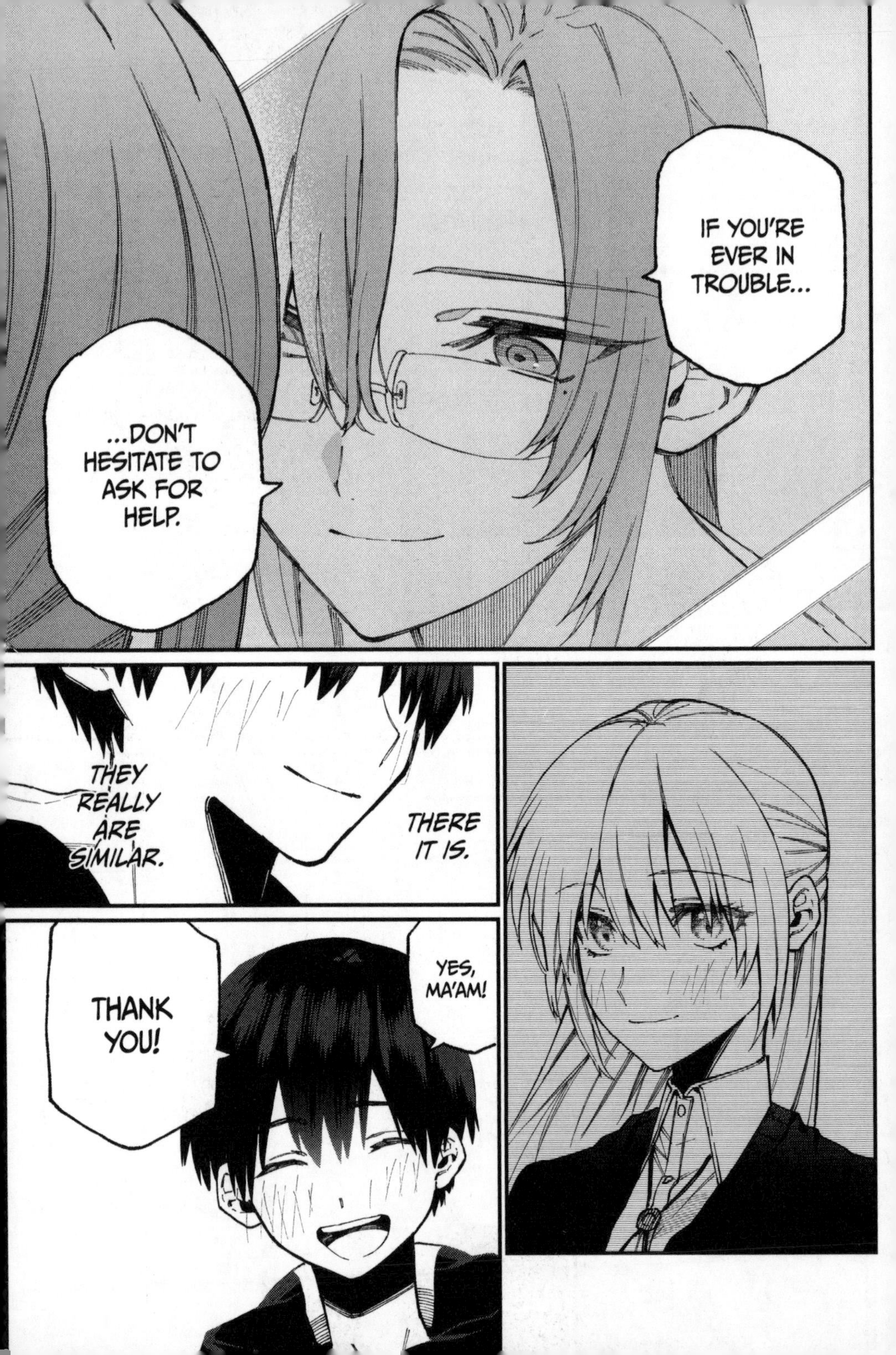
IF YOU'RE EVER IN TROUBLE...
...DON'T HESITATE TO ASK FOR HELP.
THERE IT IS.
THEY REALLY ARE SIMILAR.
YES, MA'AM!
THANK YOU!

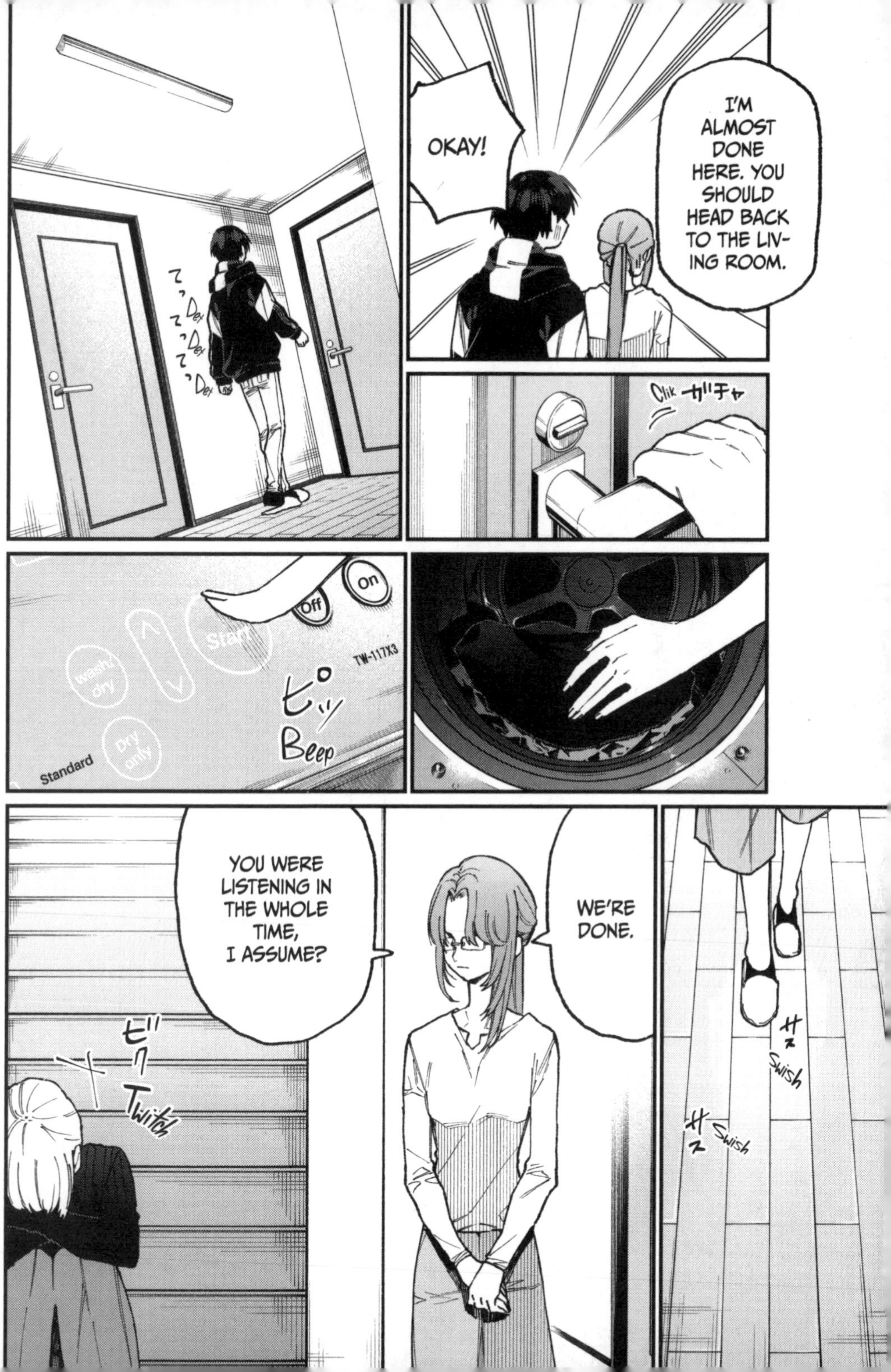
I'M ALMOST DONE HERE. YOU SHOULD HEAD BACK TO THE LIV-ING ROOM.
OKAY!
Clik ガチャ
Dex
Dex
Dex
On
Off
Start
TW-117X3
wash/dry
Dry only
Standard
ピッ Beep
ザッ Swish
ザッ Swish
WE'RE DONE.
YOU WERE LISTENING IN THE WHOLE TIME, I ASSUME?
ビクッ Twitch

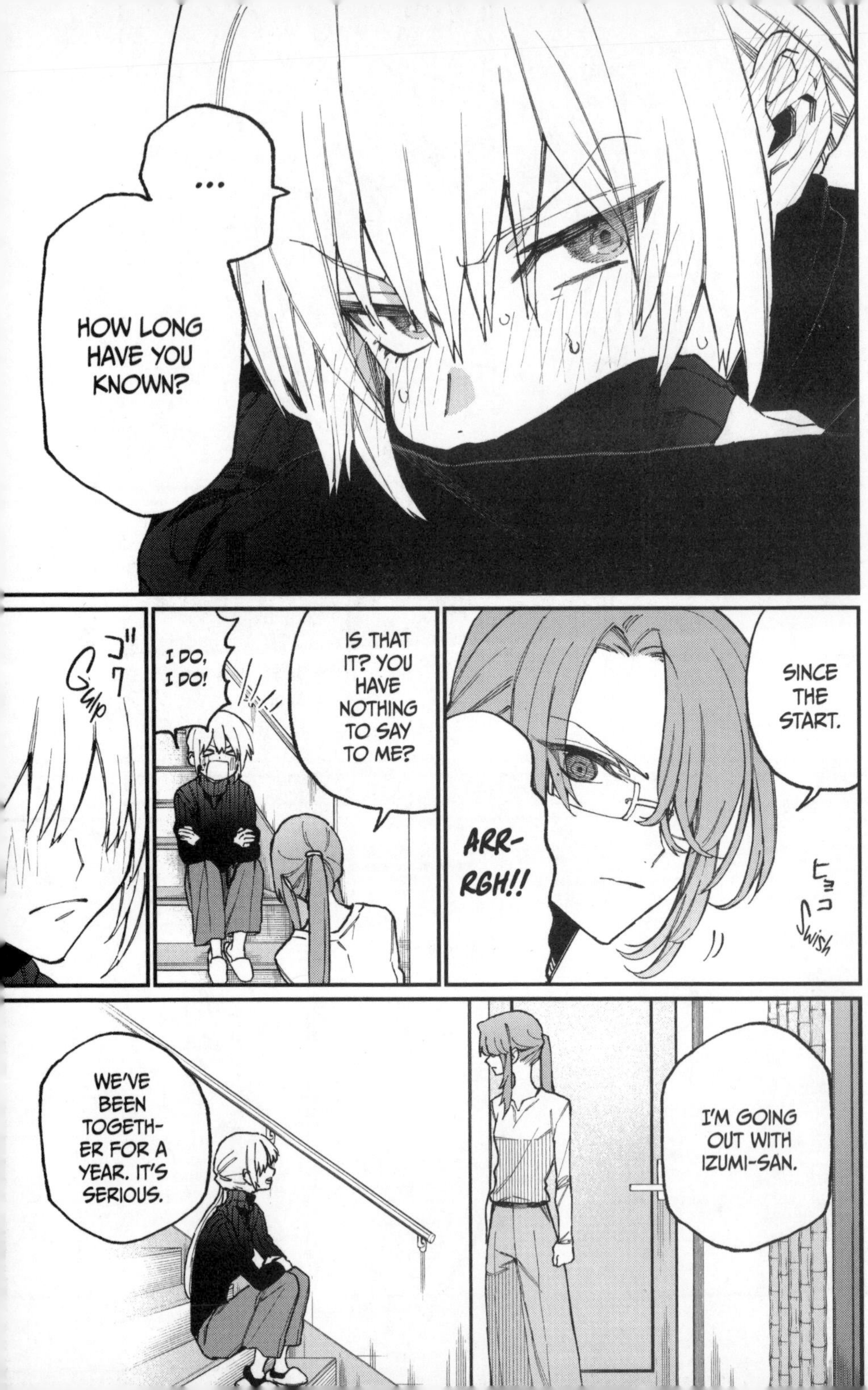
...
HOW LONG HAVE YOU KNOWN?
SINCE THE START.
ARR-RGH!!
Swish
IS THAT IT? YOU HAVE NOTHING TO SAY TO ME?
I DO, I DO!
Gulp
I'M GOING OUT WITH IZUMI-SAN.
WE'VE BEEN TOGETH-ER FOR A YEAR. IT'S SERIOUS.

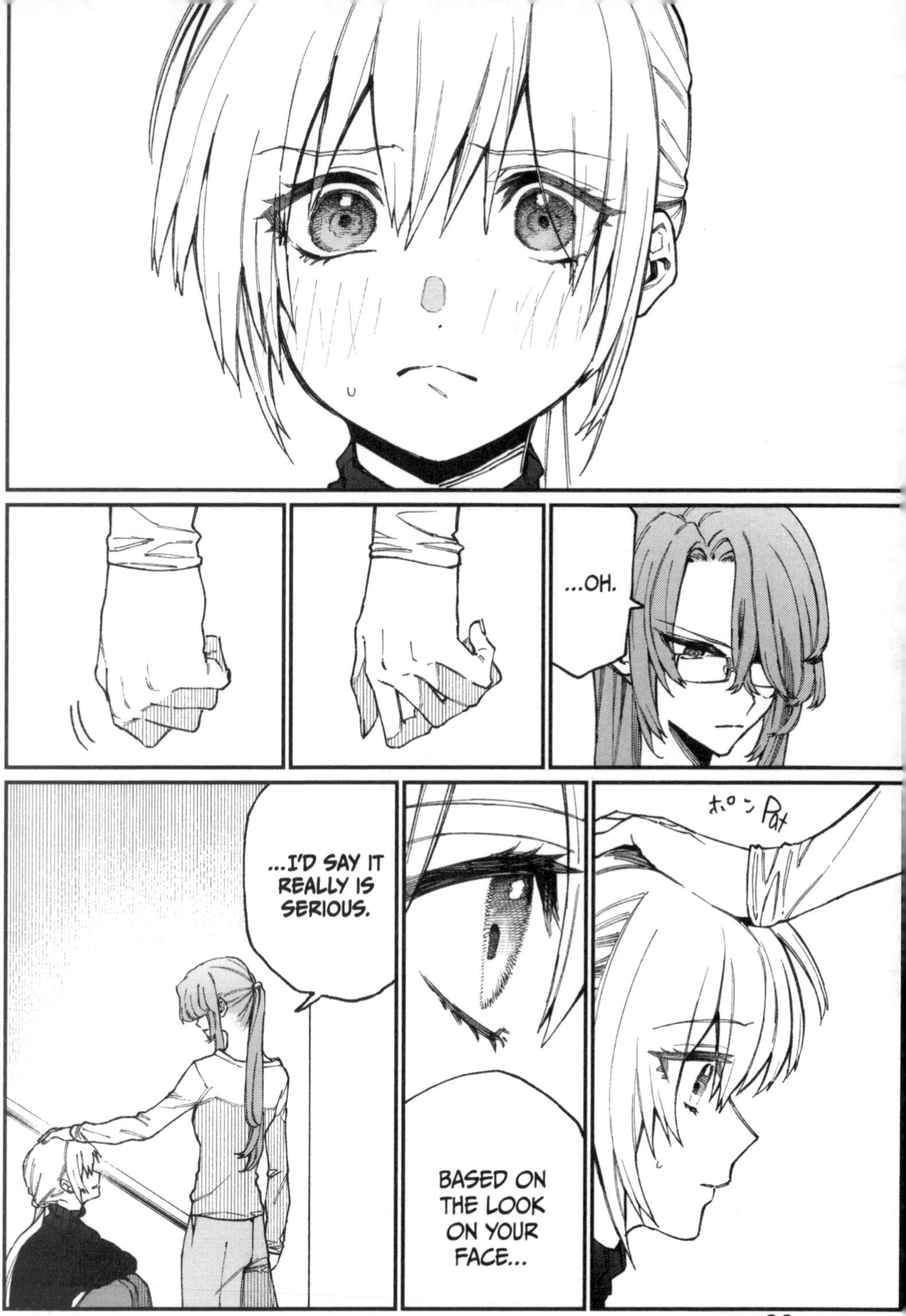
...OH.
ポン Pat
BASED ON THE LOOK ON YOUR FACE...
...I'D SAY IT REALLY IS SERIOUS.

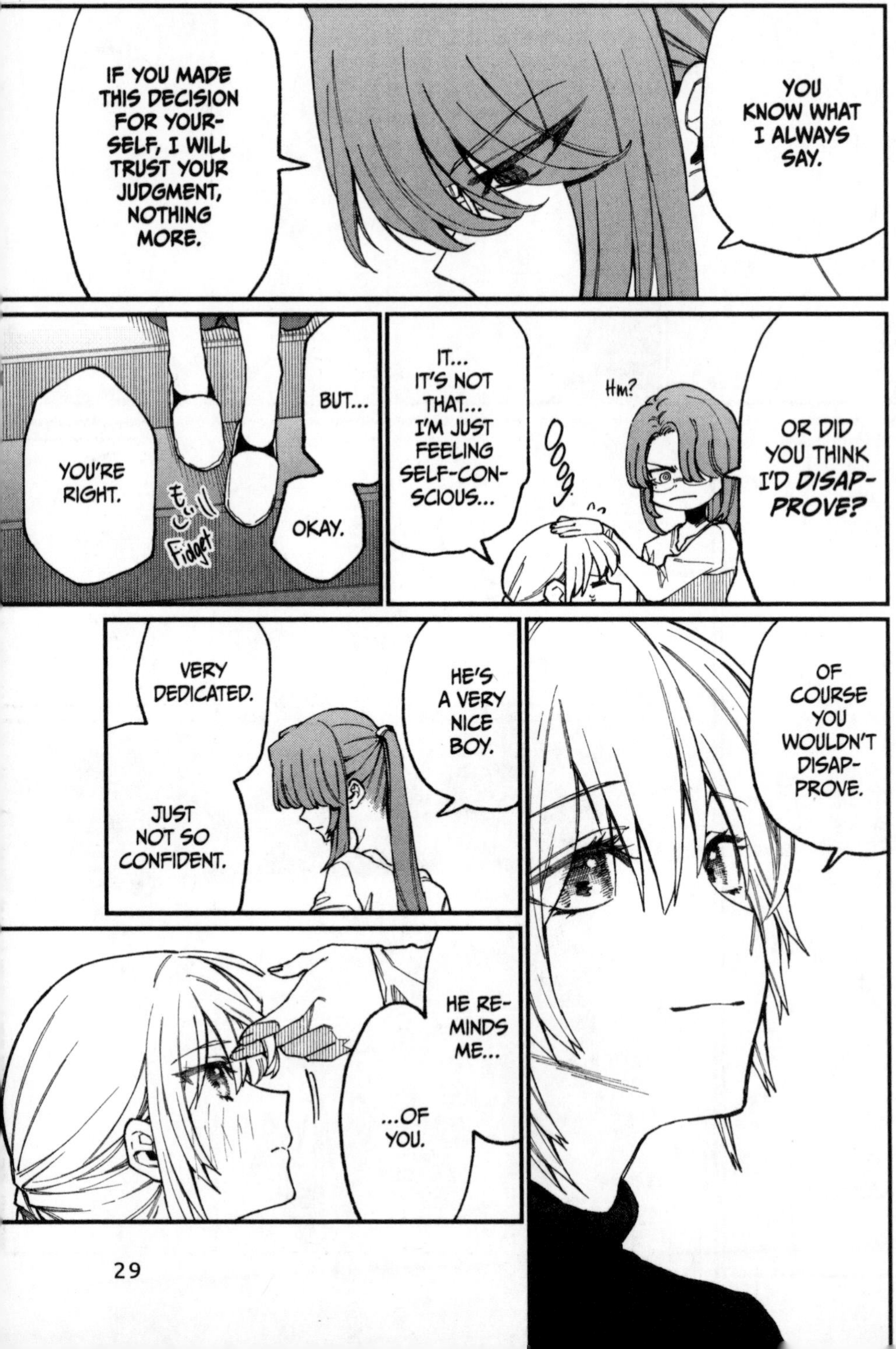
YOU KNOW WHAT I ALWAYS SAY.
IF YOU MADE THIS DECISION FOR YOUR-SELF, I WILL TRUST YOUR JUDGMENT, NOTHING MORE.
OR DID YOU THINK I'D *DISAP-PROVE?*
Hm?
IT... IT'S NOT THAT... I'M JUST FEELING SELF-CON-SCIOUS...
BUT...
OKAY.
YOU'RE RIGHT.
Fidget
OF COURSE YOU WOULDN'T DISAP-PROVE.
HE'S A VERY NICE BOY.
VERY DEDICATED.
JUST NOT SO CONFIDENT.
HE RE-MINDS ME...
...OF YOU.

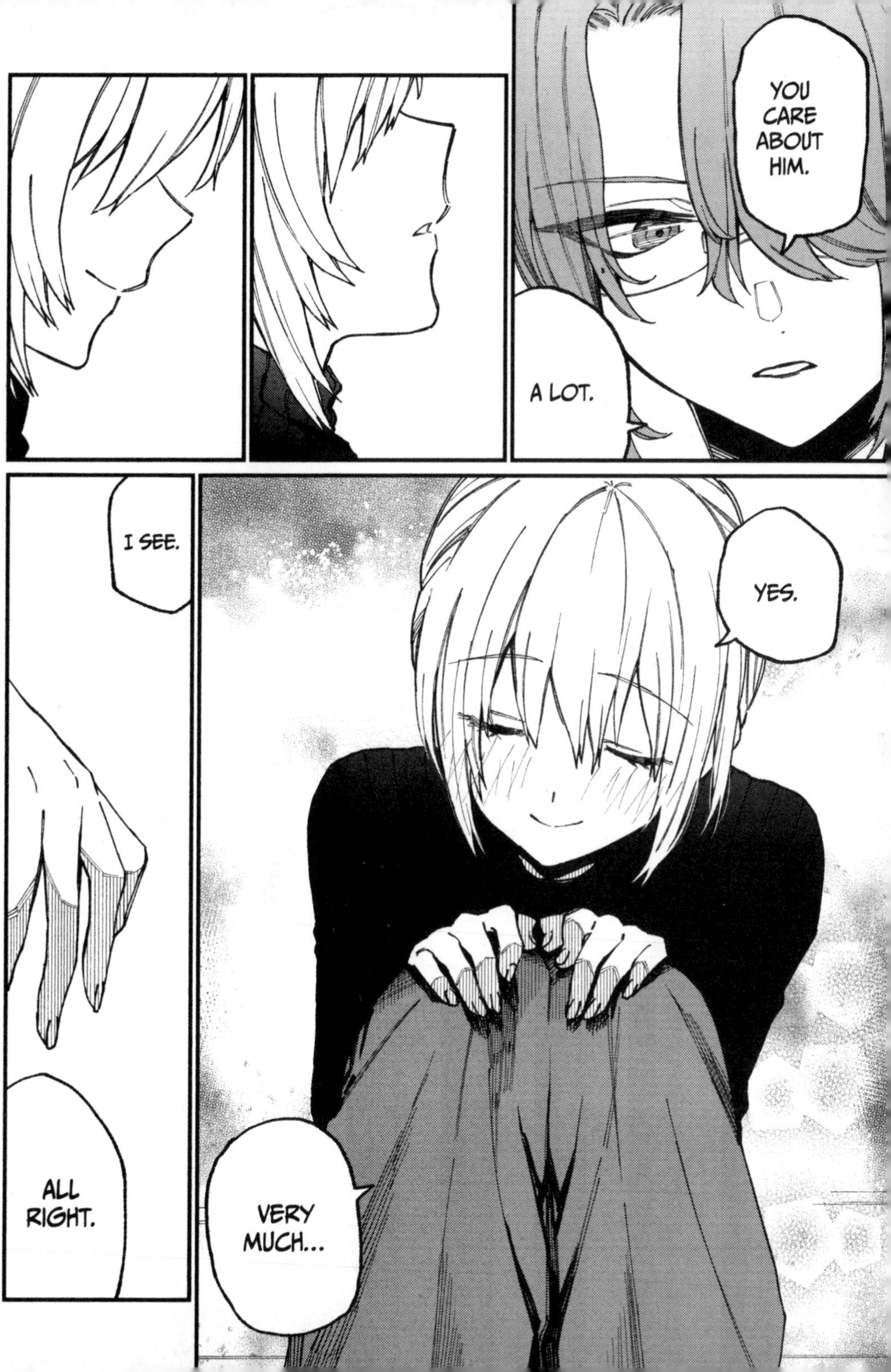
YOU CARE ABOUT HIM.
A LOT.
YES.
VERY MUCH...
I SEE.
ALL RIGHT.

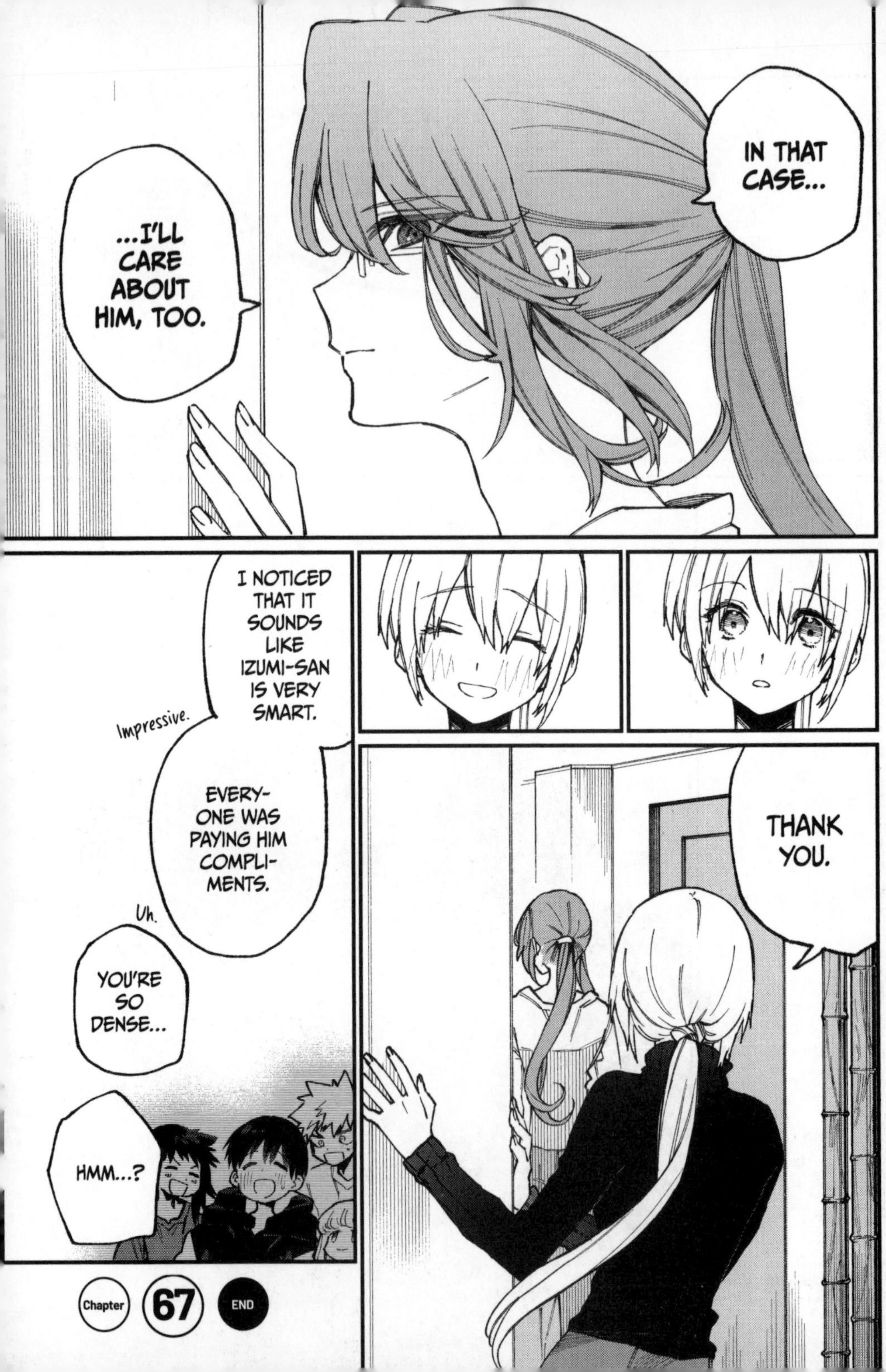
IN THAT CASE...
...I'LL CARE ABOUT HIM, TOO.
THANK YOU.
I NOTICED THAT IT SOUNDS LIKE IZUMI-SAN IS VERY SMART.
Impressive.
EVERY-ONE WAS PAYING HIM COMPLI-MENTS.
Uh.
YOU'RE SO DENSE...
HMM...?
Chapter 67 END

SHIKIMORI'S
not just a cutie

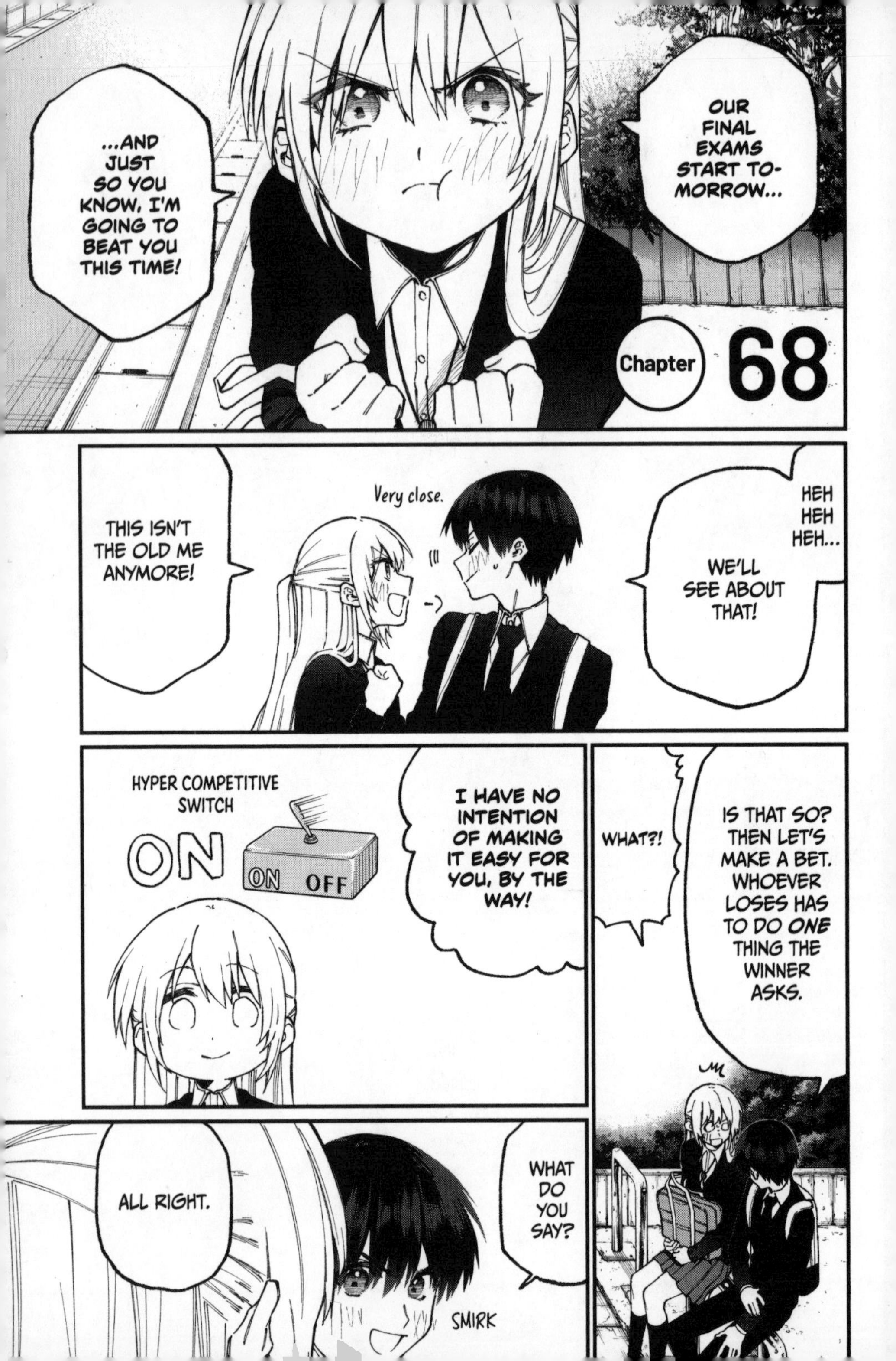
OUR FINAL EXAMS START TO-MORROW...
...AND JUST SO YOU KNOW, I'M GOING TO BEAT YOU THIS TIME!
Chapter 68
HEH HEH HEH...
WE'LL SEE ABOUT THAT!
Very close.
THIS ISN'T THE OLD ME ANYMORE!
IS THAT SO? THEN LET'S MAKE A BET. WHOEVER LOSES HAS TO DO *ONE* THING THE WINNER ASKS.
WHAT?!
I HAVE NO INTENTION OF MAKING IT EASY FOR YOU, BY THE WAY!
HYPER COMPETITIVE SWITCH
ON
ON OFF
WHAT DO YOU SAY?
ALL RIGHT.
SMIRK

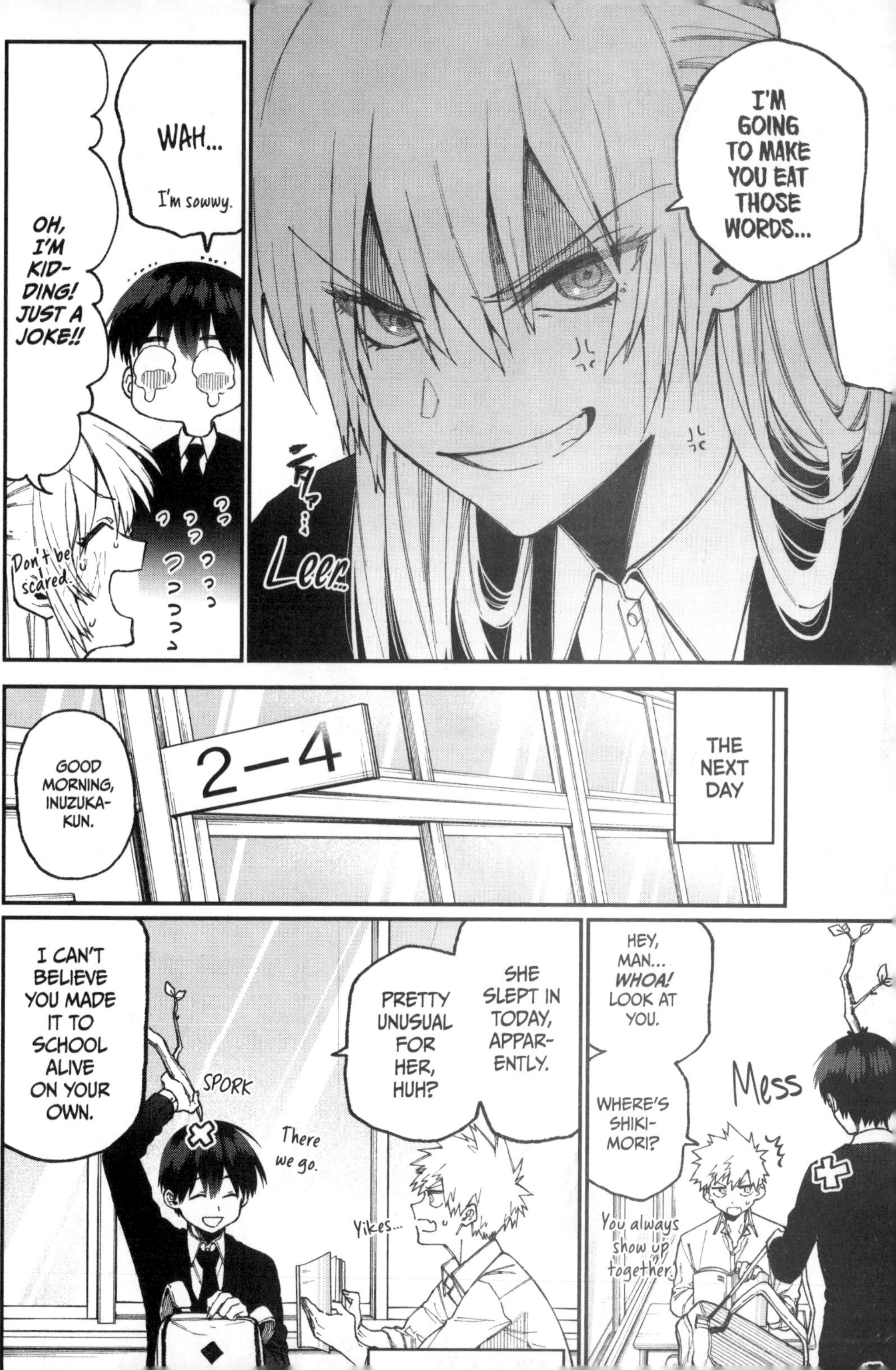
I'M GOING TO MAKE YOU EAT THOSE WORDS...
Leer...
WAH...
I'm sowwy.
OH, I'M KID-DING! JUST A JOKE!!
Don't be scared.
THE NEXT DAY
2–4
GOOD MORNING, INUZUKA-KUN.
HEY, MAN... *WHOA!* LOOK AT YOU.
Mess
WHERE'S SHIKI-MORI?
You always show up together.
SHE SLEPT IN TODAY, APPAR-ENTLY.
PRETTY UNUSUAL FOR HER, HUH?
Yikes...
I CAN'T BELIEVE YOU MADE IT TO SCHOOL ALIVE ON YOUR OWN.
SPORK
There we go.

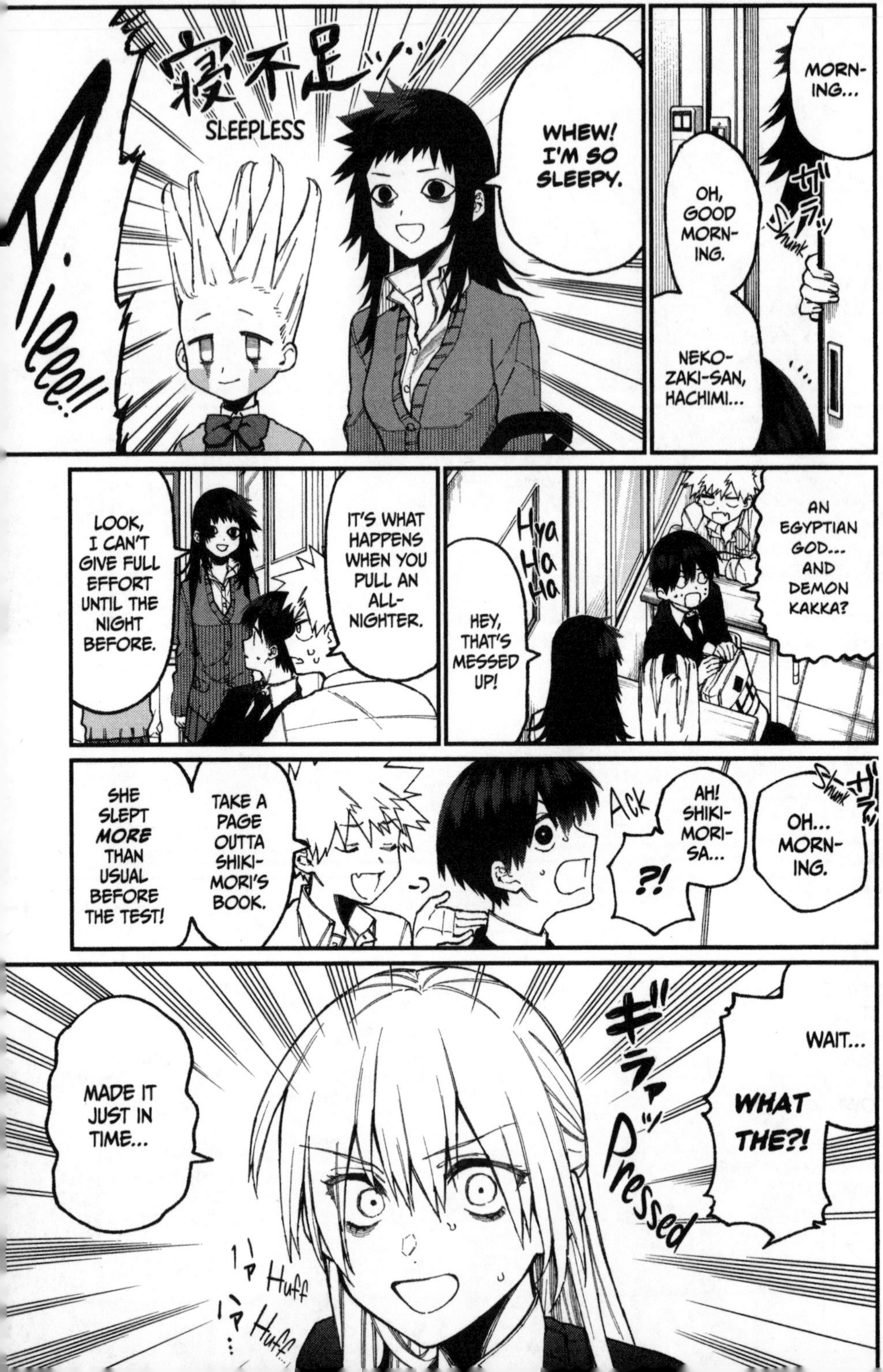

MORN-ING...
Shunk
OH, GOOD MORN-ING.
NEKO-ZAKI-SAN, HACHIMI...
寝不足ゾッ
SLEEPLESS
WHEW! I'M SO SLEEPY.
Aieee!!
AN EGYPTIAN GOD... AND DEMON KAKKA?
Hya Ha Ha
HEY, THAT'S MESSED UP!
IT'S WHAT HAPPENS WHEN YOU PULL AN ALL-NIGHTER.
LOOK, I CAN'T GIVE FULL EFFORT UNTIL THE NIGHT BEFORE.
Shunk
OH... MORN-ING.
AH! SHIKI-MORI-SA...
Ack
?!
TAKE A PAGE OUTTA SHIKI-MORI'S BOOK.
SHE SLEPT MORE THAN USUAL BEFORE THE TEST!
WAIT...
WHAT THE?!
Pressed
MADE IT JUST IN TIME...
Huff
Huff

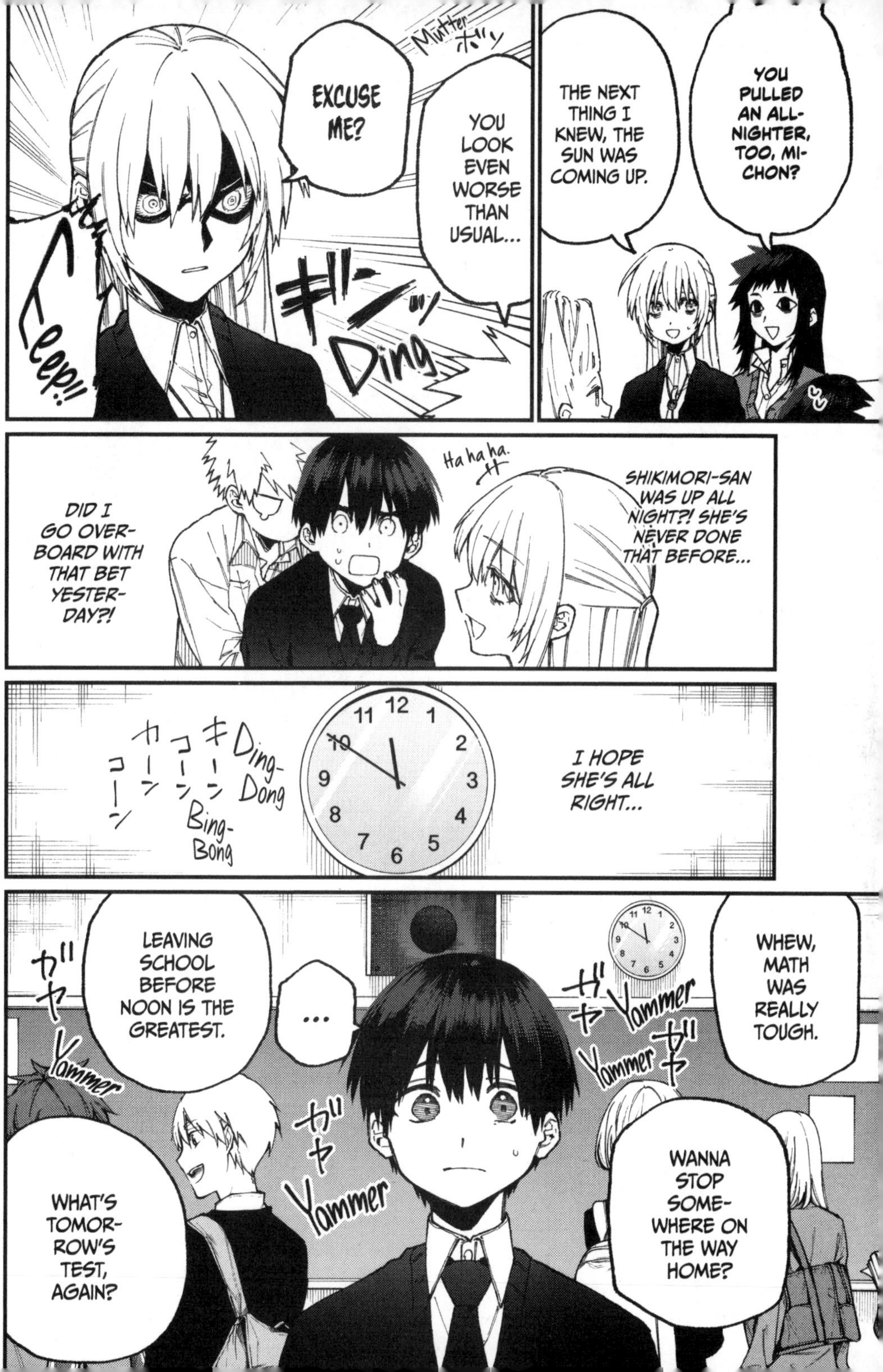
YOU PULLED AN ALL-NIGHTER, TOO, MI-CHON?
THE NEXT THING I KNEW, THE SUN WAS COMING UP.
Mutter
YOU LOOK EVEN WORSE THAN USUAL...
EXCUSE ME?
Ding
Eep!!
SHIKIMORI-SAN WAS UP ALL NIGHT?! SHE'S NEVER DONE THAT BEFORE...
Ha ha ha.
DID I GO OVER-BOARD WITH THAT BET YESTER-DAY?!
I HOPE SHE'S ALL RIGHT...
Ding-Dong
Bing-Bong
WHEW, MATH WAS REALLY TOUGH.
Yammer
Yammer
LEAVING SCHOOL BEFORE NOON IS THE GREATEST.
...
WANNA STOP SOME-WHERE ON THE WAY HOME?
Yammer
Yammer
WHAT'S TOMOR-ROW'S TEST, AGAIN?

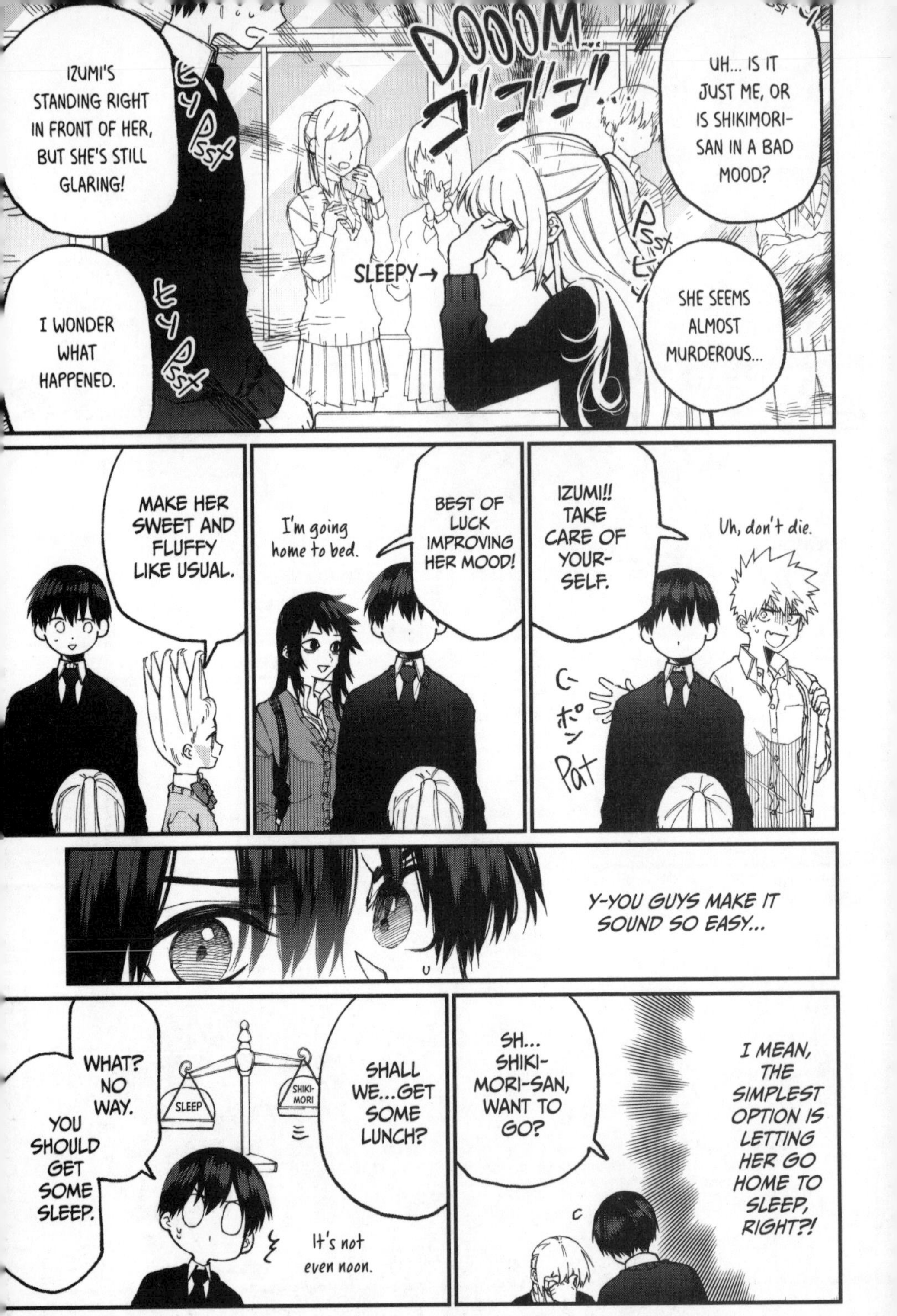
UH... IS IT JUST ME, OR IS SHIKIMORI-SAN IN A BAD MOOD?
Pssst
SHE SEEMS ALMOST MURDEROUS...
DOOOM
SLEEPY→
IZUMI'S STANDING RIGHT IN FRONT OF HER, BUT SHE'S STILL GLARING!
Pssst
Pssst
I WONDER WHAT HAPPENED.
Uh, don't die.
IZUMI!! TAKE CARE OF YOURSELF.
Pat
BEST OF LUCK IMPROVING HER MOOD!
I'm going home to bed.
MAKE HER SWEET AND FLUFFY LIKE USUAL.
Y-YOU GUYS MAKE IT SOUND SO EASY...
I MEAN, THE SIMPLEST OPTION IS LETTING HER GO HOME TO SLEEP, RIGHT?!
SH... SHIKI-MORI-SAN, WANT TO GO?
SHALL WE...GET SOME LUNCH?
SHIKI-MORI
SLEEP
WHAT? NO WAY.
YOU SHOULD GET SOME SLEEP.
It's not even noon.

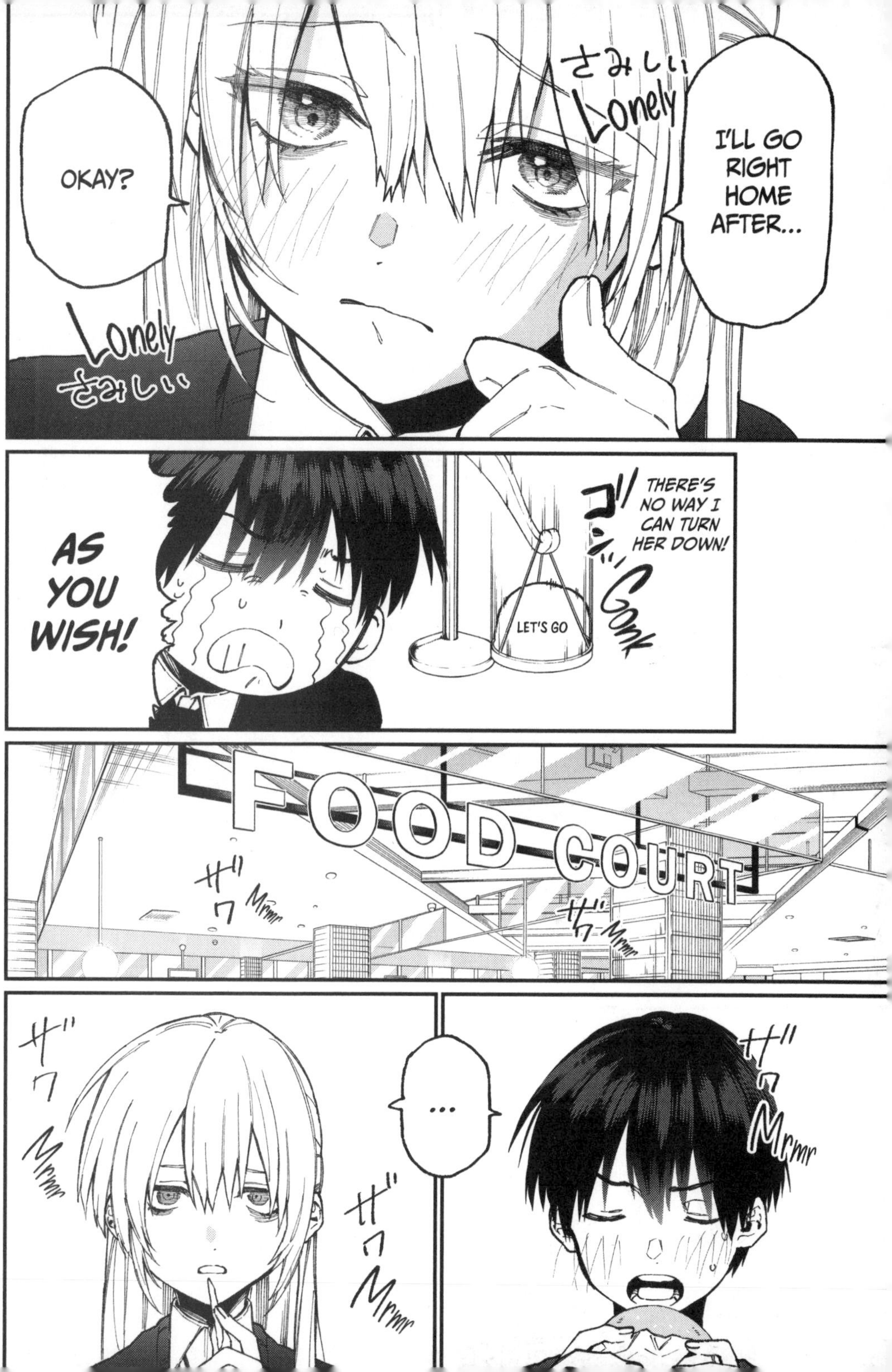

さみしい
Lonely
I'LL GO RIGHT HOME AFTER...
OKAY?
Lonely
さみしい
THERE'S NO WAY I CAN TURN HER DOWN!
ゴン
Gonk
LET'S GO
AS YOU WISH!
FOOD COURT
ザワ
Mrmr
ザワ
Mrmr
ザワ
Mrmr
...
ザワ
Mrmr
ザワ
Mrmr

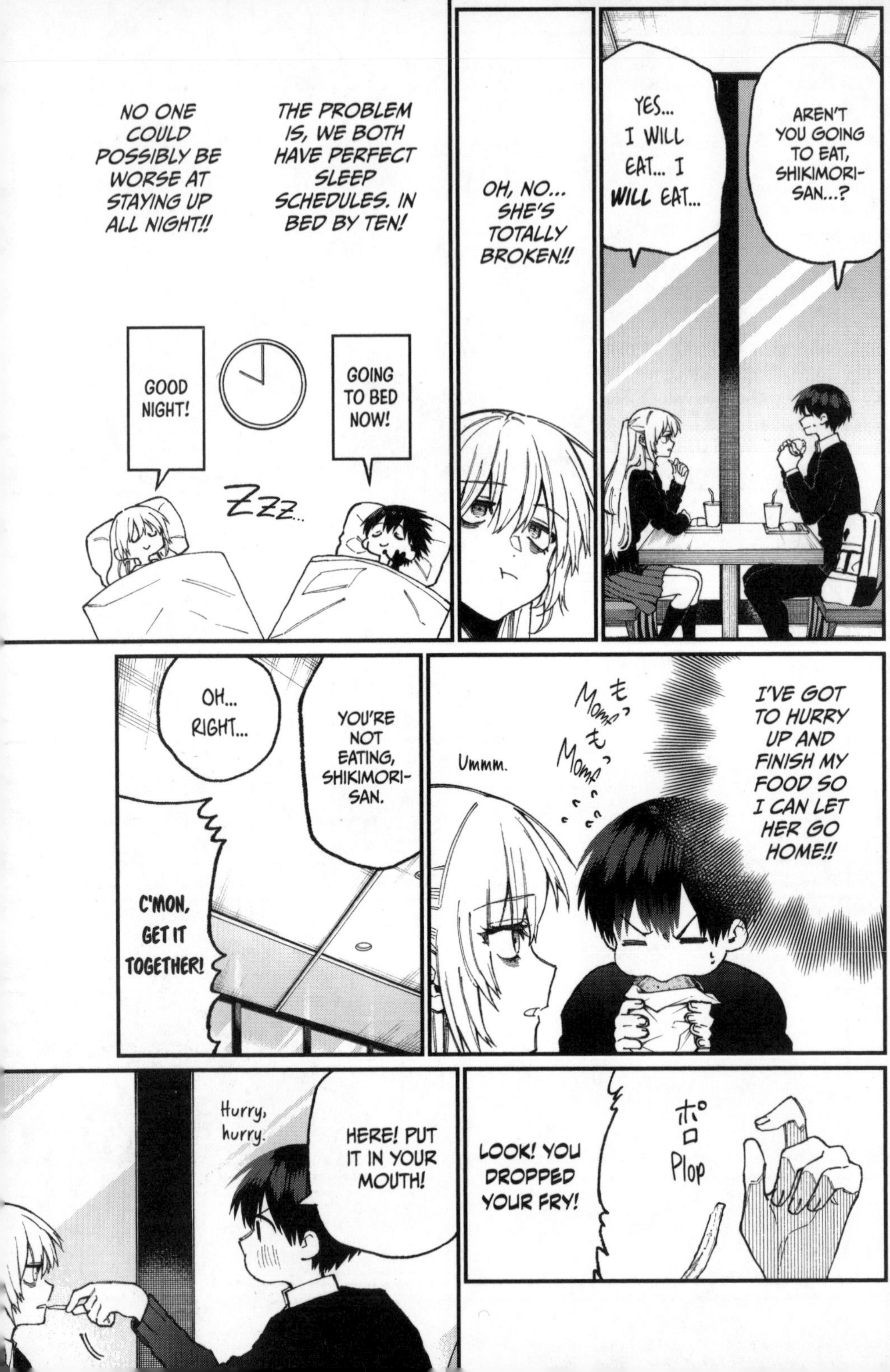

AREN'T YOU GOING TO EAT, SHIKIMORI-SAN...?
YES... I WILL EAT... I **WILL** EAT...
OH, NO... SHE'S TOTALLY BROKEN!!
THE PROBLEM IS, WE BOTH HAVE PERFECT SLEEP SCHEDULES. IN BED BY TEN!
NO ONE COULD POSSIBLY BE WORSE AT STAYING UP ALL NIGHT!!
GOING TO BED NOW!
GOOD NIGHT!
ZZZ...
I'VE GOT TO HURRY UP AND FINISH MY FOOD SO I CAN LET HER GO HOME!!
もっ Momf
もっ Momf
Ummm.
YOU'RE NOT EATING, SHIKIMORI-SAN.
OH... RIGHT...
C'MON, GET IT TOGETHER!
ポロ Plop
LOOK! YOU DROPPED YOUR FRY!
HERE! PUT IT IN YOUR MOUTH!
Hurry, hurry.

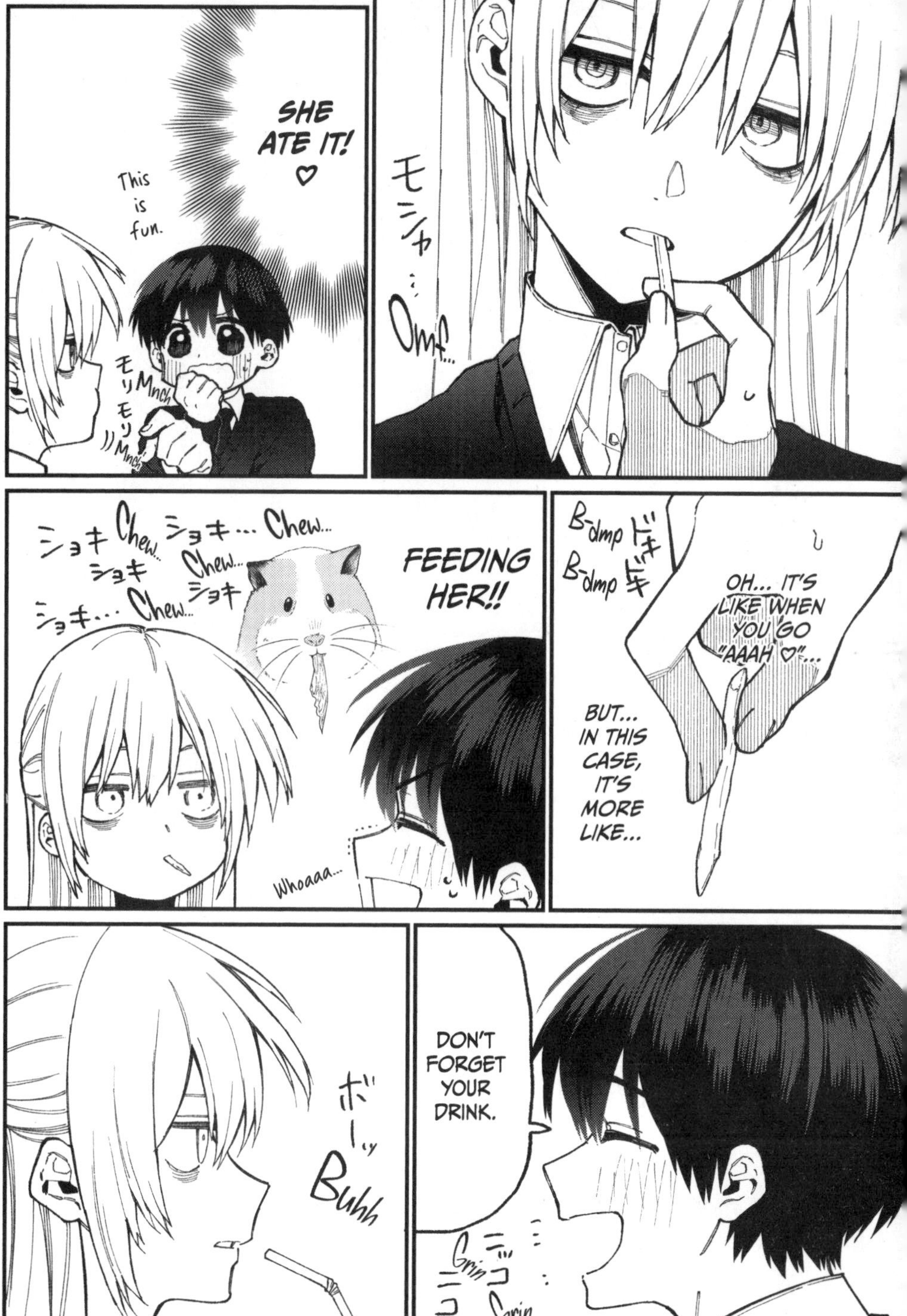
モシャ…
Omf…
SHE ATE IT! ♡
This is fun.
モリモリ
Mnch Mnch
B-dmp B-dmp
ドキ ドキ
OH… IT'S LIKE WHEN YOU GO "AAAH ♡"…
BUT… IN THIS CASE, IT'S MORE LIKE…
FEEDING HER!!
ショキ… Chew…
ショキ Chew…
ショキ Chew…
ショキ… Chew…
Whoaaa…
DON'T FORGET YOUR DRINK.
ニコッ ニコ
Grin Grin
ボーッ
Buhh

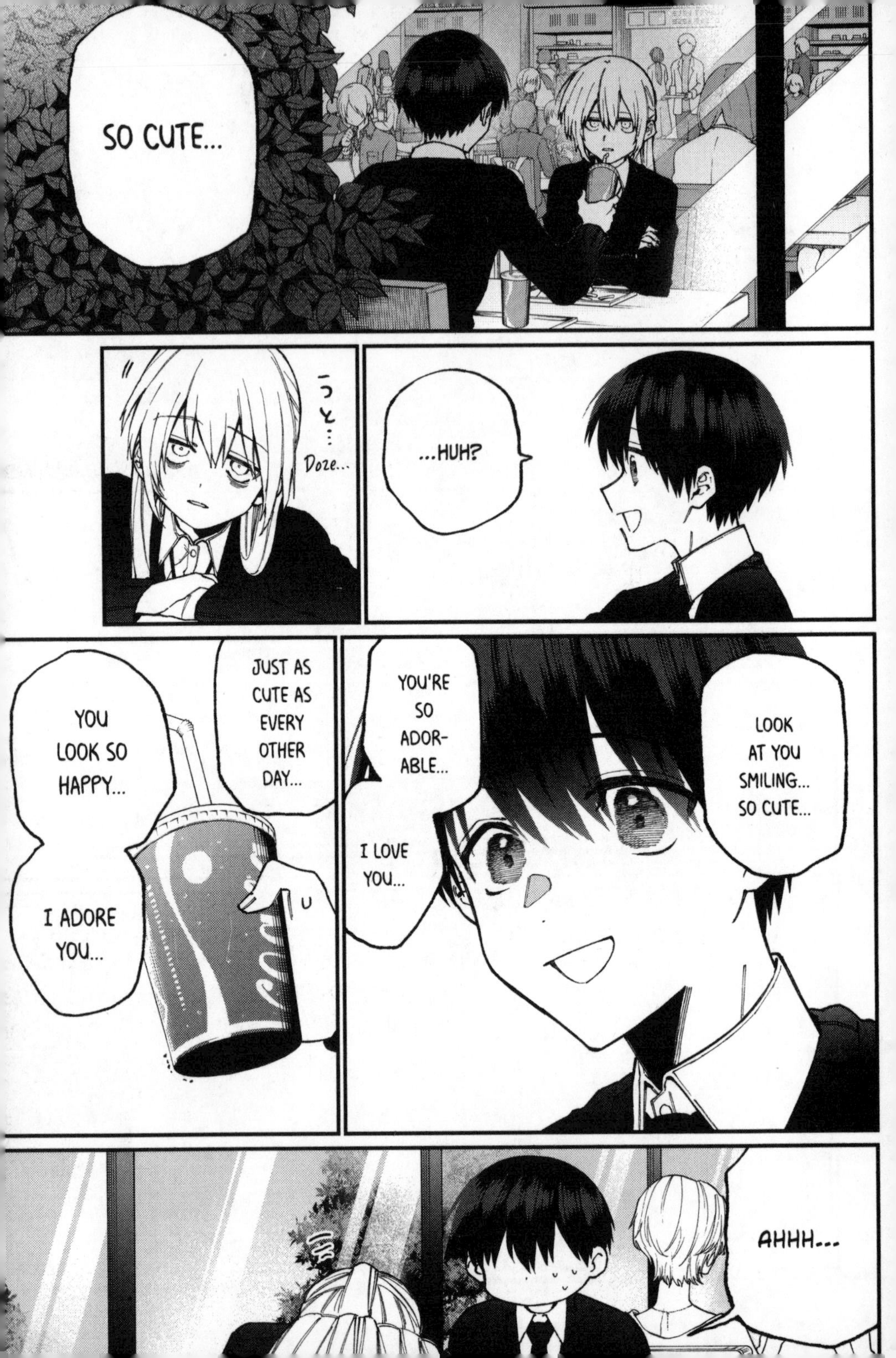
SO CUTE...
...HUH?
うと…
Doze...
LOOK AT YOU SMILING... SO CUTE...
YOU'RE SO ADOR-ABLE...
I LOVE YOU...
JUST AS CUTE AS EVERY OTHER DAY...
YOU LOOK SO HAPPY...
I ADORE YOU...
AHHH...

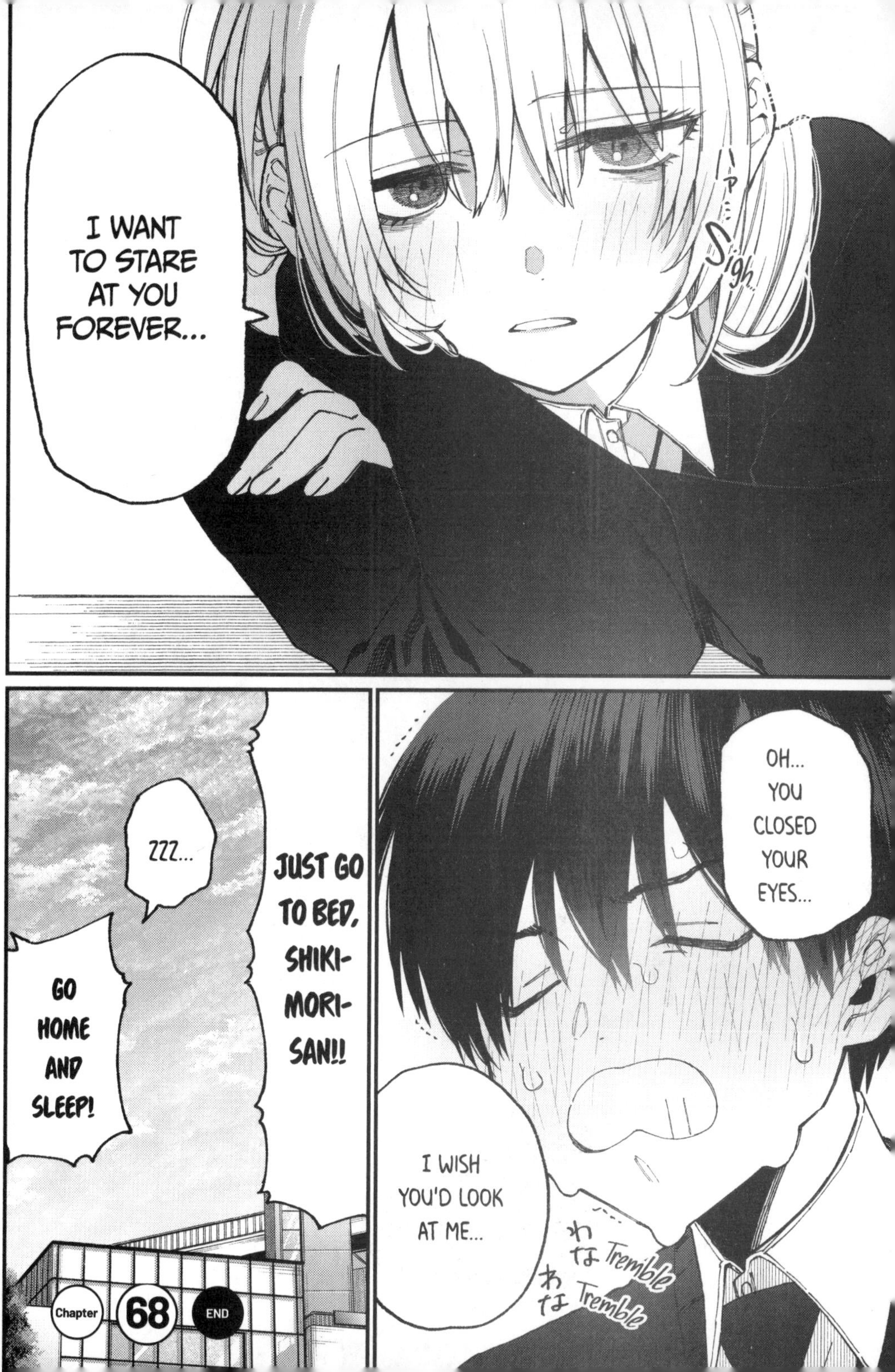
I WANT TO STARE AT YOU FOREVER...
Sigh...
OH... YOU CLOSED YOUR EYES...
I WISH YOU'D LOOK AT ME...
わな Tremble
わな Tremble
JUST GO TO BED, SHIKIMORI-SAN!!
ZZZ...
GO HOME AND SLEEP!
Chapter 68 END

SHIKIMORI'S not just a cutie

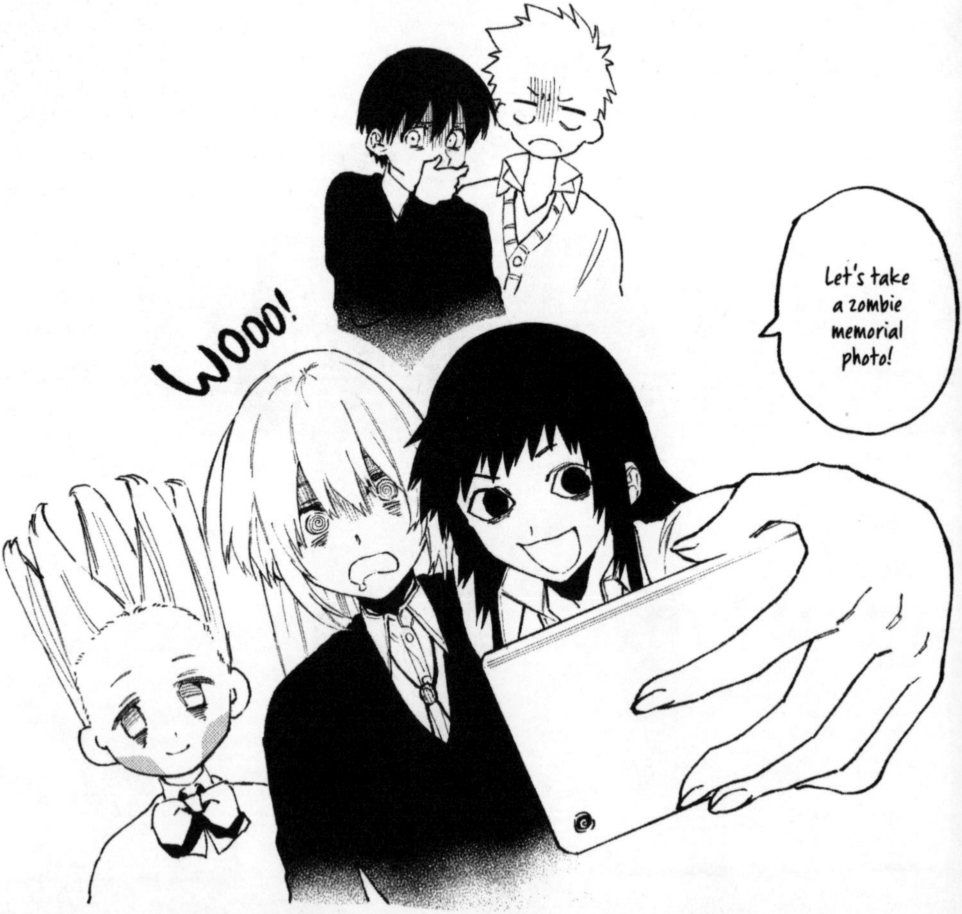
Let's take a zombie memorial photo!
WOOO!

SHIKIMORI'S
Not just a cutie

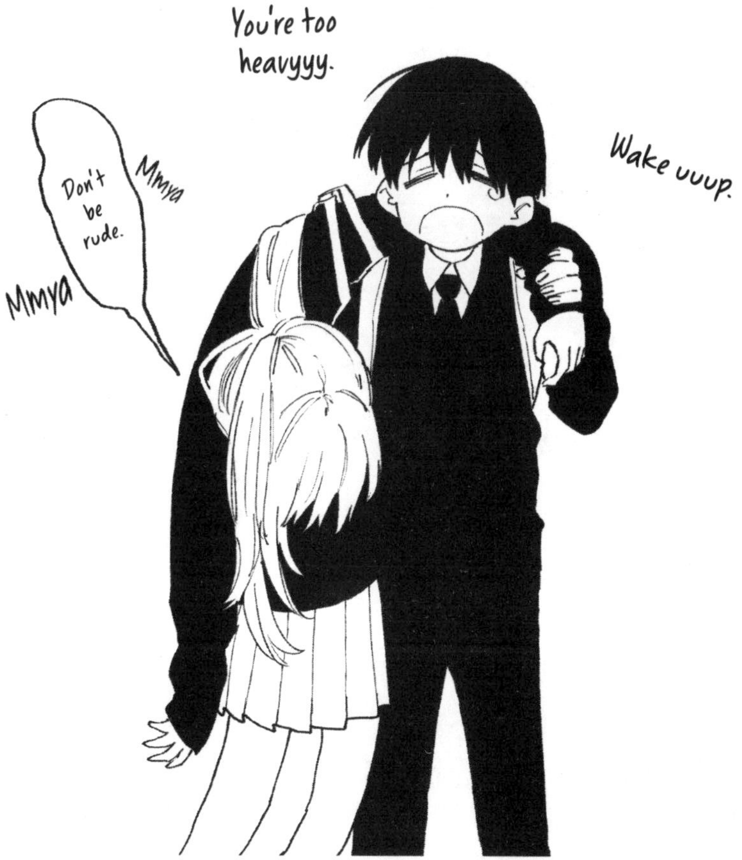

You're too heavyyy.
Wake uuup.
Mmya
Don't be rude.
Mmya

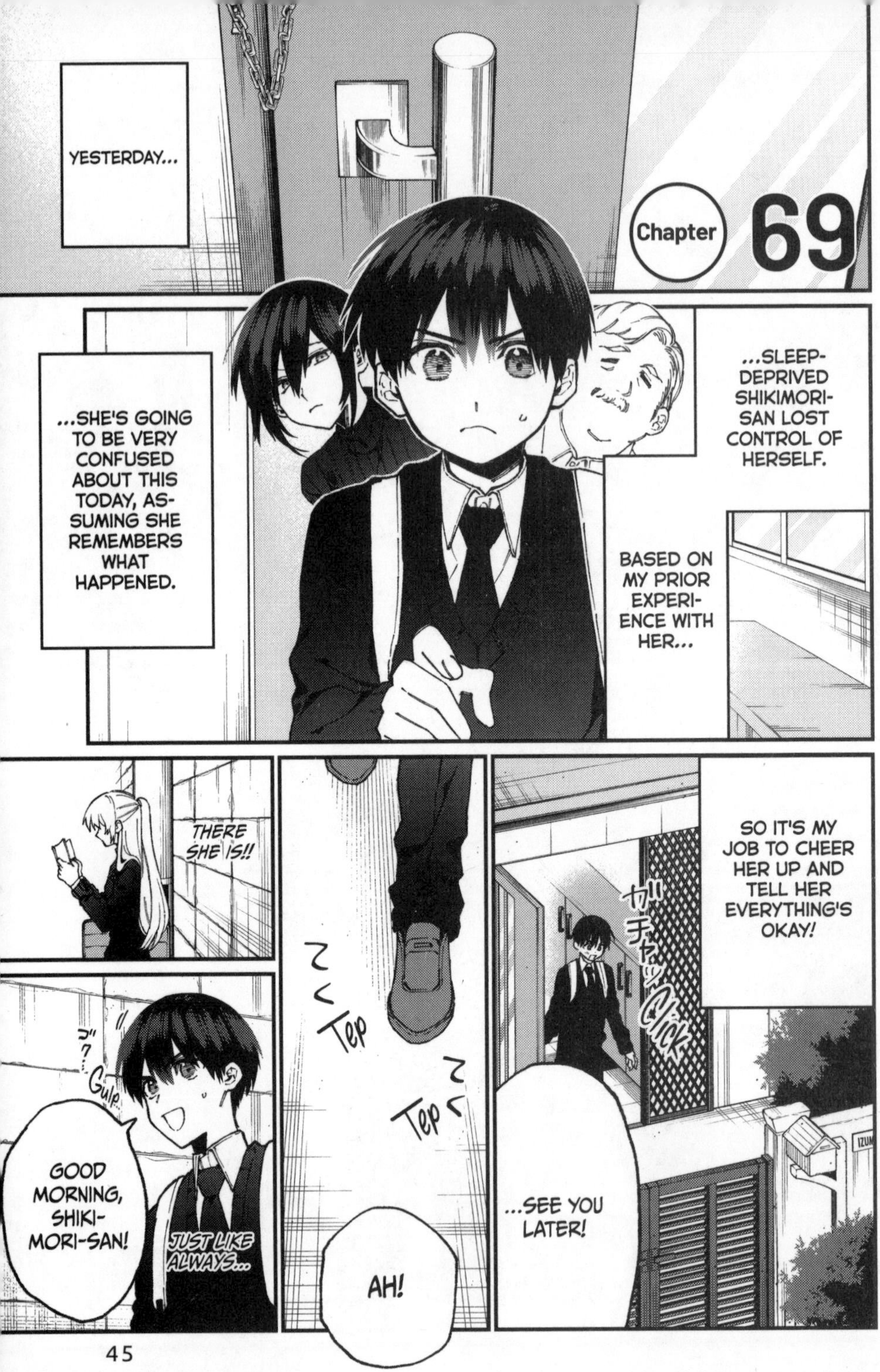
Chapter 69
YESTERDAY...
...SLEEP-DEPRIVED SHIKIMORI-SAN LOST CONTROL OF HERSELF.
BASED ON MY PRIOR EXPERIENCE WITH HER...
...SHE'S GOING TO BE VERY CONFUSED ABOUT THIS TODAY, AS-SUMING SHE REMEMBERS WHAT HAPPENED.
SO IT'S MY JOB TO CHEER HER UP AND TELL HER EVERYTHING'S OKAY!
CLICK
...SEE YOU LATER!
AH!
Tep
Tep
THERE SHE IS!!
Gulp
GOOD MORNING, SHIKI-MORI-SAN!
JUST LIKE ALWAYS...

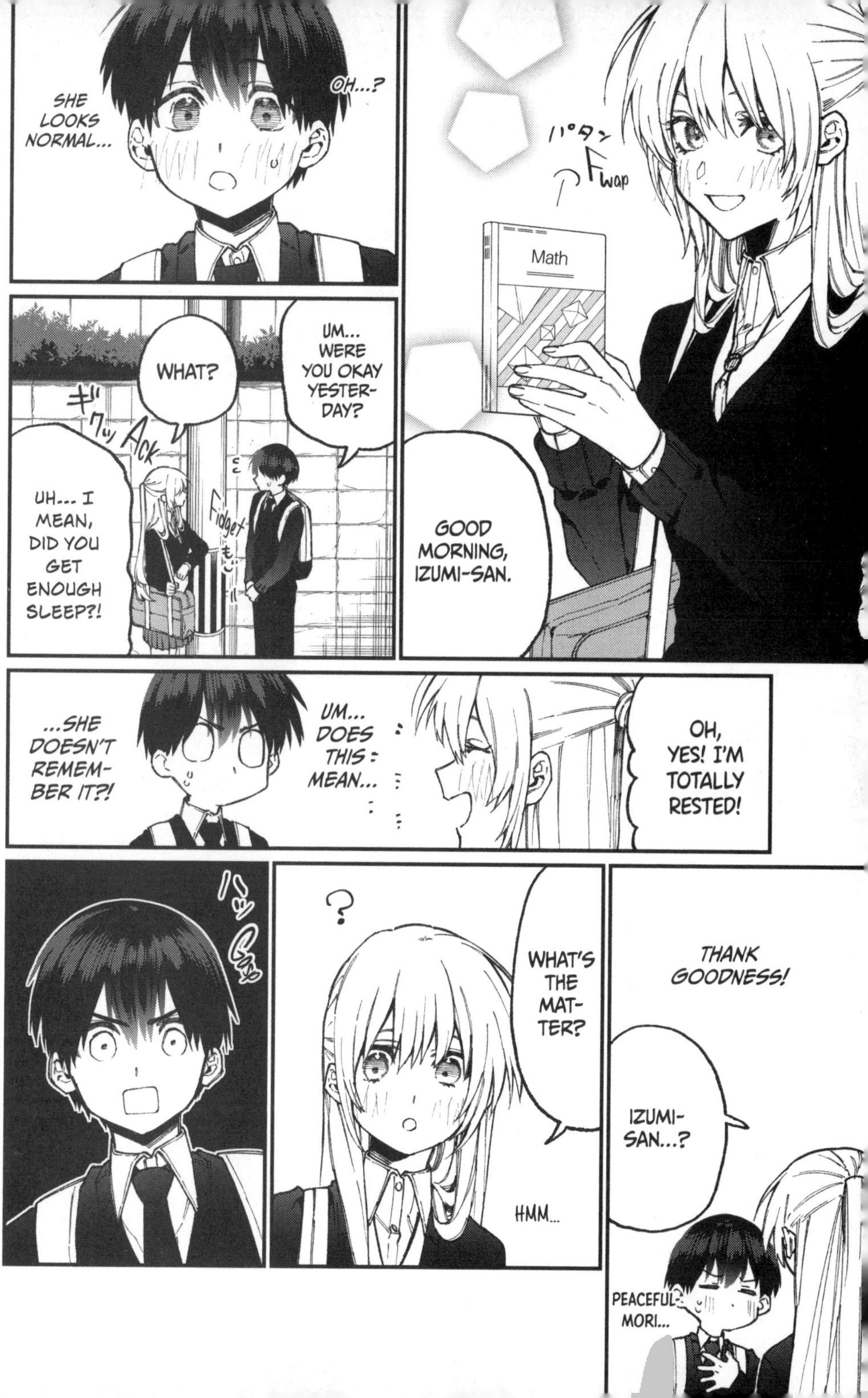

パタン
Fwap
Math
GOOD MORNING, IZUMI-SAN.
OH...?
SHE LOOKS NORMAL...
UM... WERE YOU OKAY YESTER-DAY?
WHAT?
ギクッ
Ack
UH... I MEAN, DID YOU GET ENOUGH SLEEP?!
Fidget
もじ
OH, YES! I'M TOTALLY RESTED!
UM... DOES THIS MEAN...
...SHE DOESN'T REMEMBER IT?!
THANK GOODNESS!
IZUMI-SAN...?
PEACEFUL-MORI...
WHAT'S THE MAT-TER?
?
HMM...
ハッ

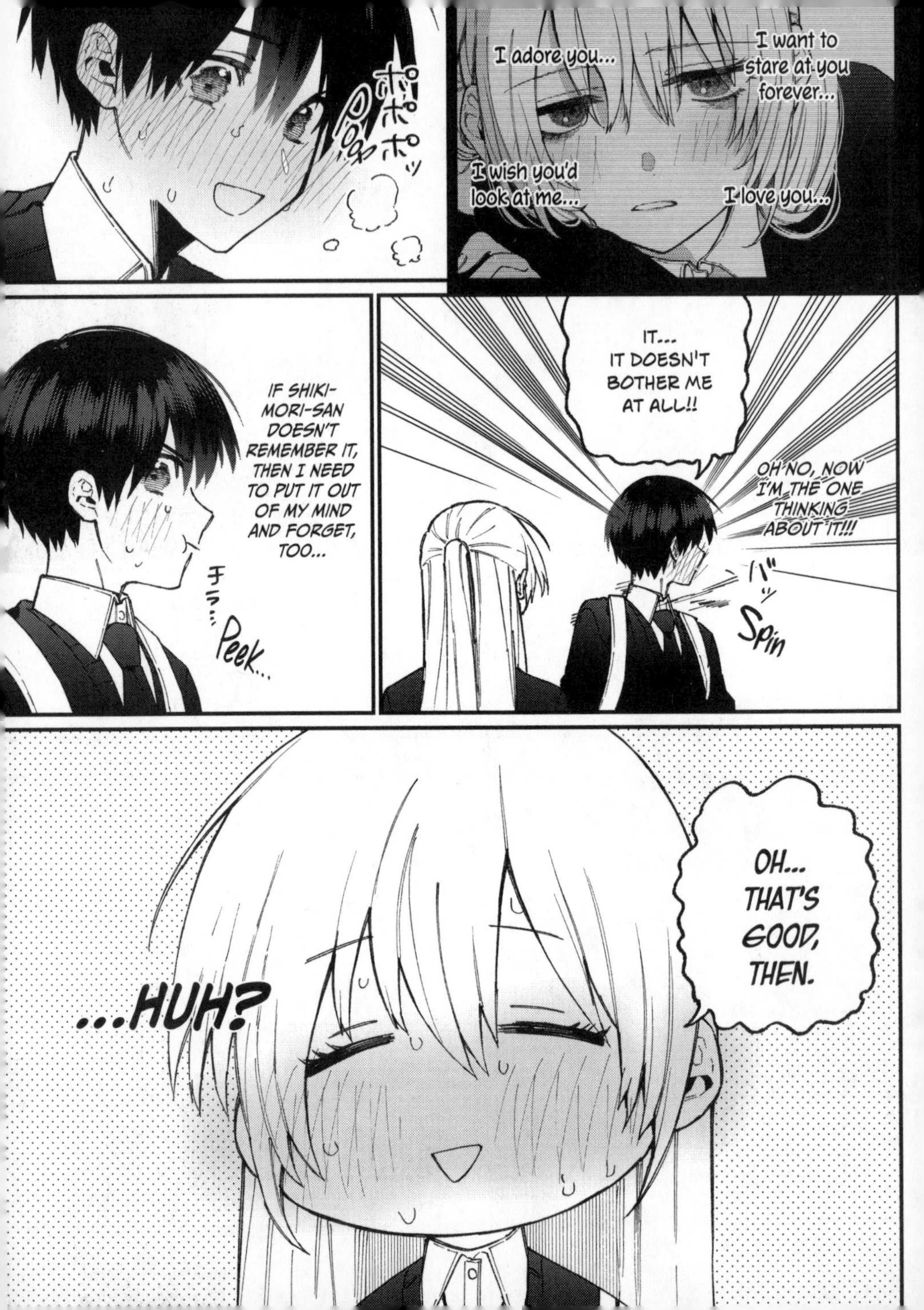

I want to stare at you forever...
I adore you...
I love you...
I wish you'd look at me...
ポポポッ
Pop
IT... IT DOESN'T BOTHER ME AT ALL!!
OH NO, NOW I'M THE ONE THINKING ABOUT IT!!!
バッ
Spin
IF SHIKIMORI-SAN DOESN'T REMEMBER IT, THEN I NEED TO PUT IT OUT OF MY MIND AND FORGET, TOO...
チラ...
Peek...
OH... THAT'S GOOD, THEN.
...HUH?

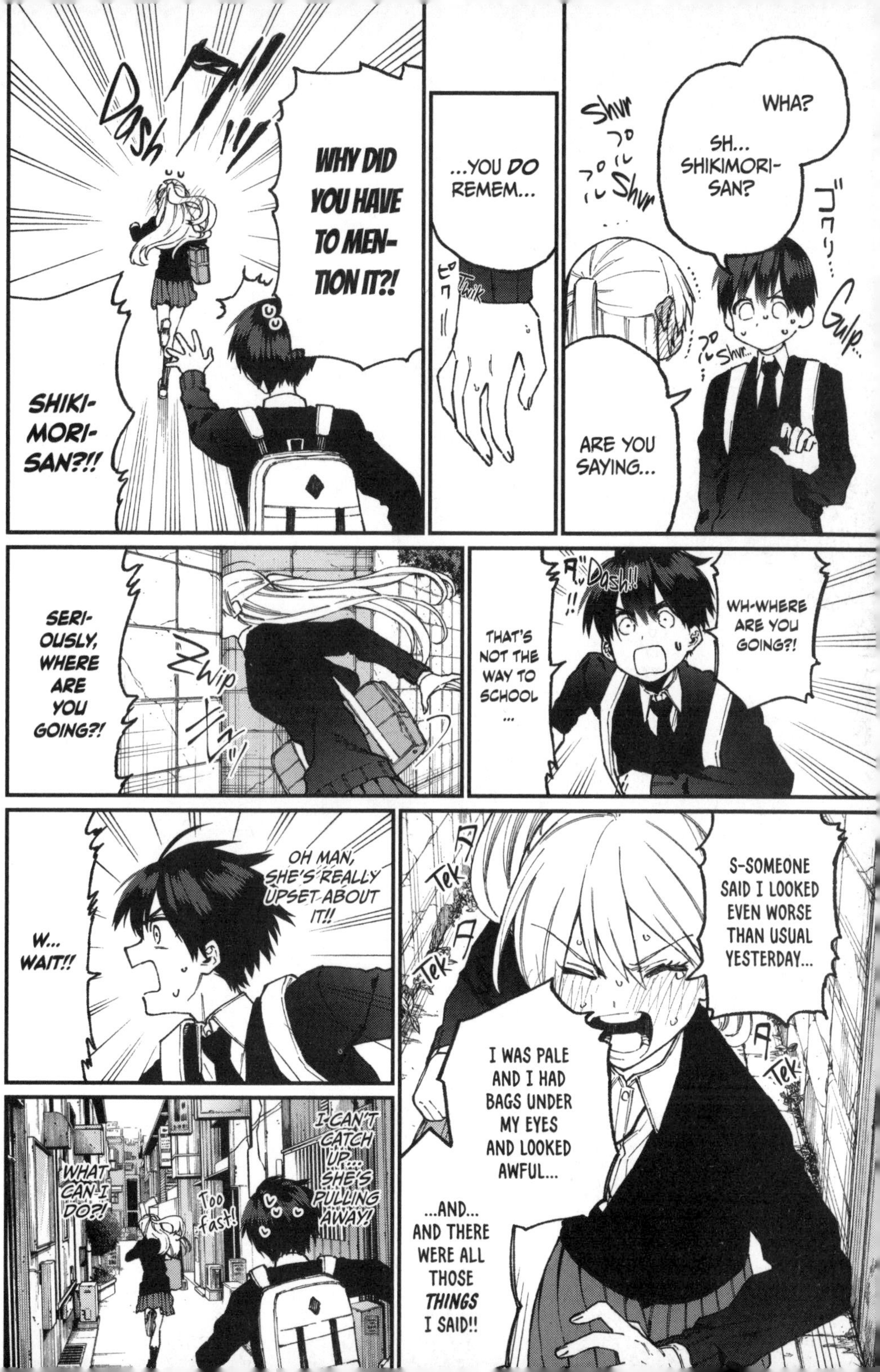

WHA?
SH... SHIKIMORI-SAN?
Shvr
Shvr
Gulp...
Shvr...
ARE YOU SAYING...
...YOU DO REMEM...
Twik
Dash
WHY DID YOU HAVE TO MEN-TION IT?!
SHIKI-MORI-SAN?!!
Dash!!
WH-WHERE ARE YOU GOING?!
THAT'S NOT THE WAY TO SCHOOL ...
Zwip
SERI-OUSLY, WHERE ARE YOU GOING?!
Tek
Tek
S-SOMEONE SAID I LOOKED EVEN WORSE THAN USUAL YESTERDAY...
Tek
I WAS PALE AND I HAD BAGS UNDER MY EYES AND LOOKED AWFUL...
...AND... AND THERE WERE ALL THOSE THINGS I SAID!!
OH MAN, SHE'S REALLY UPSET ABOUT IT!!
W... WAIT!!
I CAN'T CATCH UP... SHE'S PULLING AWAY!
Too fast!
WHAT CAN I DO?!

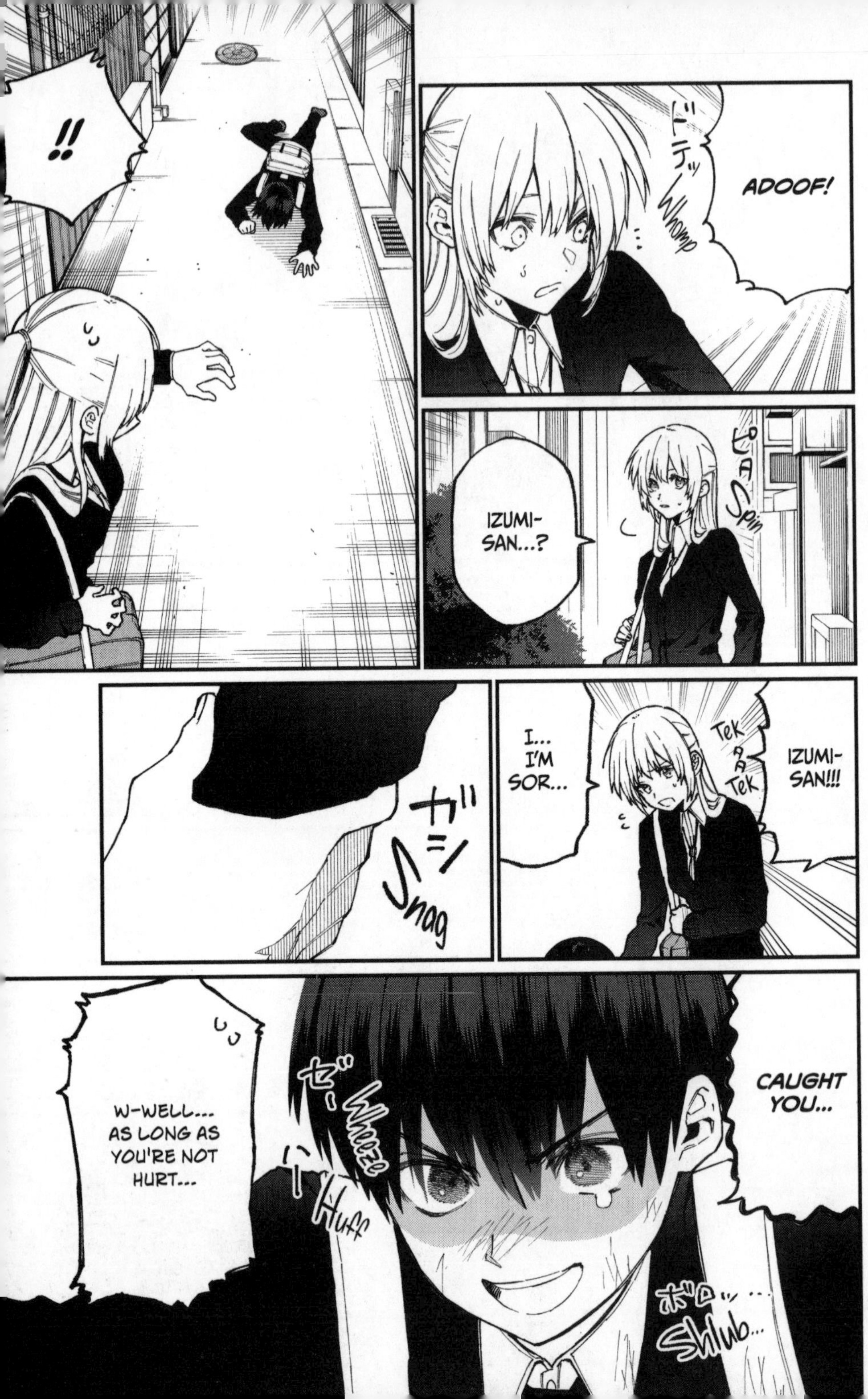
ドテッ
Whomp
ADOOF!
ピタ
Spin
IZUMI-SAN...?
!!
IZUMI-SAN!!!
Tek Tek
I... I'M SOR...
ガシ
Snag
CAUGHT YOU...
ぜー
Wheeze
ハー
Huff
ボロッ...
Shlub...
W-WELL... AS LONG AS YOU'RE NOT HURT...

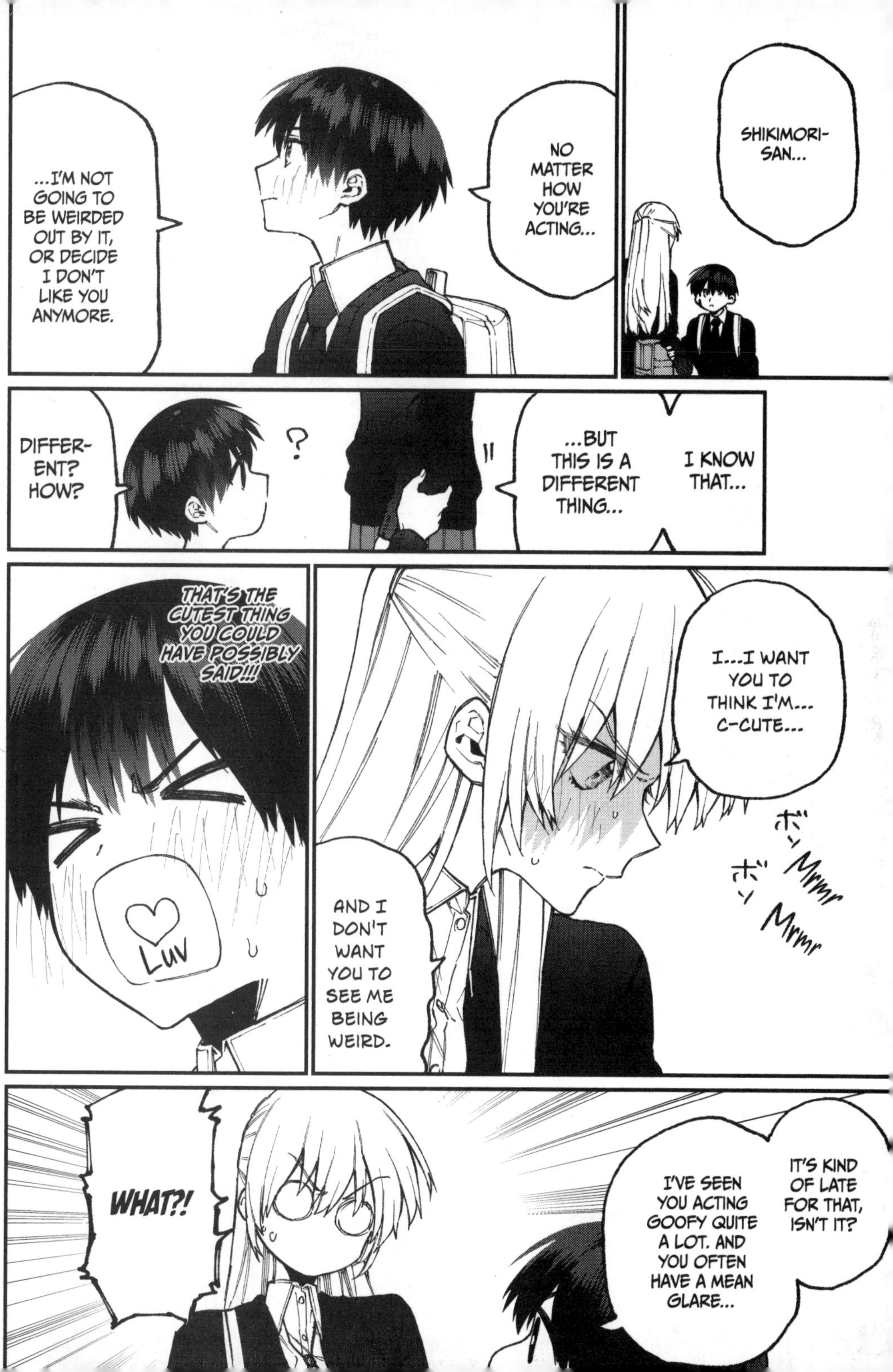
SHIKIMORI-SAN...
NO MATTER HOW YOU'RE ACTING...
...I'M NOT GOING TO BE WEIRDED OUT BY IT, OR DECIDE I DON'T LIKE YOU ANYMORE.
I KNOW THAT...
...BUT THIS IS A DIFFERENT THING...
DIFFER-ENT? HOW?
I...I WANT YOU TO THINK I'M... C-CUTE...
Mrmr
Mrmr
AND I DON'T WANT YOU TO SEE ME BEING WEIRD.
THAT'S THE CUTEST THING YOU COULD HAVE POSSIBLY SAID!!!
Luv
IT'S KIND OF LATE FOR THAT, ISN'T IT?
I'VE SEEN YOU ACTING GOOFY QUITE A LOT. AND YOU OFTEN HAVE A MEAN GLARE...
WHAT?!

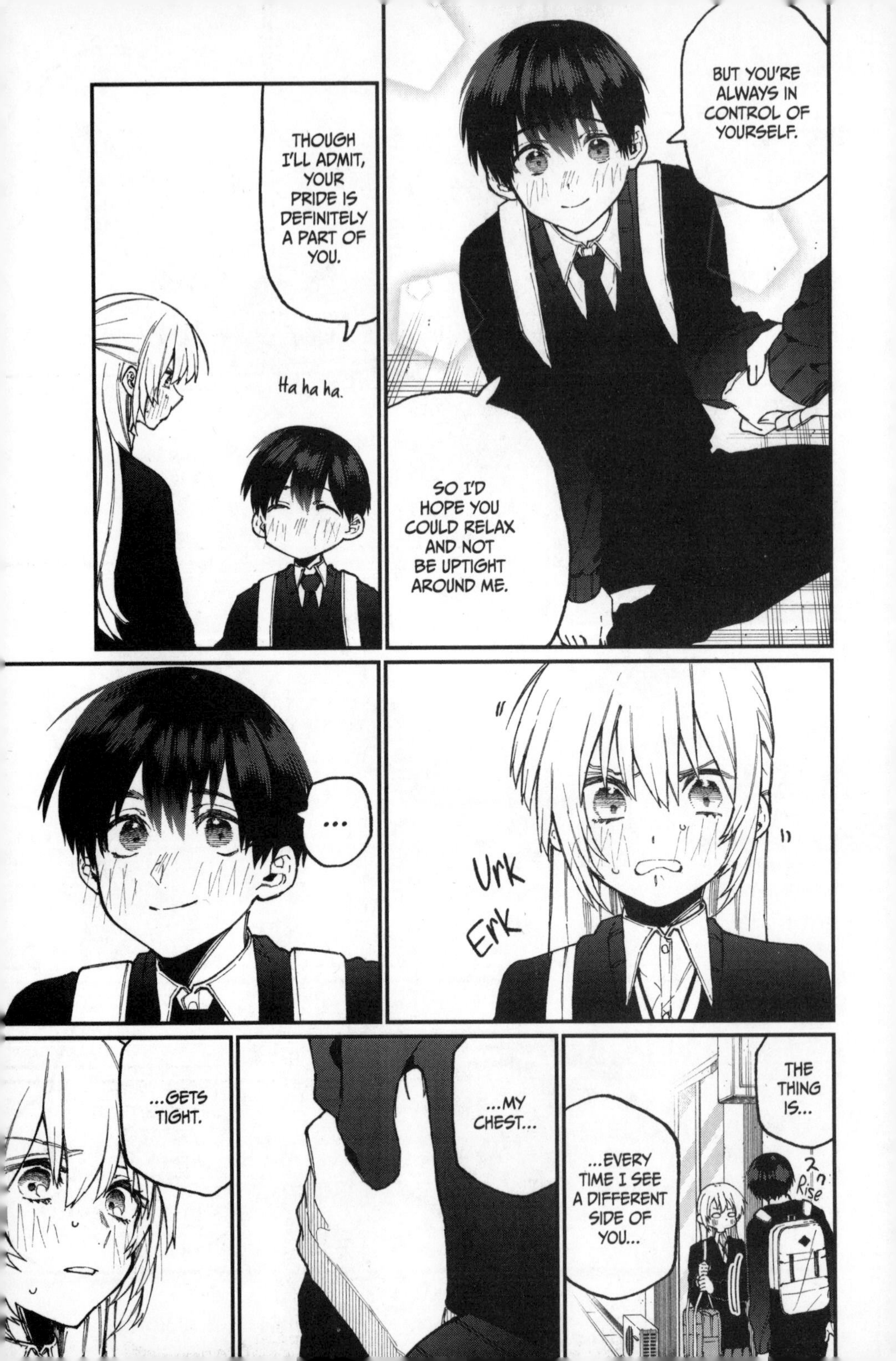
BUT YOU'RE ALWAYS IN CONTROL OF YOURSELF.
SO I'D HOPE YOU COULD RELAX AND NOT BE UPTIGHT AROUND ME.
THOUGH I'LL ADMIT, YOUR PRIDE IS DEFINITELY A PART OF YOU.
Ha ha ha.
Urk
Erk
...
THE THING IS...
Rise
...EVERY TIME I SEE A DIFFERENT SIDE OF YOU...
...MY CHEST...
...GETS TIGHT.

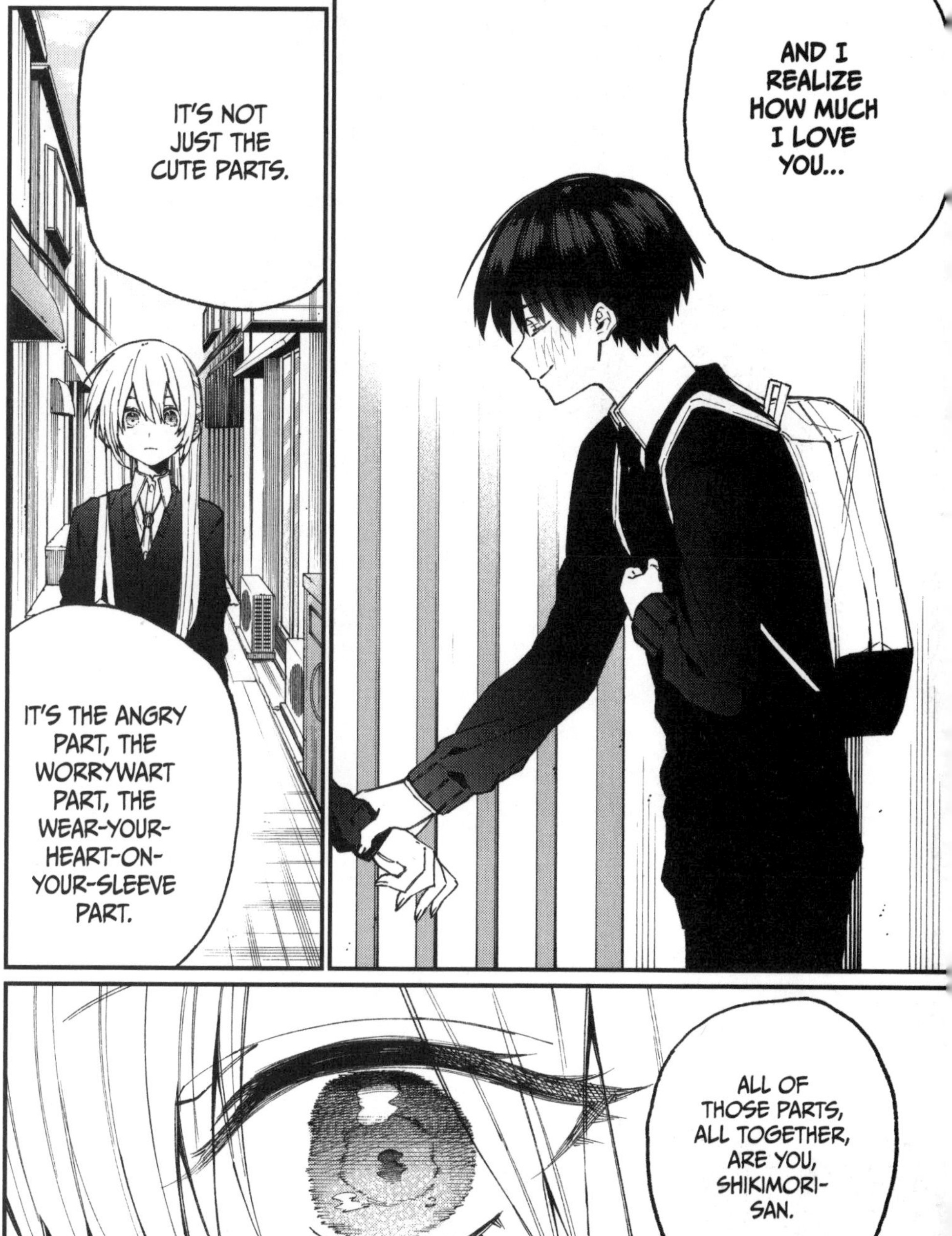
AND I REALIZE HOW MUCH I LOVE YOU...
IT'S NOT JUST THE CUTE PARTS.
IT'S THE ANGRY PART, THE WORRYWART PART, THE WEAR-YOUR-HEART-ON-YOUR-SLEEVE PART.
ALL OF THOSE PARTS, ALL TOGETHER, ARE YOU, SHIKIMORI-SAN.

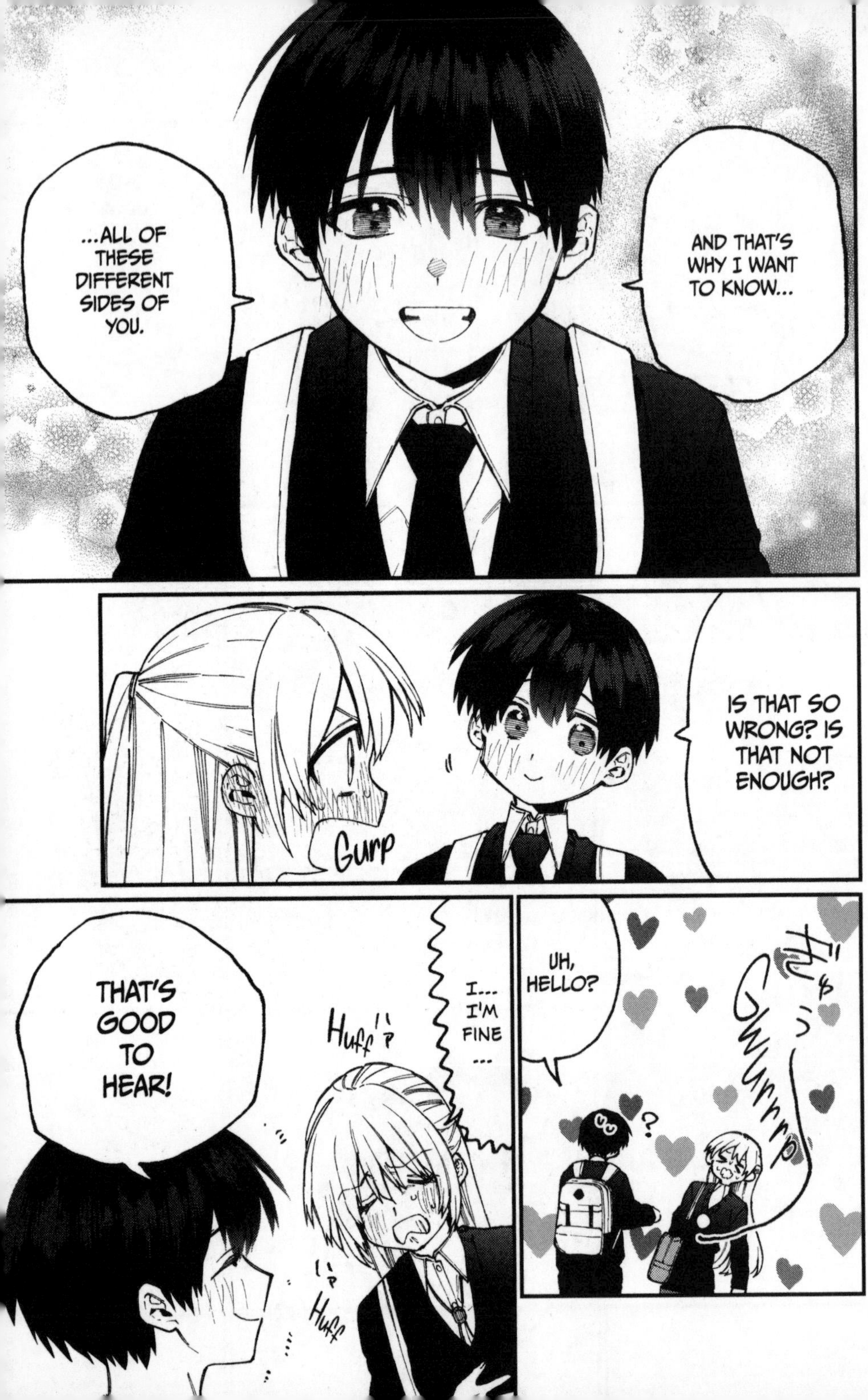
AND THAT'S WHY I WANT TO KNOW...
...ALL OF THESE DIFFERENT SIDES OF YOU.
IS THAT SO WRONG? IS THAT NOT ENOUGH?
Gurp
UH, HELLO?
GWurrrp
I... I'M FINE ...
Huff
THAT'S GOOD TO HEAR!
Huff

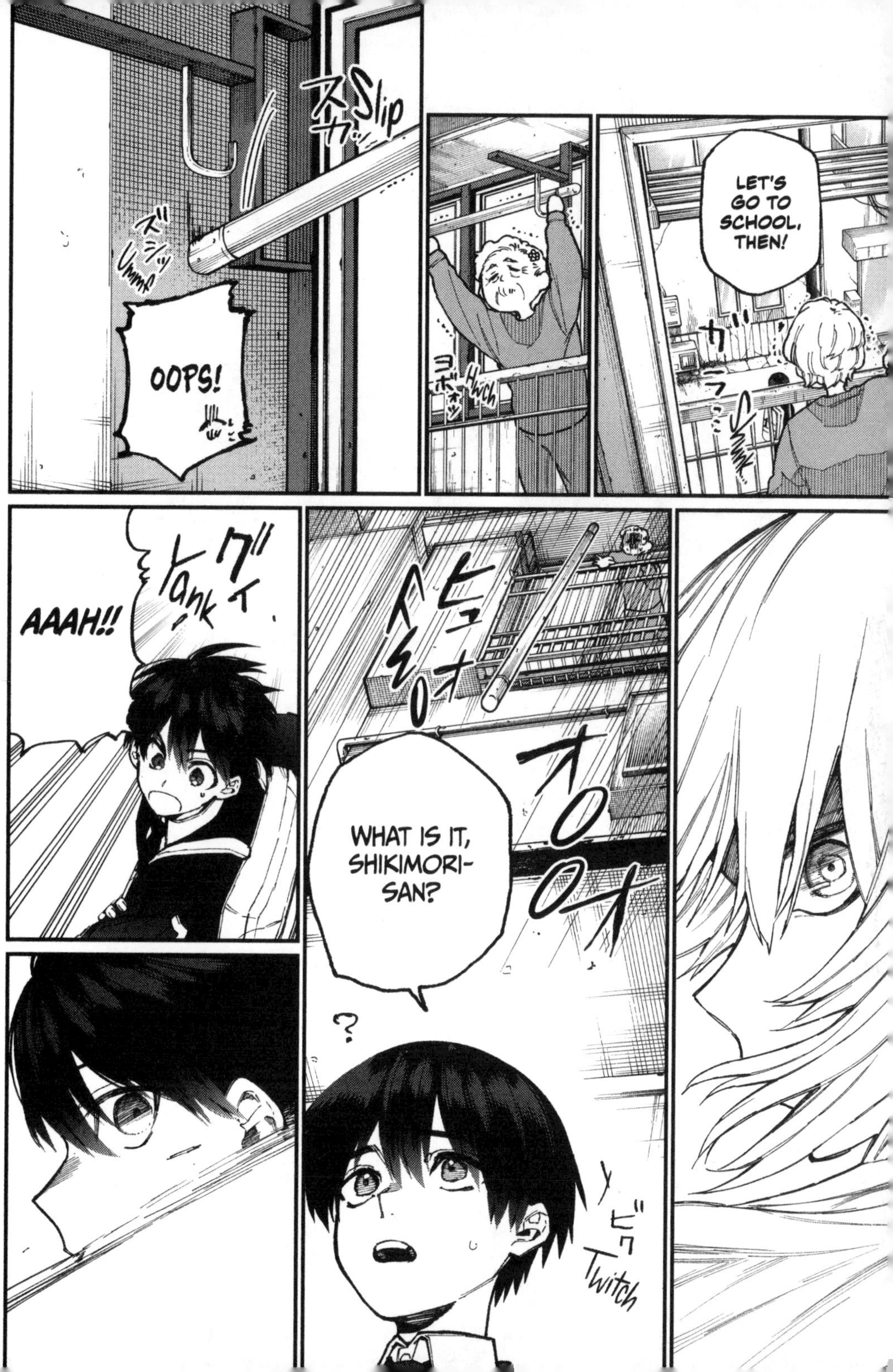
LET'S GO TO SCHOOL, THEN!
Slip
OOPS!
WHAT IS IT, SHIKIMORI-SAN?
?
Twitch
Yank
AAAH!!

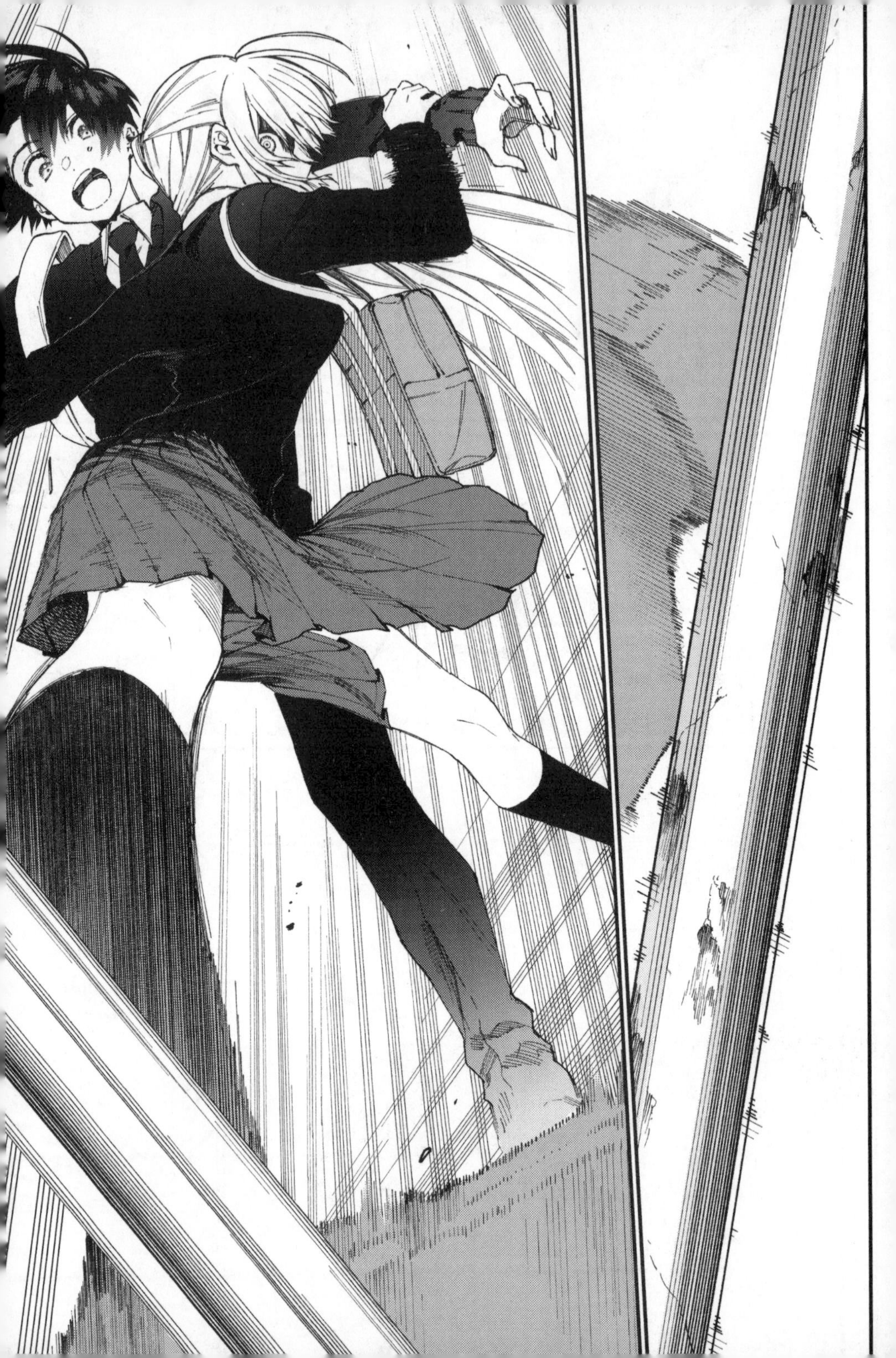

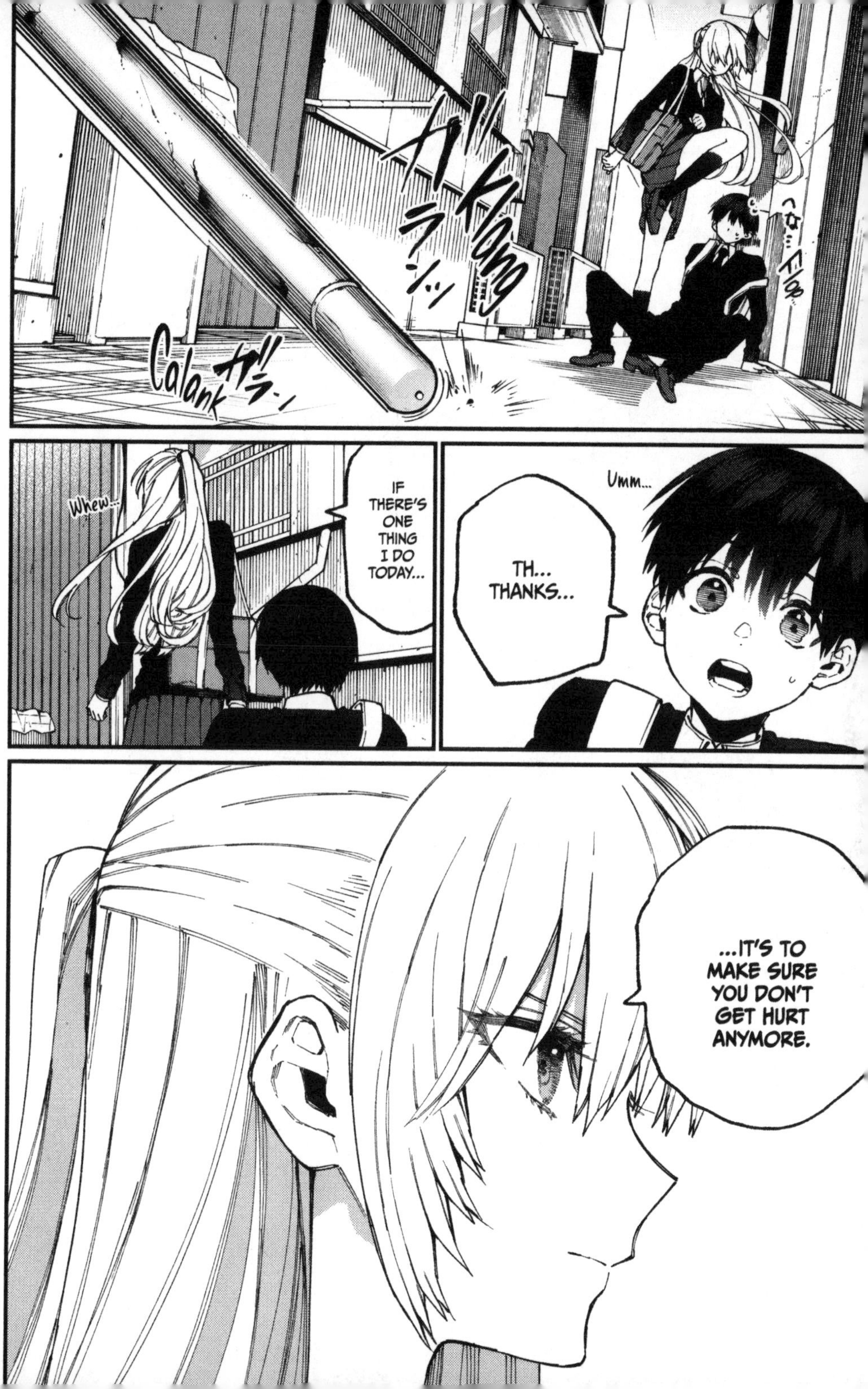

Flop
へな…
Klang
Calank
Umm...
TH... THANKS...
Whew...
IF THERE'S ONE THING I DO TODAY...
...IT'S TO MAKE SURE YOU DON'T GET HURT ANYMORE.

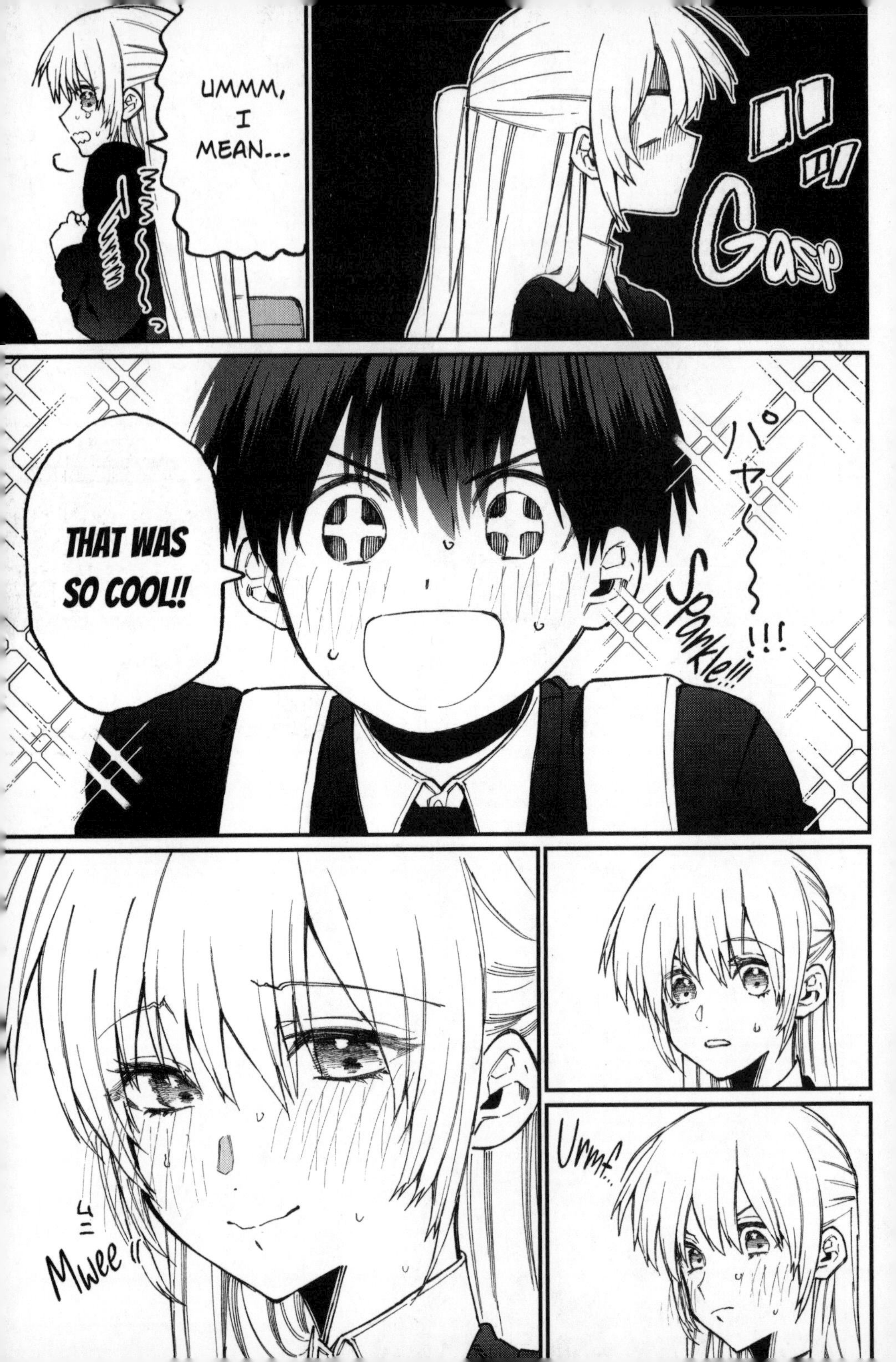
Gasp
UMMM, I MEAN...
Mm~ Turrrn~
パァ〜!!!
Sparkle!!!
THAT WAS SO COOL!!
Urmf..
ムニ
Mwee!!

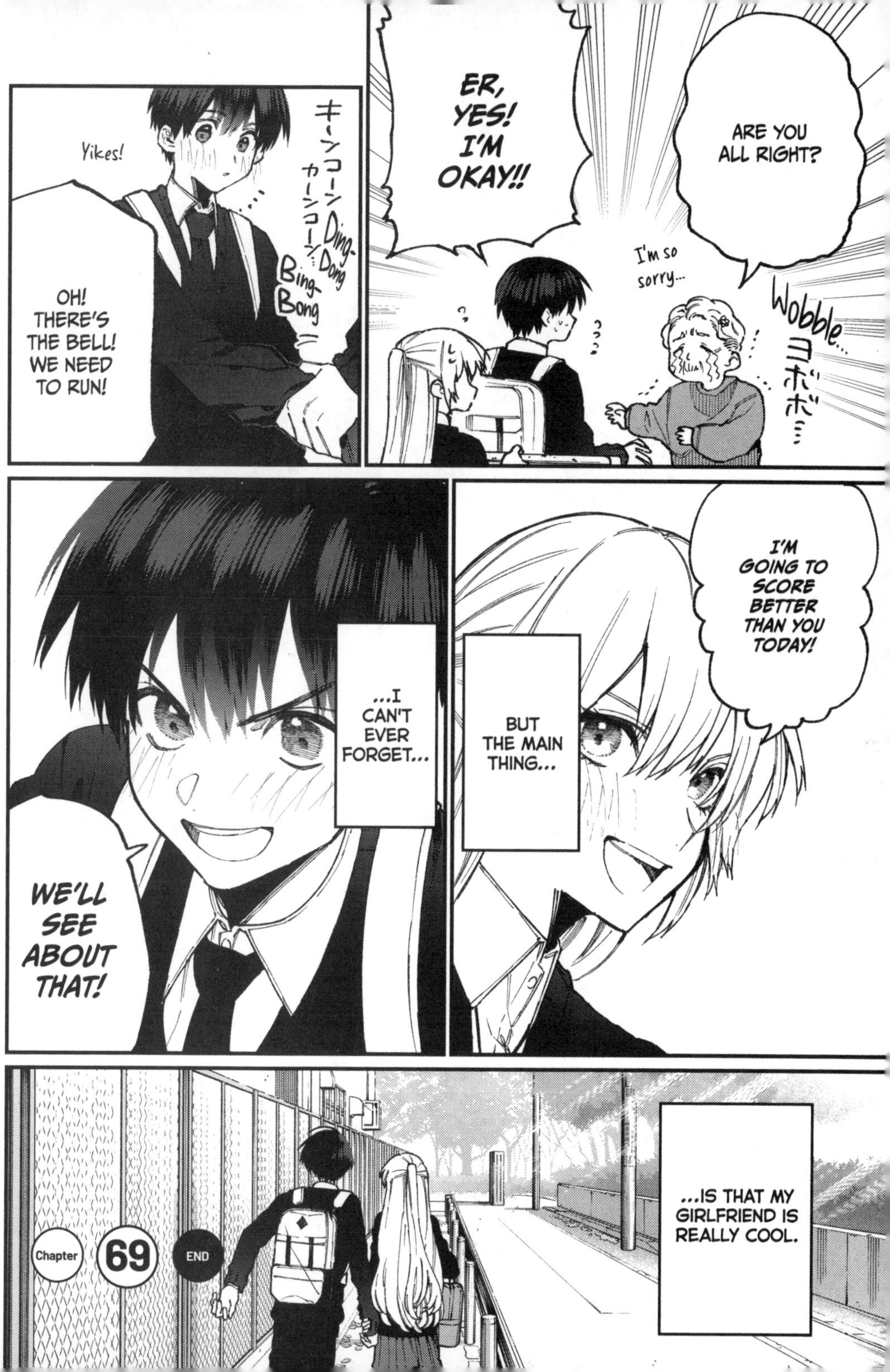
ARE YOU ALL RIGHT?
ER, YES! I'M OKAY!!
I'm so sorry...
Wobble...
ヨボボ…
キーンコーン
カーンコーン
Ding-Dong
Bing-Bong
Yikes!
OH! THERE'S THE BELL! WE NEED TO RUN!
I'M GOING TO SCORE BETTER THAN YOU TODAY!
BUT THE MAIN THING...
...I CAN'T EVER FORGET...
WE'LL SEE ABOUT THAT!
...IS THAT MY GIRLFRIEND IS REALLY COOL.
Chapter 69 END

SHIKIMORI'S not just a cutie

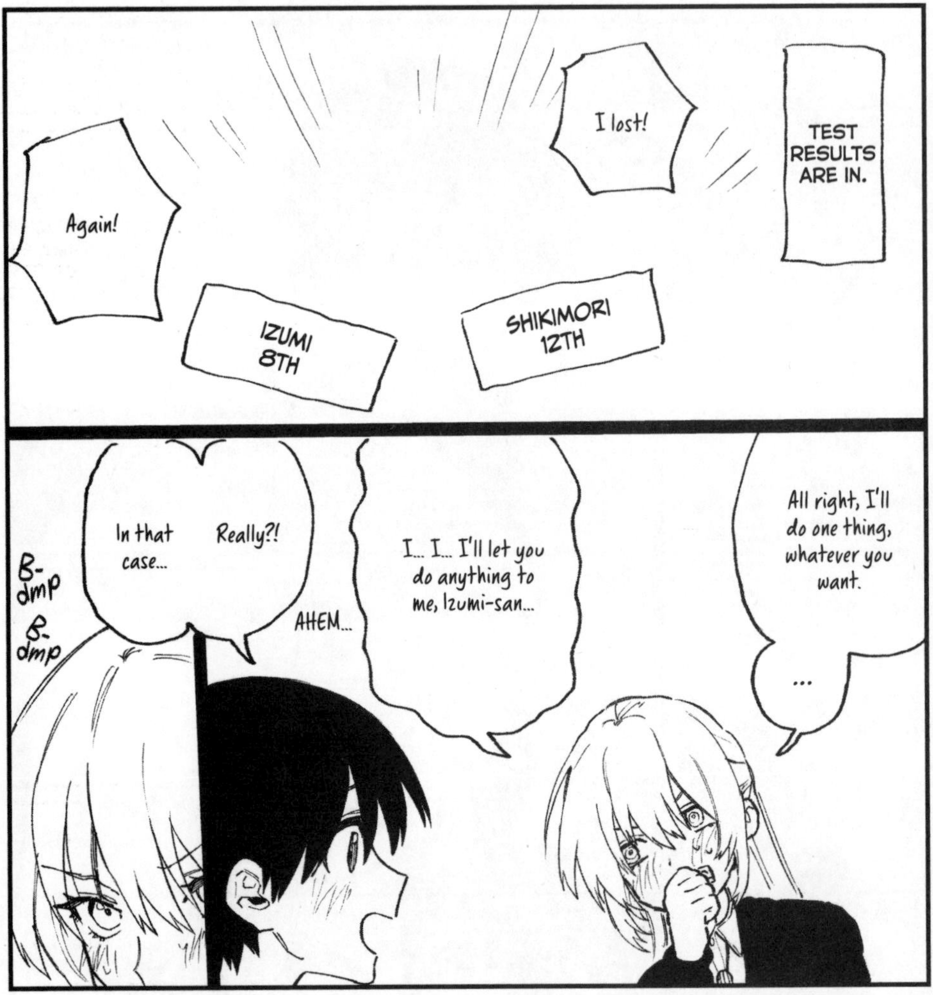
TEST RESULTS ARE IN.
I lost!
SHIKIMORI 12TH
Again!
IZUMI 8TH
All right, I'll do one thing, whatever you want.
...
I... I... I'll let you do anything to me, Izumi-san...
AHEM...
Really?!
In that case...
B-dmp
B-dmp

SHIKIMORI'S Not just a cutie

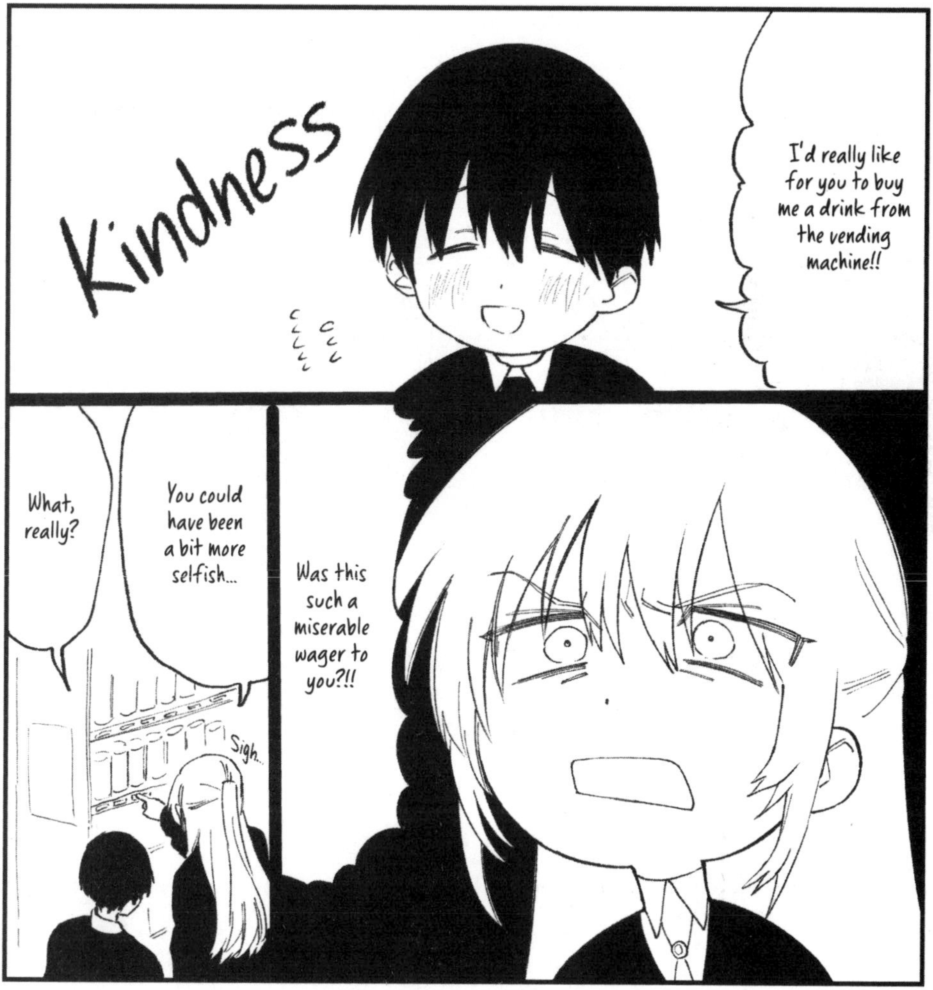
Kindness
I'd really like for you to buy me a drink from the vending machine!!
Was this such a miserable wager to you?!!
You could have been a bit more selfish...
What, really?
Sigh...

Chapter 70

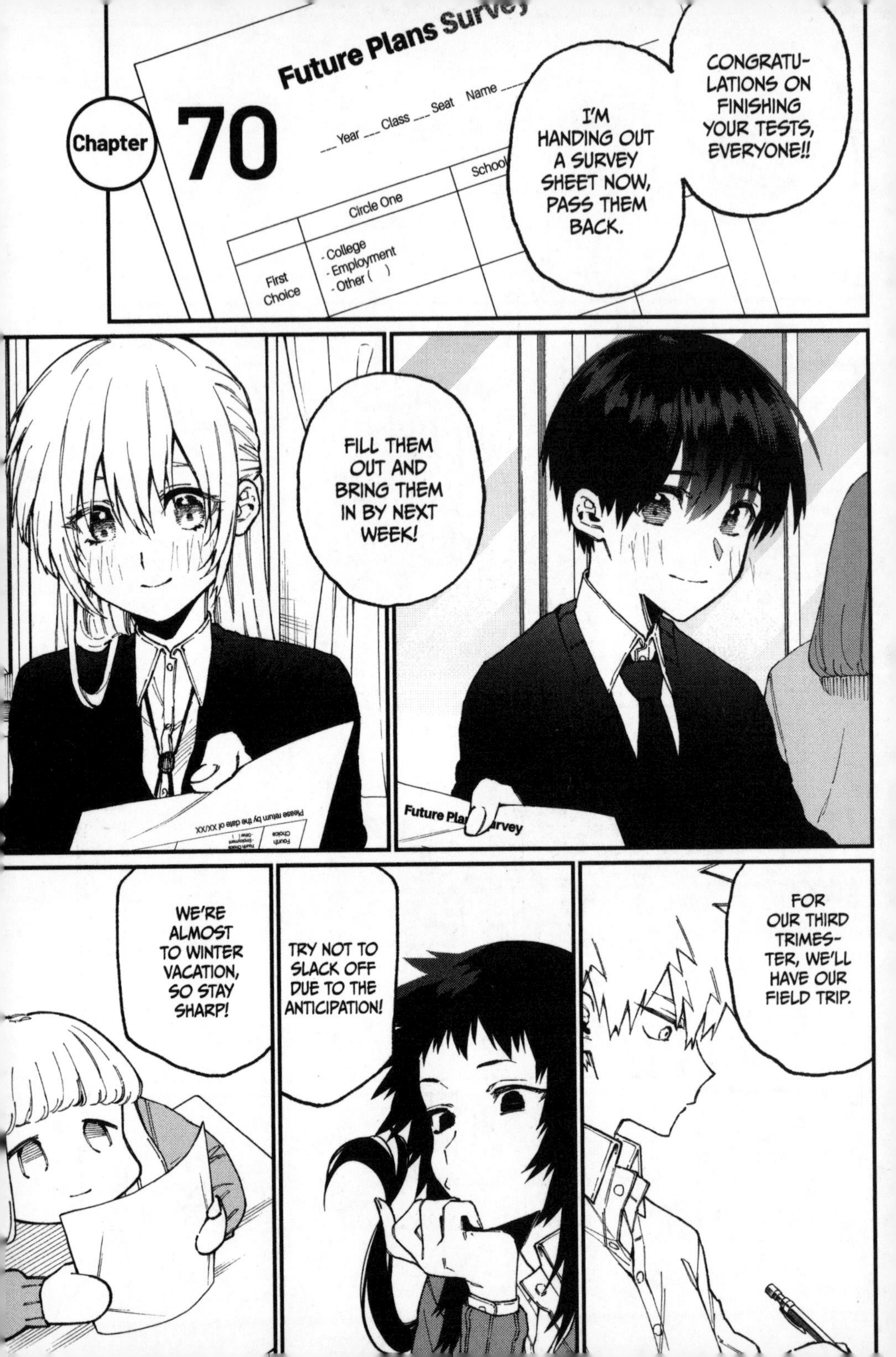
Chapter
70
Future Plans Survey
___ Year ___ Class ___ Seat Name
School
Circle One
First Choice
- College
- Employment
- Other ( )
CONGRATULATIONS ON FINISHING YOUR TESTS, EVERYONE!!
I'M HANDING OUT A SURVEY SHEET NOW, PASS THEM BACK.
Future Plans Survey
FILL THEM OUT AND BRING THEM IN BY NEXT WEEK!
Please return by the date of XX/XX
Fourth Choice
FOR OUR THIRD TRIMESTER, WE'LL HAVE OUR FIELD TRIP.
TRY NOT TO SLACK OFF DUE TO THE ANTICIPATION!
WE'RE ALMOST TO WINTER VACATION, SO STAY SHARP!

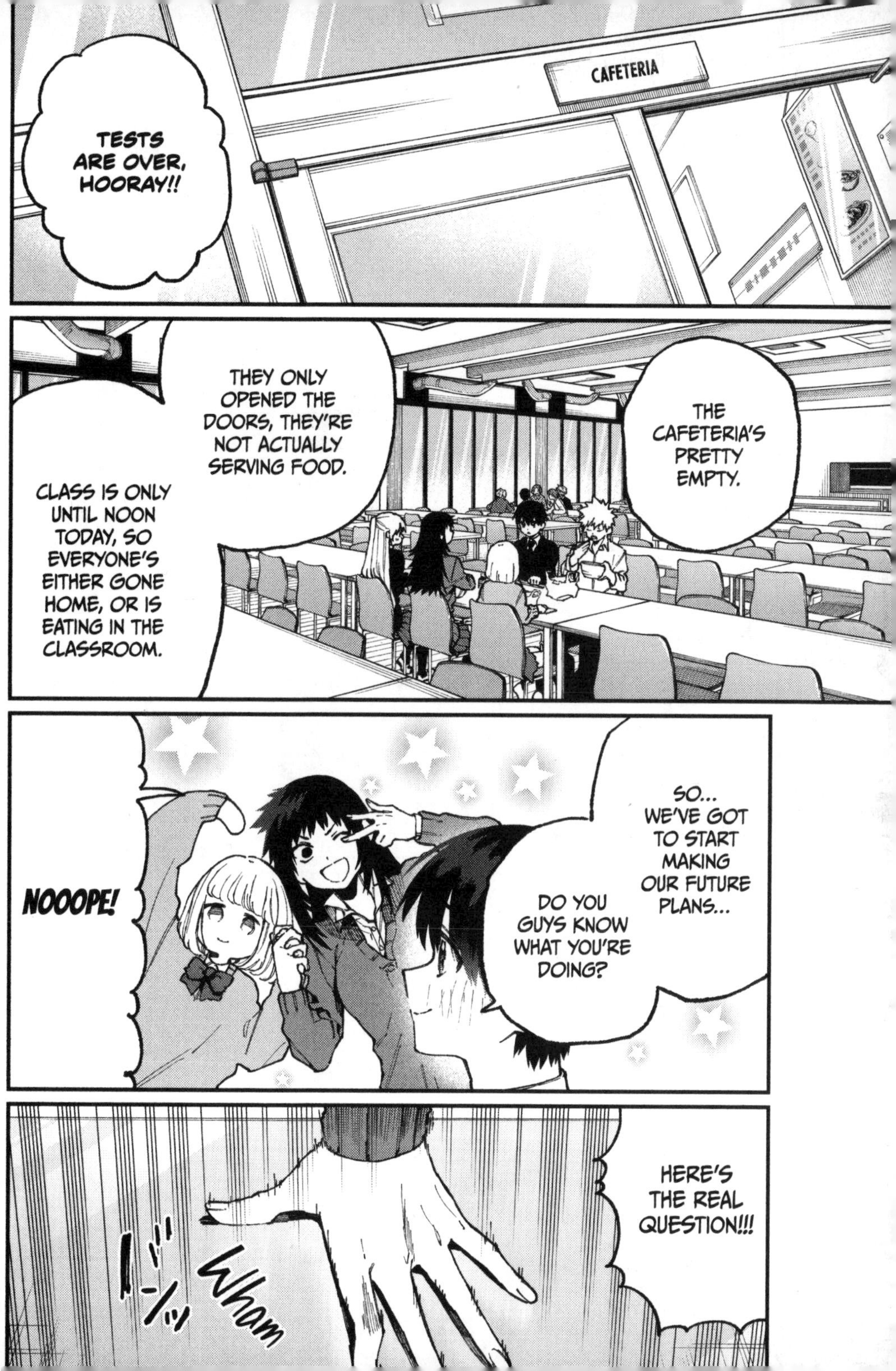
CAFETERIA
TESTS ARE OVER, HOORAY!!
THE CAFETERIA'S PRETTY EMPTY.
THEY ONLY OPENED THE DOORS, THEY'RE NOT ACTUALLY SERVING FOOD.
CLASS IS ONLY UNTIL NOON TODAY, SO EVERYONE'S EITHER GONE HOME, OR IS EATING IN THE CLASSROOM.
SO... WE'VE GOT TO START MAKING OUR FUTURE PLANS...
DO YOU GUYS KNOW WHAT YOU'RE DOING?
NOOOPE!
HERE'S THE REAL QUESTION!!!
Wham

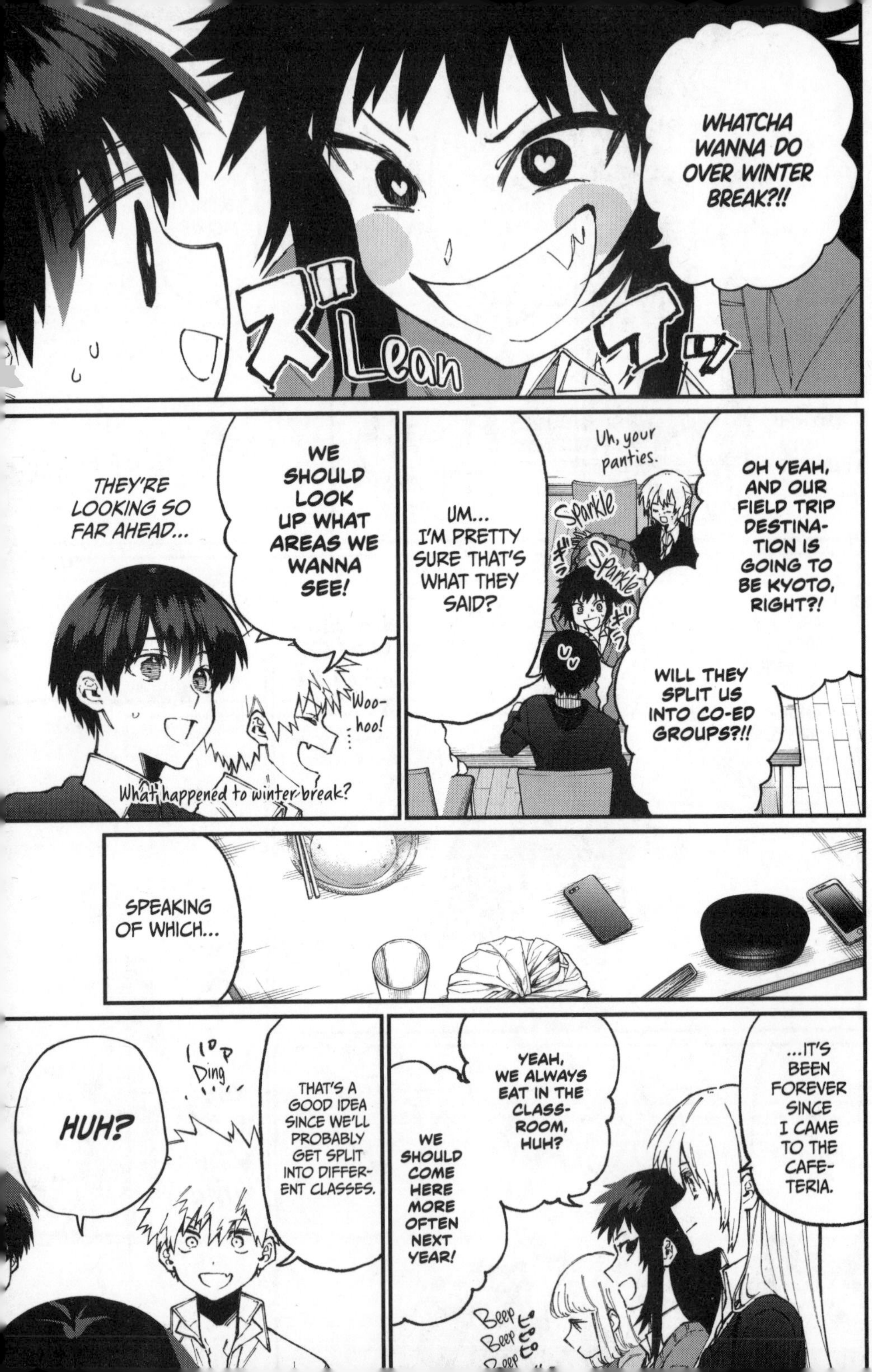
WHATCHA WANNA DO OVER WINTER BREAK?!!
Lean
OH YEAH, AND OUR FIELD TRIP DESTINATION IS GOING TO BE KYOTO, RIGHT?!
Uh, your panties.
Sparkle
Sparkle
WILL THEY SPLIT US INTO CO-ED GROUPS?!!
UM... I'M PRETTY SURE THAT'S WHAT THEY SAID?
WE SHOULD LOOK UP WHAT AREAS WE WANNA SEE!
THEY'RE LOOKING SO FAR AHEAD...
Woo-hoo!
What happened to winter break?
SPEAKING OF WHICH...
...IT'S BEEN FOREVER SINCE I CAME TO THE CAFETERIA.
YEAH, WE ALWAYS EAT IN THE CLASSROOM, HUH?
WE SHOULD COME HERE MORE OFTEN NEXT YEAR!
Beep
Beep
THAT'S A GOOD IDEA SINCE WE'LL PROBABLY GET SPLIT INTO DIFFERENT CLASSES.
Ding
HUH?

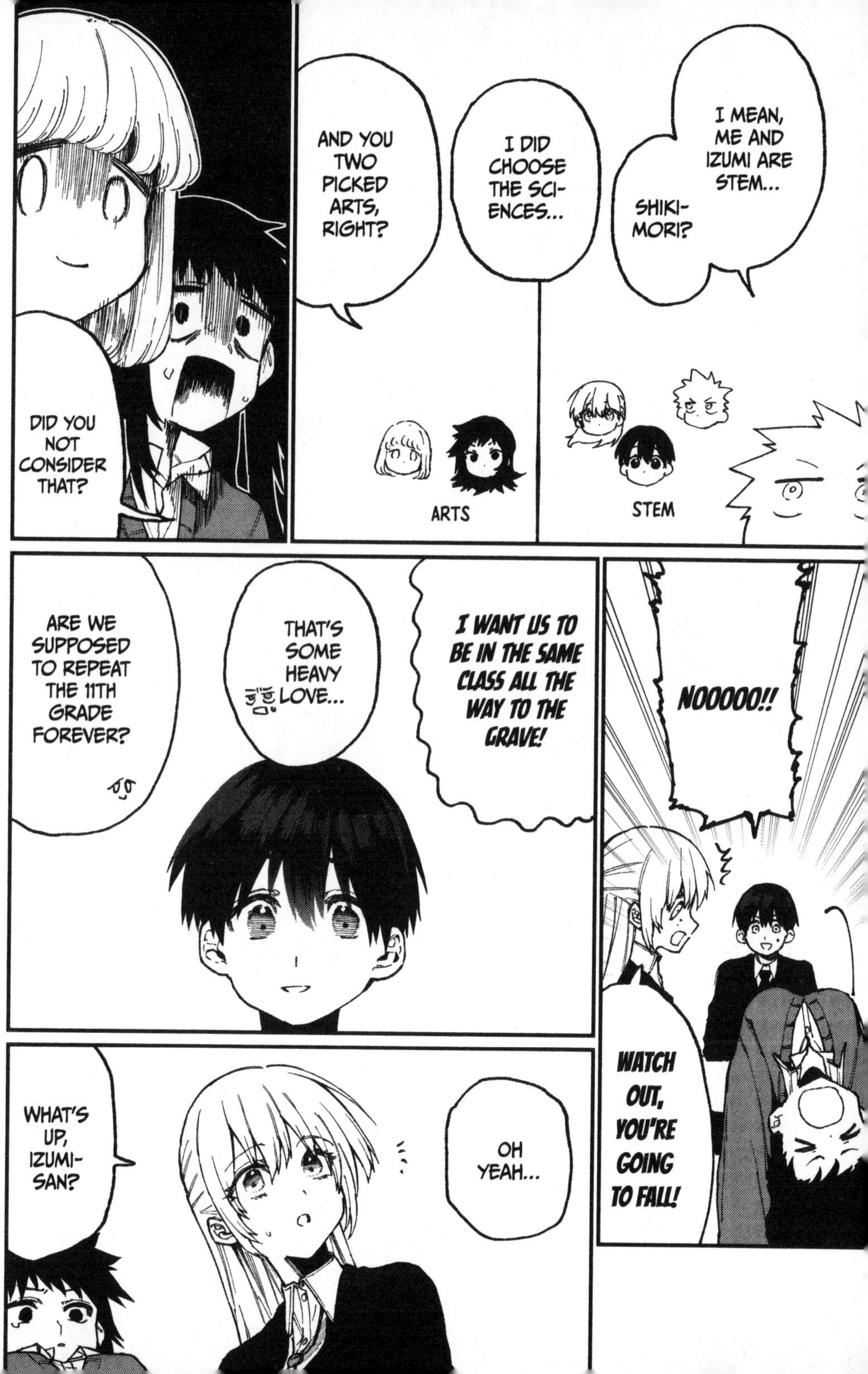
I MEAN, ME AND IZUMI ARE STEM...
SHIKI-MORI?
STEM
I DID CHOOSE THE SCI-ENCES...
AND YOU TWO PICKED ARTS, RIGHT?
ARTS
DID YOU NOT CONSIDER THAT?
NOOOOO!!
WATCH OUT, YOU'RE GOING TO FALL!
I WANT US TO BE IN THE SAME CLASS ALL THE WAY TO THE GRAVE!
THAT'S SOME HEAVY LOVE...
ARE WE SUPPOSED TO REPEAT THE 11TH GRADE FOREVER?
OH YEAH...
WHAT'S UP, IZUMI-SAN?

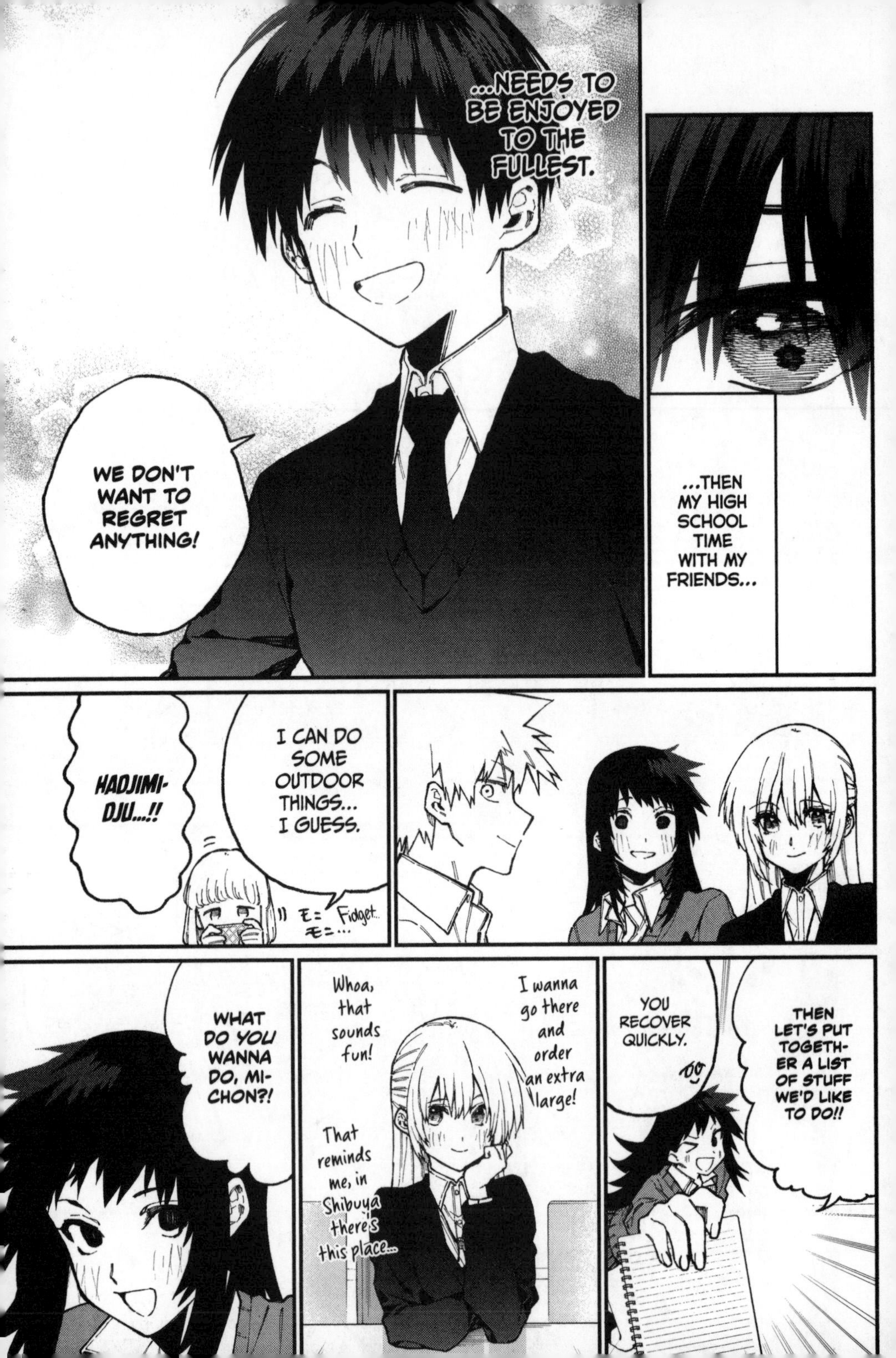
...THEN MY HIGH SCHOOL TIME WITH MY FRIENDS...
...NEEDS TO BE ENJOYED TO THE FULLEST.
WE DON'T WANT TO REGRET ANYTHING!
I CAN DO SOME OUTDOOR THINGS... I GUESS.
モニ モニ... Fidget...
HADJIMI-DJU...!!
THEN LET'S PUT TOGETH-ER A LIST OF STUFF WE'D LIKE TO DO!!
YOU RECOVER QUICKLY.
I wanna go there and order an extra large!
Whoa, that sounds fun!
That reminds me, in Shibuya there's this place...
WHAT DO YOU WANNA DO, MI-CHON?!

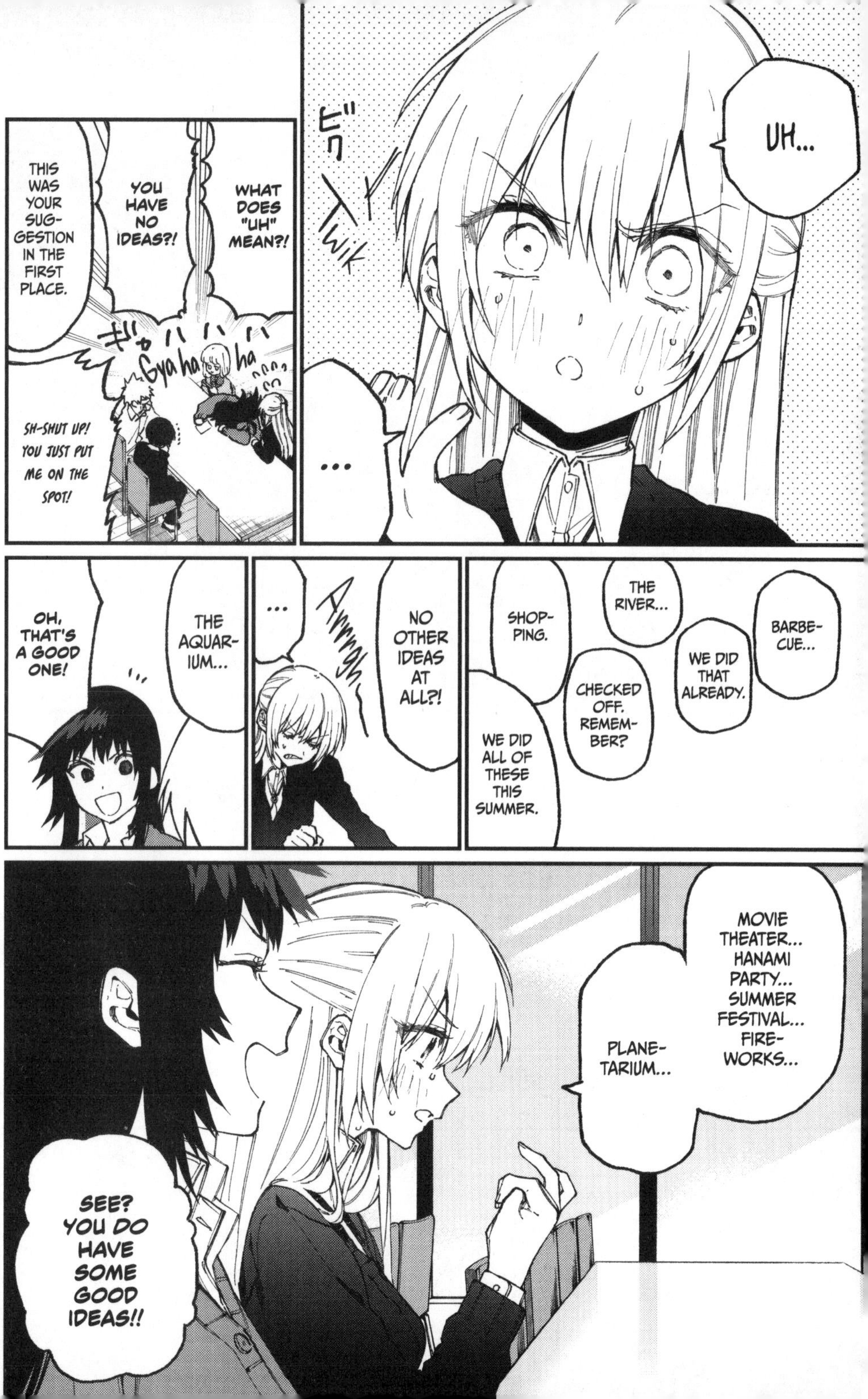
UH...
Twik
...
WHAT DOES "UH" MEAN?!
YOU HAVE NO IDEAS?!
THIS WAS YOUR SUGGESTION IN THE FIRST PLACE.
Gya ha ha ha
SH-SHUT UP! YOU JUST PUT ME ON THE SPOT!
BARBECUE...
THE RIVER...
WE DID THAT ALREADY.
SHOPPING.
CHECKED OFF. REMEMBER?
WE DID ALL OF THESE THIS SUMMER.
NO OTHER IDEAS AT ALL?!
Arrrgh
...
THE AQUARIUM...
OH, THAT'S A GOOD ONE!
MOVIE THEATER... HANAMI PARTY... SUMMER FESTIVAL... FIREWORKS...
PLANETARIUM...
SEE? YOU DO HAVE SOME GOOD IDEAS!!

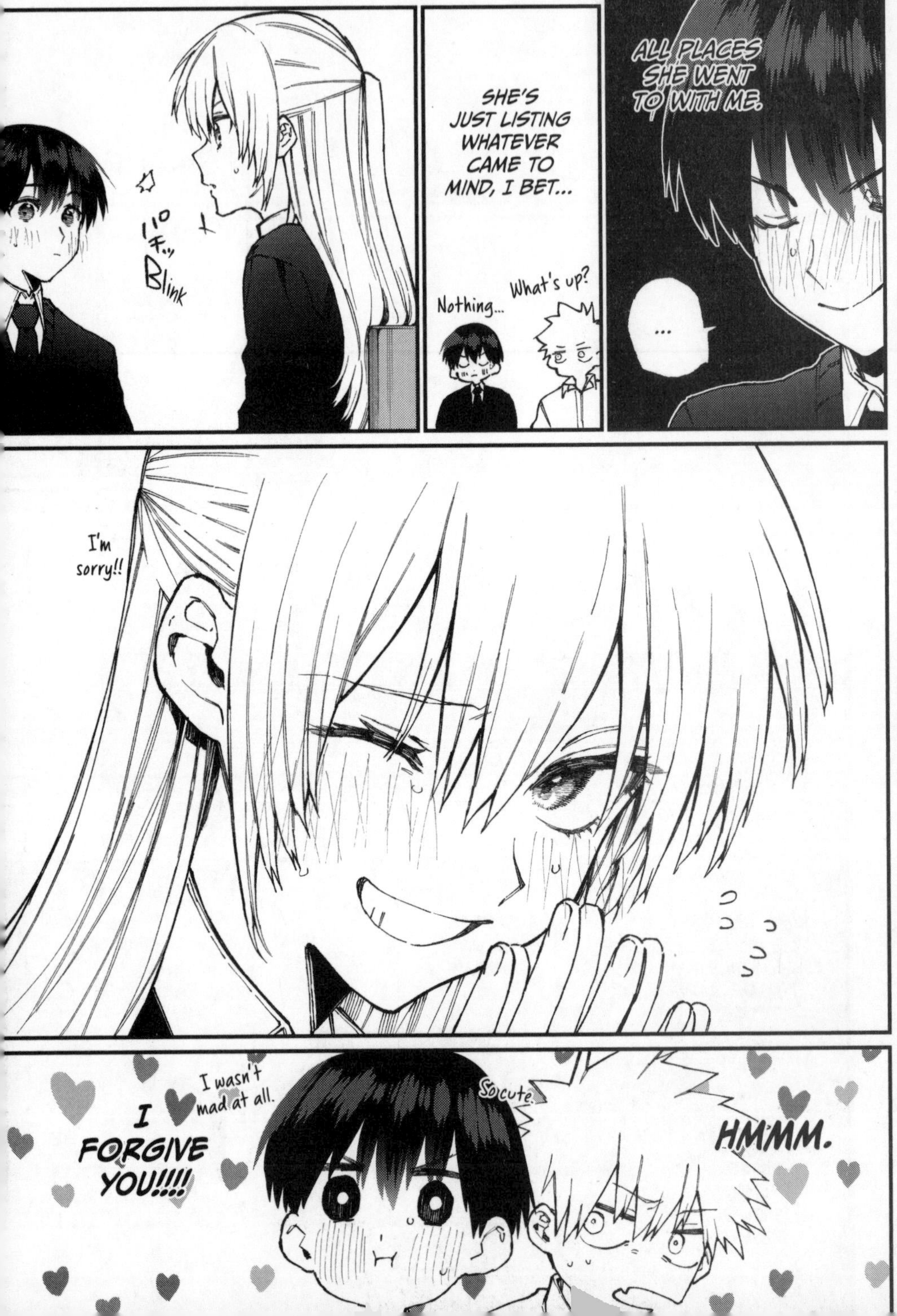
ALL PLACES SHE WENT TO WITH ME.
...
SHE'S JUST LISTING WHATEVER CAME TO MIND, I BET...
What's up?
Nothing...
パチッ
Blink
I'm sorry!!
HMMM.
So cute.
I wasn't mad at all.
I FORGIVE YOU!!!!

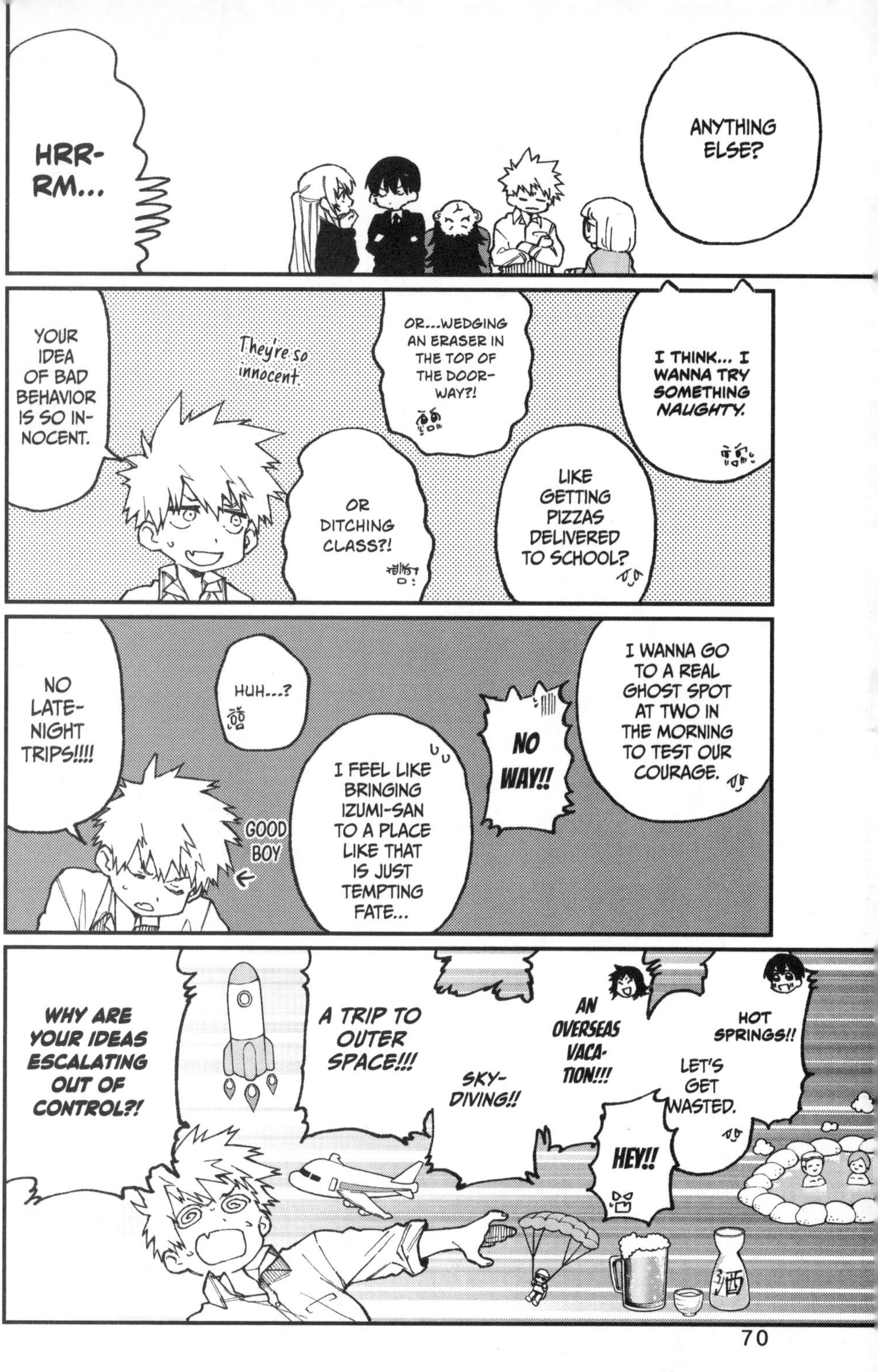
ANYTHING ELSE?
HRR-RM...
I THINK... I WANNA TRY SOMETHING NAUGHTY.
OR...WEDGING AN ERASER IN THE TOP OF THE DOOR-WAY?!
LIKE GETTING PIZZAS DELIVERED TO SCHOOL?
OR DITCHING CLASS?!
They're so innocent
YOUR IDEA OF BAD BEHAVIOR IS SO IN-NOCENT.
I WANNA GO TO A REAL GHOST SPOT AT TWO IN THE MORNING TO TEST OUR COURAGE.
NO WAY!!
HUH...?
I FEEL LIKE BRINGING IZUMI-SAN TO A PLACE LIKE THAT IS JUST TEMPTING FATE...
GOOD BOY
NO LATE-NIGHT TRIPS!!!!
HOT SPRINGS!!
LET'S GET WASTED.
AN OVERSEAS VACA-TION!!!
HEY!!
SKY-DIVING!!
A TRIP TO OUTER SPACE!!!
WHY ARE YOUR IDEAS ESCALATING OUT OF CONTROL?!

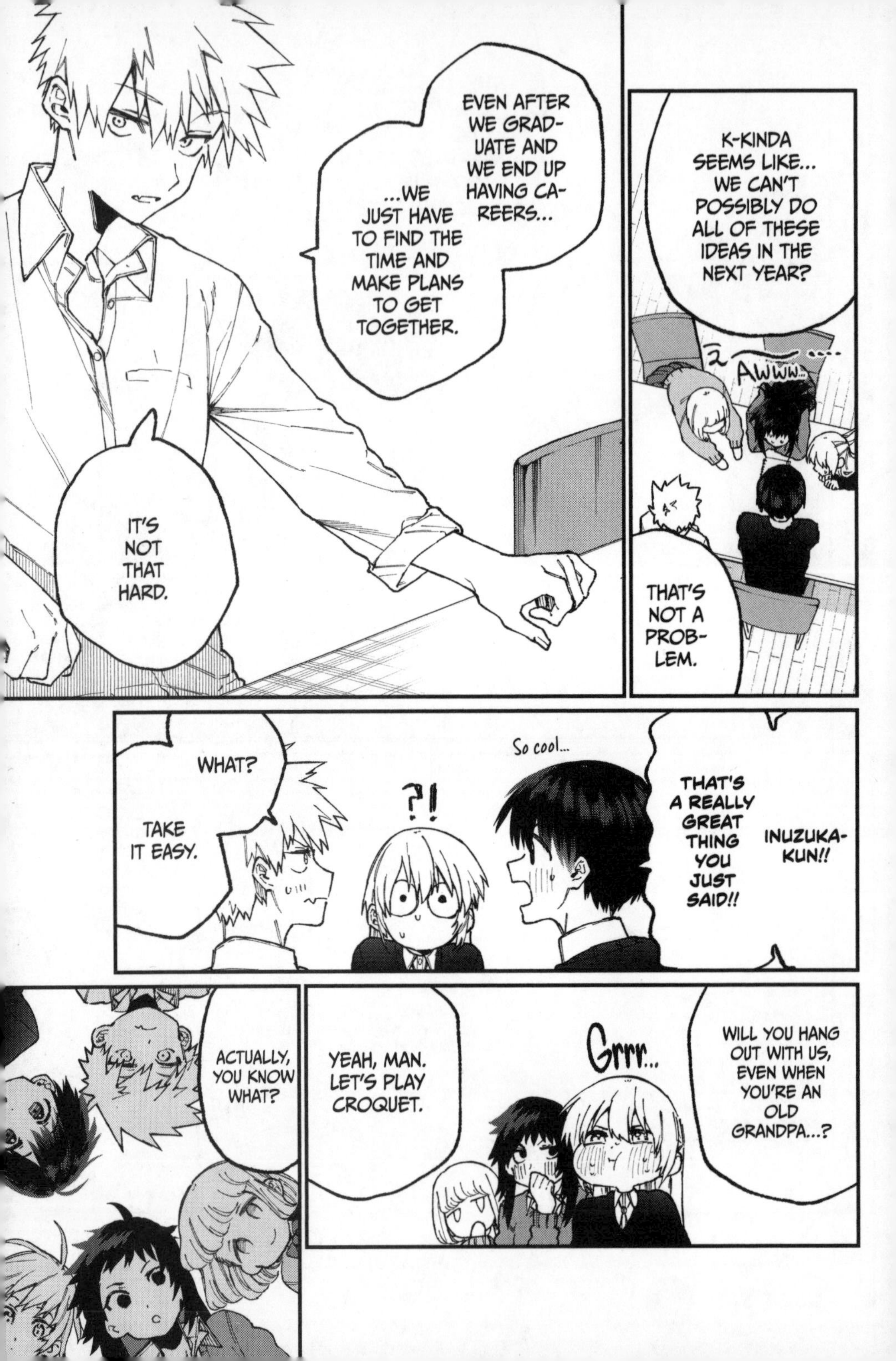
K-KINDA SEEMS LIKE... WE CAN'T POSSIBLY DO ALL OF THESE IDEAS IN THE NEXT YEAR?
AWWW...
THAT'S NOT A PROB-LEM.
EVEN AFTER WE GRAD-UATE AND WE END UP HAVING CA-REERS...
...WE JUST HAVE TO FIND THE TIME AND MAKE PLANS TO GET TOGETHER.
IT'S NOT THAT HARD.
THAT'S A REALLY GREAT THING YOU JUST SAID!!
INUZUKA-KUN!!
So cool...
?!
WHAT?
TAKE IT EASY.
WILL YOU HANG OUT WITH US, EVEN WHEN YOU'RE AN OLD GRANDPA...?
Grrr...
YEAH, MAN. LET'S PLAY CROQUET.
ACTUALLY, YOU KNOW WHAT?

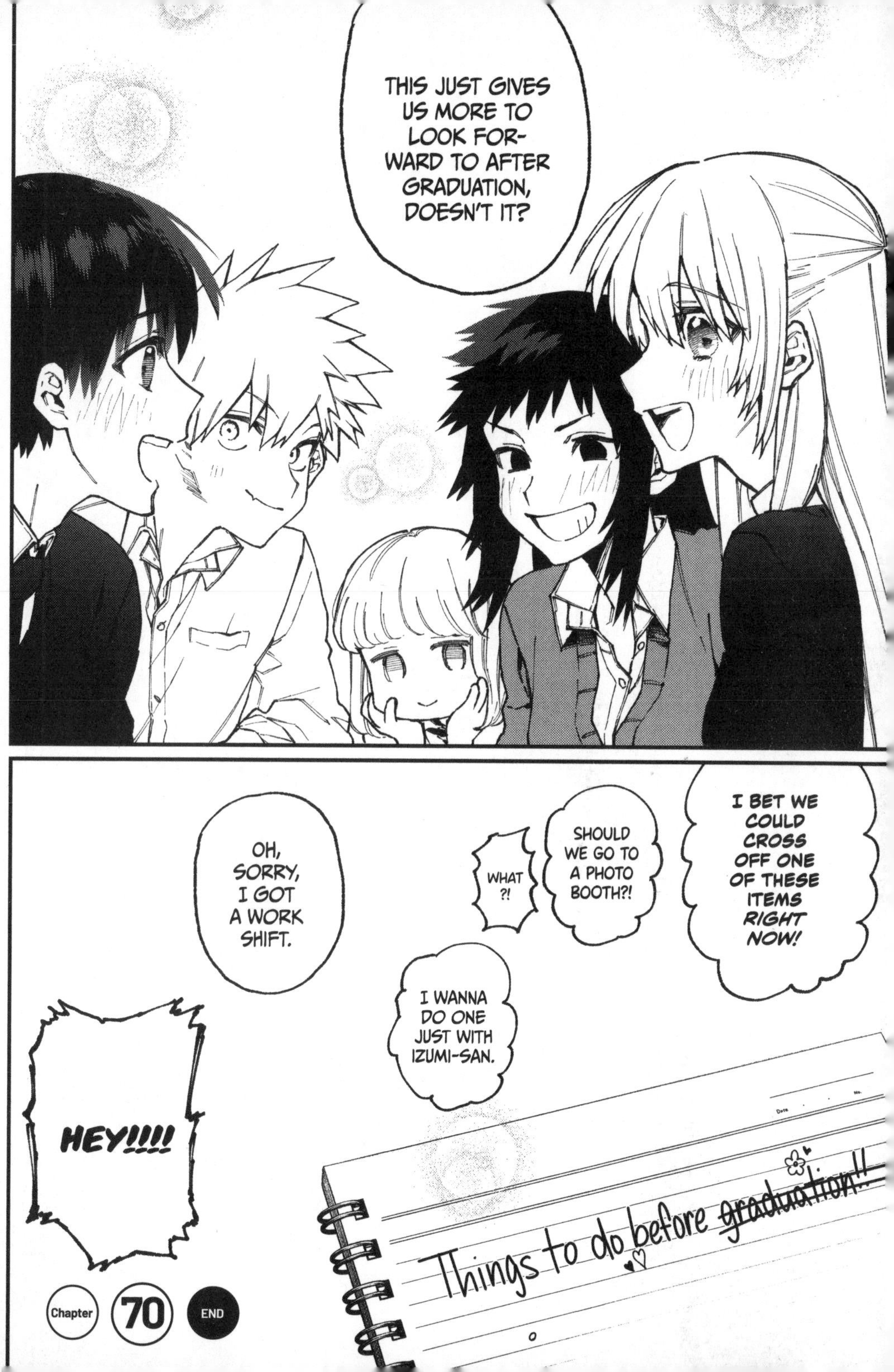
THIS JUST GIVES US MORE TO LOOK FOR-WARD TO AFTER GRADUATION, DOESN'T IT?
I BET WE COULD CROSS OFF ONE OF THESE ITEMS *RIGHT NOW!*
SHOULD WE GO TO A PHOTO BOOTH?!
WHAT ?!
OH, SORRY, I GOT A WORK SHIFT.
I WANNA DO ONE JUST WITH IZUMI-SAN.
HEY!!!!
Things to do before ~~graduation~~!!
Chapter 70 END

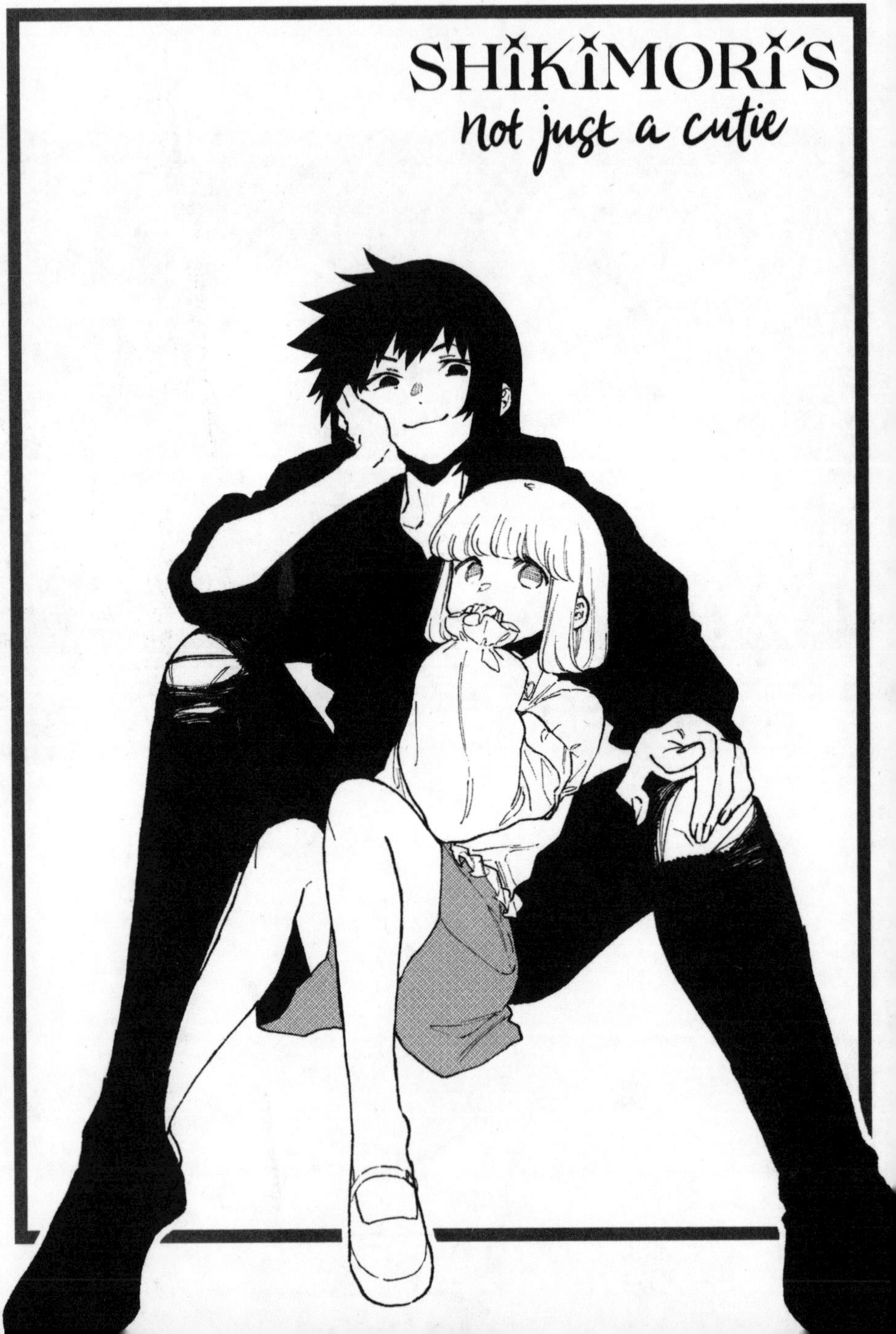
SHIKIMORI'S
Not just a cutie

SHIKIMORI'S *not just a cutie*

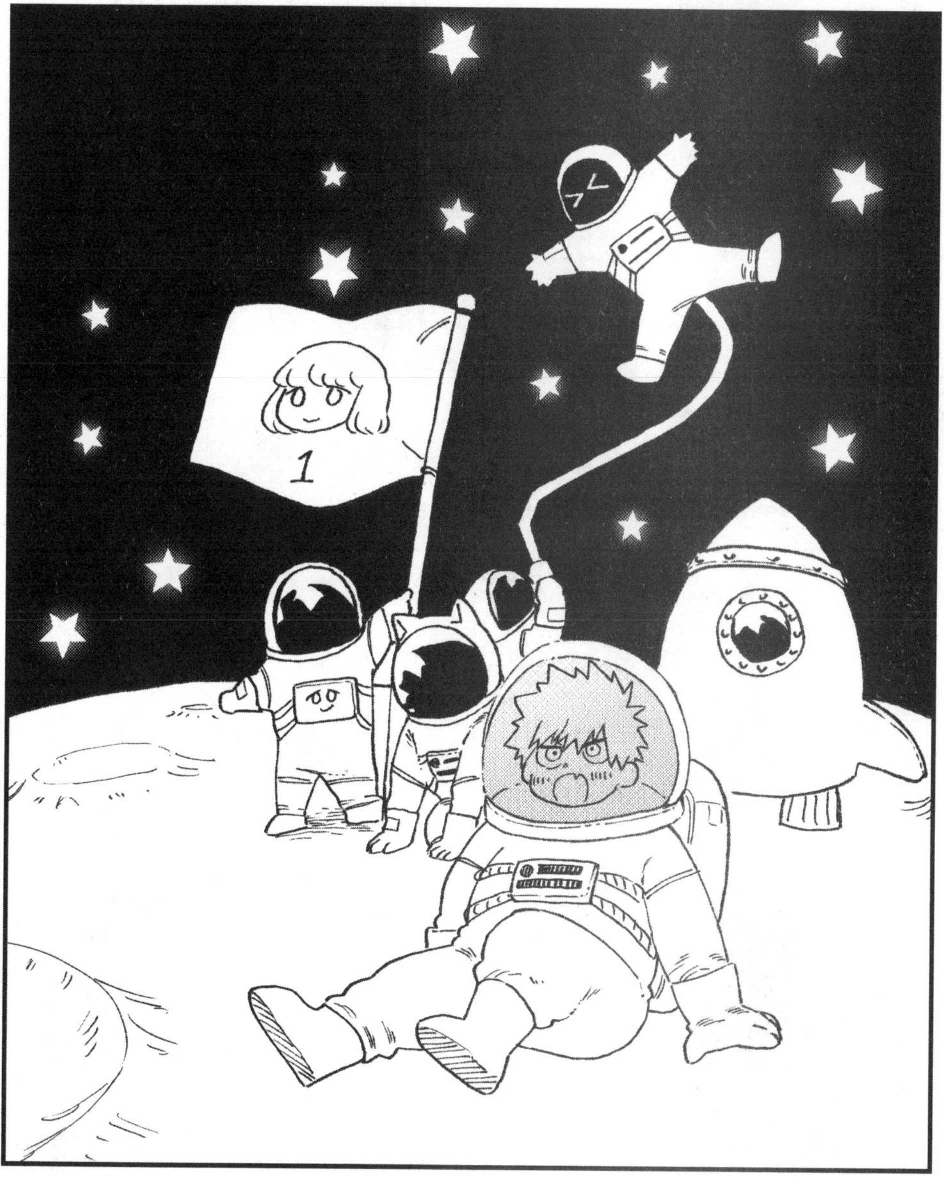
1

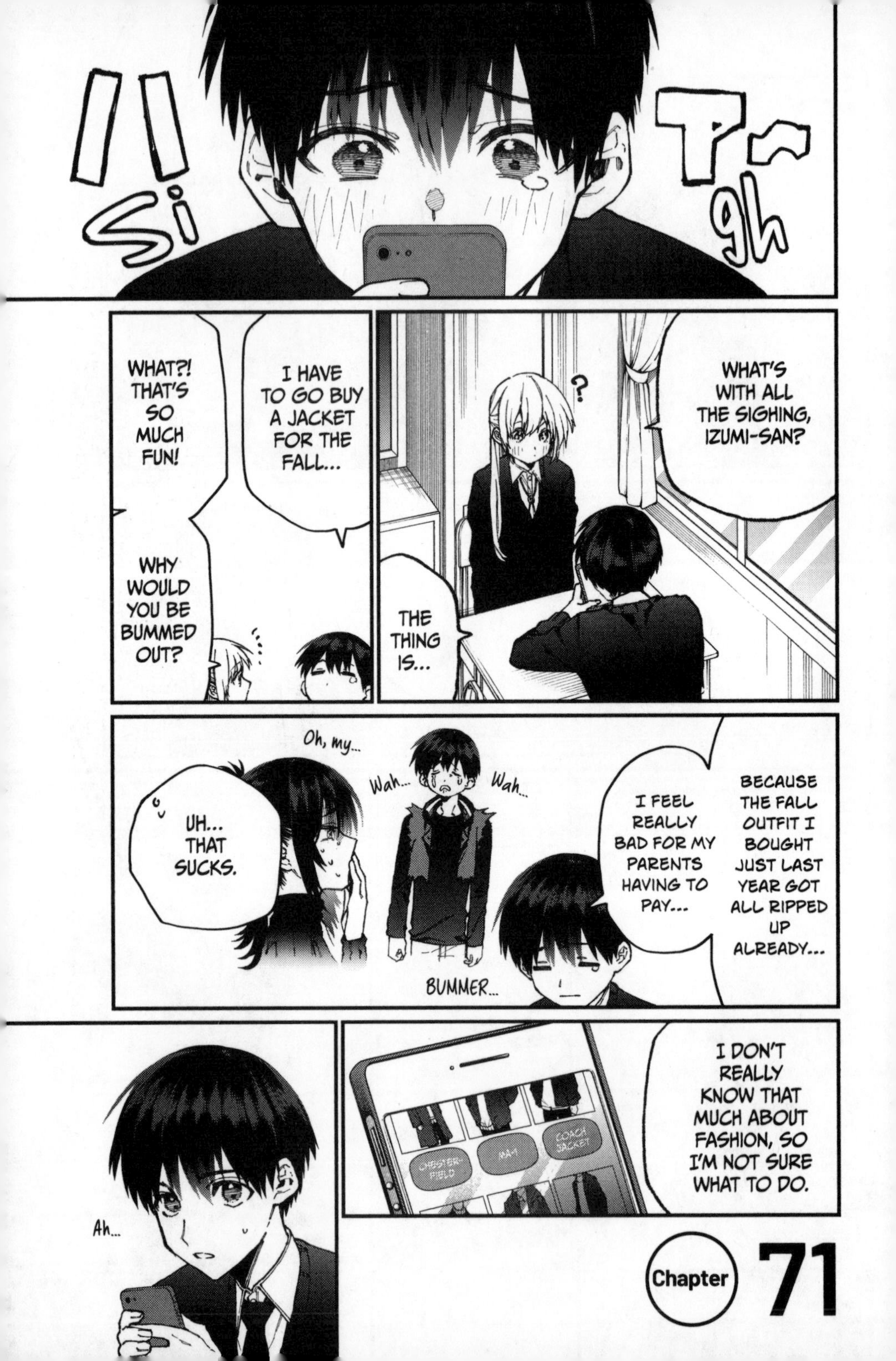
ハ
Si
ア~
gh
WHAT'S WITH ALL THE SIGHING, IZUMI-SAN?
?
THE THING IS...
I HAVE TO GO BUY A JACKET FOR THE FALL...
WHAT?! THAT'S SO MUCH FUN!
WHY WOULD YOU BE BUMMED OUT?
BECAUSE THE FALL OUTFIT I BOUGHT JUST LAST YEAR GOT ALL RIPPED UP ALREADY...
I FEEL REALLY BAD FOR MY PARENTS HAVING TO PAY...
Wah...
Wah...
BUMMER...
Oh, my...
UH... THAT SUCKS.
I DON'T REALLY KNOW THAT MUCH ABOUT FASHION, SO I'M NOT SURE WHAT TO DO.
COACH JACKET
CHESTER-FIELD
Ah...
Chapter 71

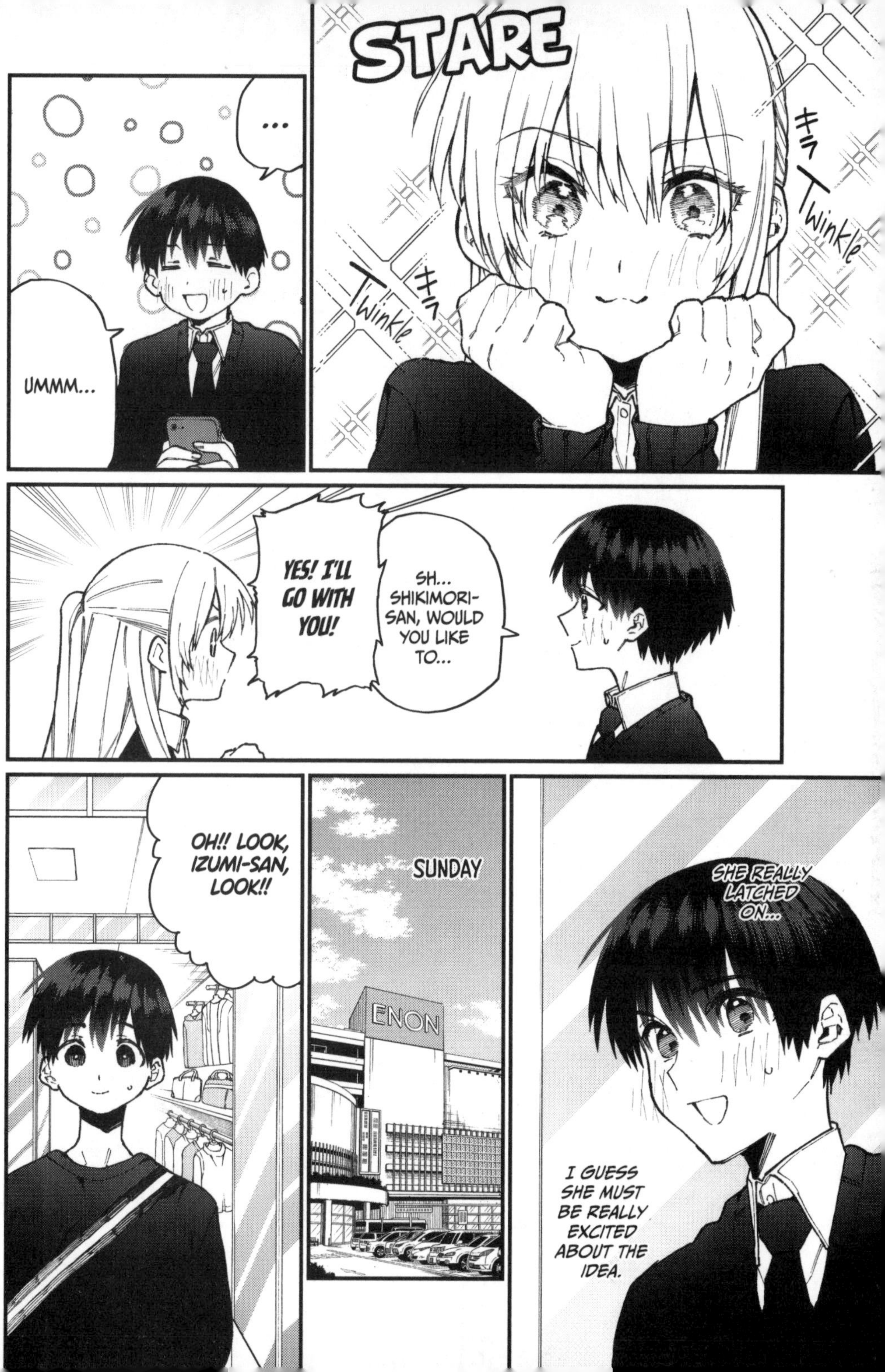
STARE
キラ Twinkle
キラ Twinkle
...
UMMM...
SH... SHIKIMORI-SAN, WOULD YOU LIKE TO...
YES! I'LL GO WITH YOU!
SHE REALLY LATCHED ON...
I GUESS SHE MUST BE REALLY EXCITED ABOUT THE IDEA.
SUNDAY
ENON
OH!! LOOK, IZUMI-SAN, LOOK!!

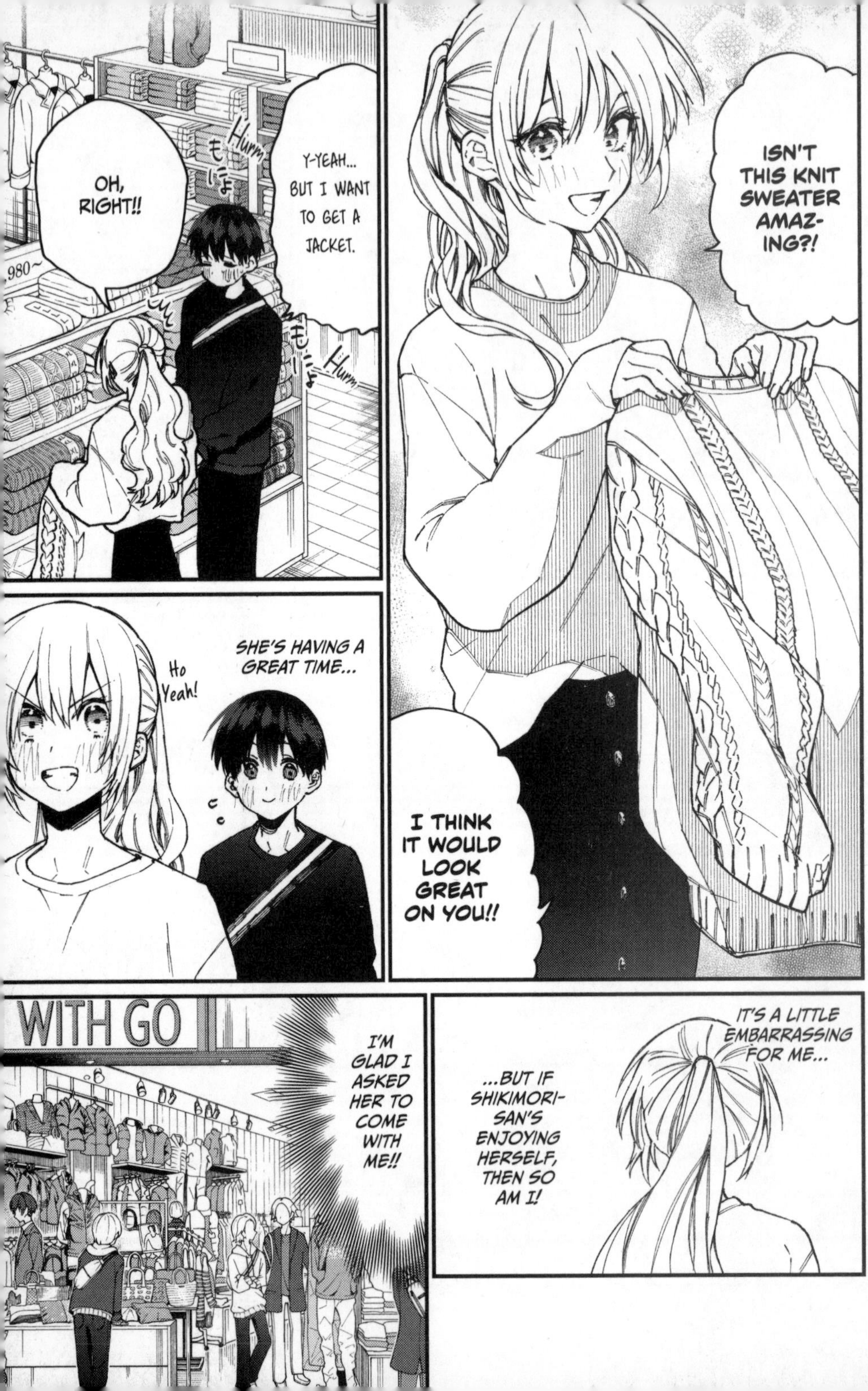
ISN'T THIS KNIT SWEATER AMAZ-ING?!
I THINK IT WOULD LOOK GREAT ON YOU!!
Y-YEAH... BUT I WANT TO GET A JACKET.
Hurm
もじょ
Hurm
もじょ
OH, RIGHT!!
980~
SHE'S HAVING A GREAT TIME...
Ho Yeah!
IT'S A LITTLE EMBARRASSING FOR ME...
...BUT IF SHIKIMORI-SAN'S ENJOYING HERSELF, THEN SO AM I!
WITH GO
I'M GLAD I ASKED HER TO COME WITH ME!!

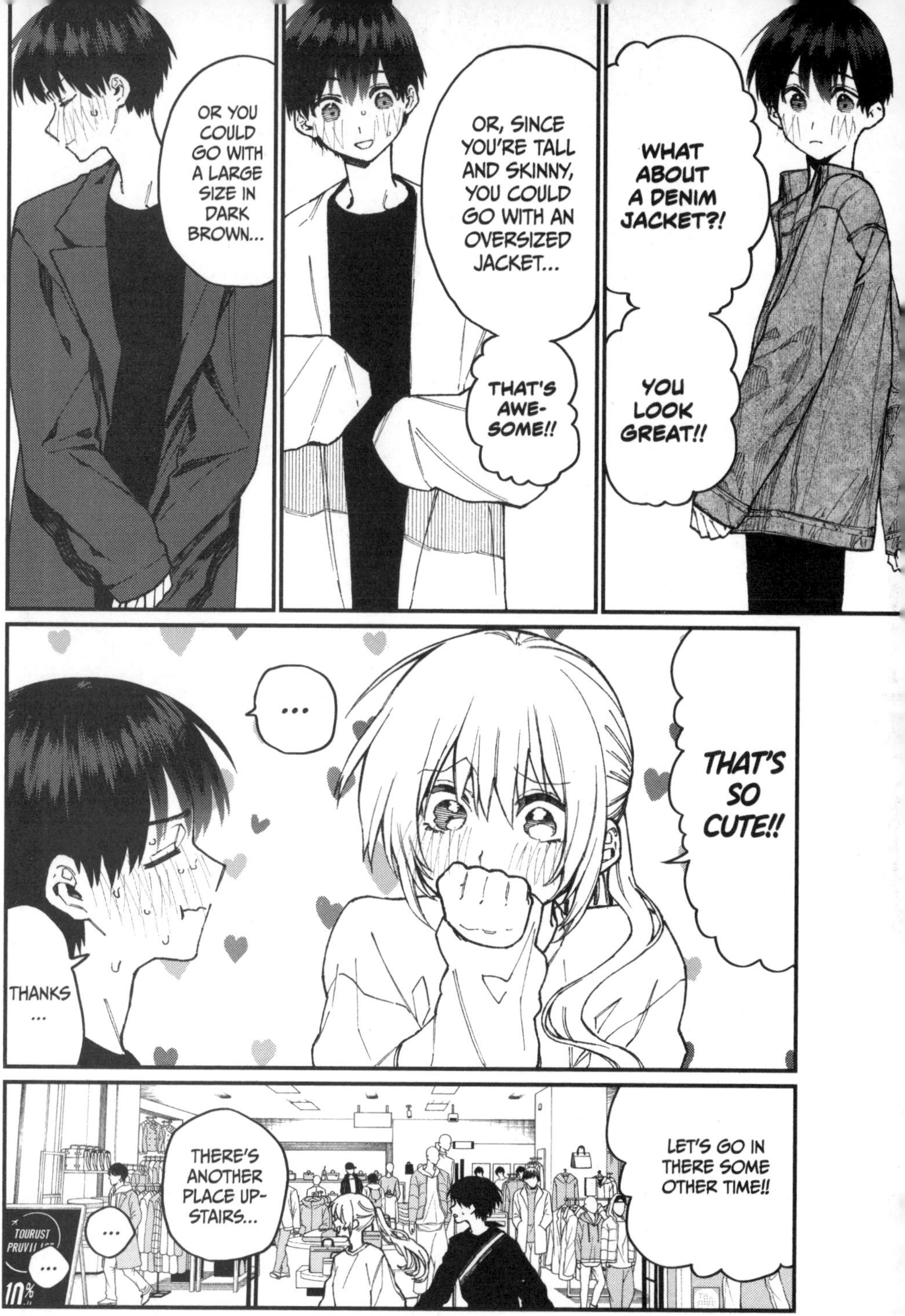
WHAT ABOUT A DENIM JACKET?!
YOU LOOK GREAT!!
OR, SINCE YOU'RE TALL AND SKINNY, YOU COULD GO WITH AN OVERSIZED JACKET...
THAT'S AWE-SOME!!
OR YOU COULD GO WITH A LARGE SIZE IN DARK BROWN...
THAT'S SO CUTE!!
...
THANKS...
LET'S GO IN THERE SOME OTHER TIME!!
THERE'S ANOTHER PLACE UP-STAIRS...
...
...
TOURUST
10%

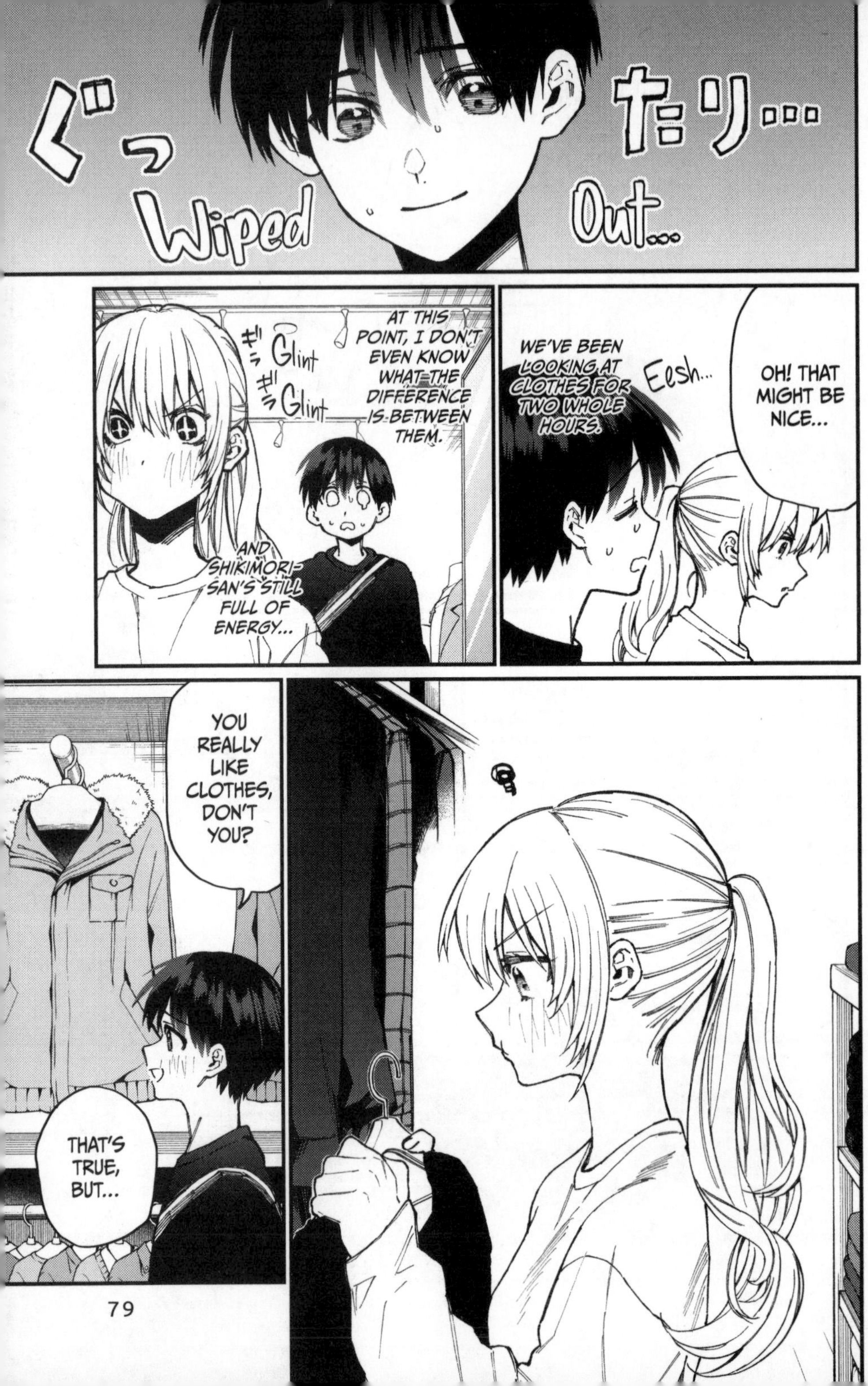

ぐっ
Wiped
たり…
Out…
OH! THAT MIGHT BE NICE...
Eesh...
WE'VE BEEN LOOKING AT CLOTHES FOR TWO WHOLE HOURS.
AT THIS POINT, I DON'T EVEN KNOW WHAT THE DIFFERENCE IS BETWEEN THEM.
ギラ Glint
ギラ Glint
AND SHIKIMORI-SAN'S STILL FULL OF ENERGY...
YOU REALLY LIKE CLOTHES, DON'T YOU?
THAT'S TRUE, BUT...

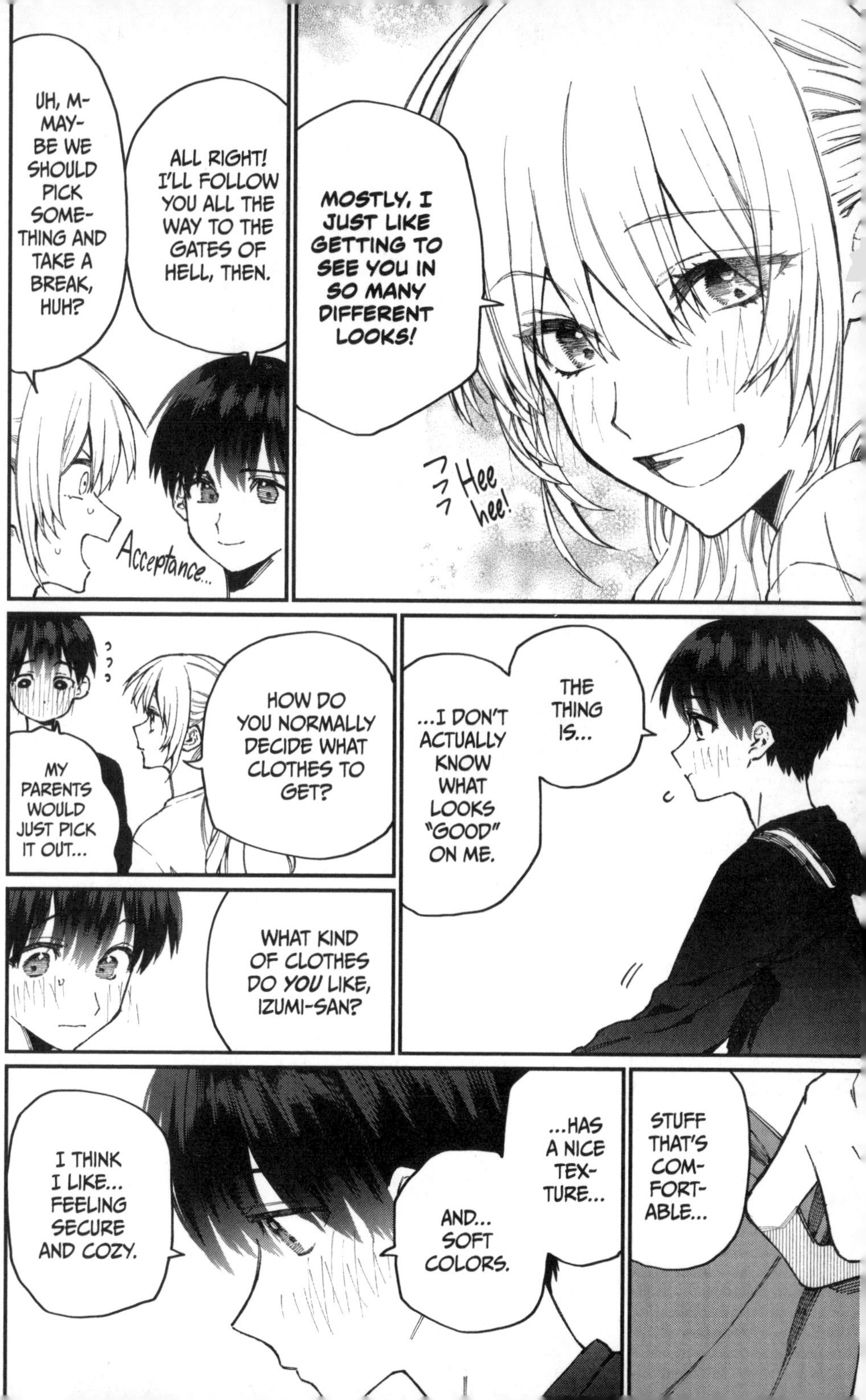
MOSTLY, I JUST LIKE GETTING TO SEE YOU IN SO MANY DIFFERENT LOOKS!
Hee hee!
ALL RIGHT! I'LL FOLLOW YOU ALL THE WAY TO THE GATES OF HELL, THEN.
UH, M-MAYBE WE SHOULD PICK SOMETHING AND TAKE A BREAK, HUH?
Acceptance...
THE THING IS...
...I DON'T ACTUALLY KNOW WHAT LOOKS "GOOD" ON ME.
HOW DO YOU NORMALLY DECIDE WHAT CLOTHES TO GET?
MY PARENTS WOULD JUST PICK IT OUT...
WHAT KIND OF CLOTHES DO YOU LIKE, IZUMI-SAN?
STUFF THAT'S COMFORTABLE...
...HAS A NICE TEXTURE...
AND... SOFT COLORS.
I THINK I LIKE... FEELING SECURE AND COZY.

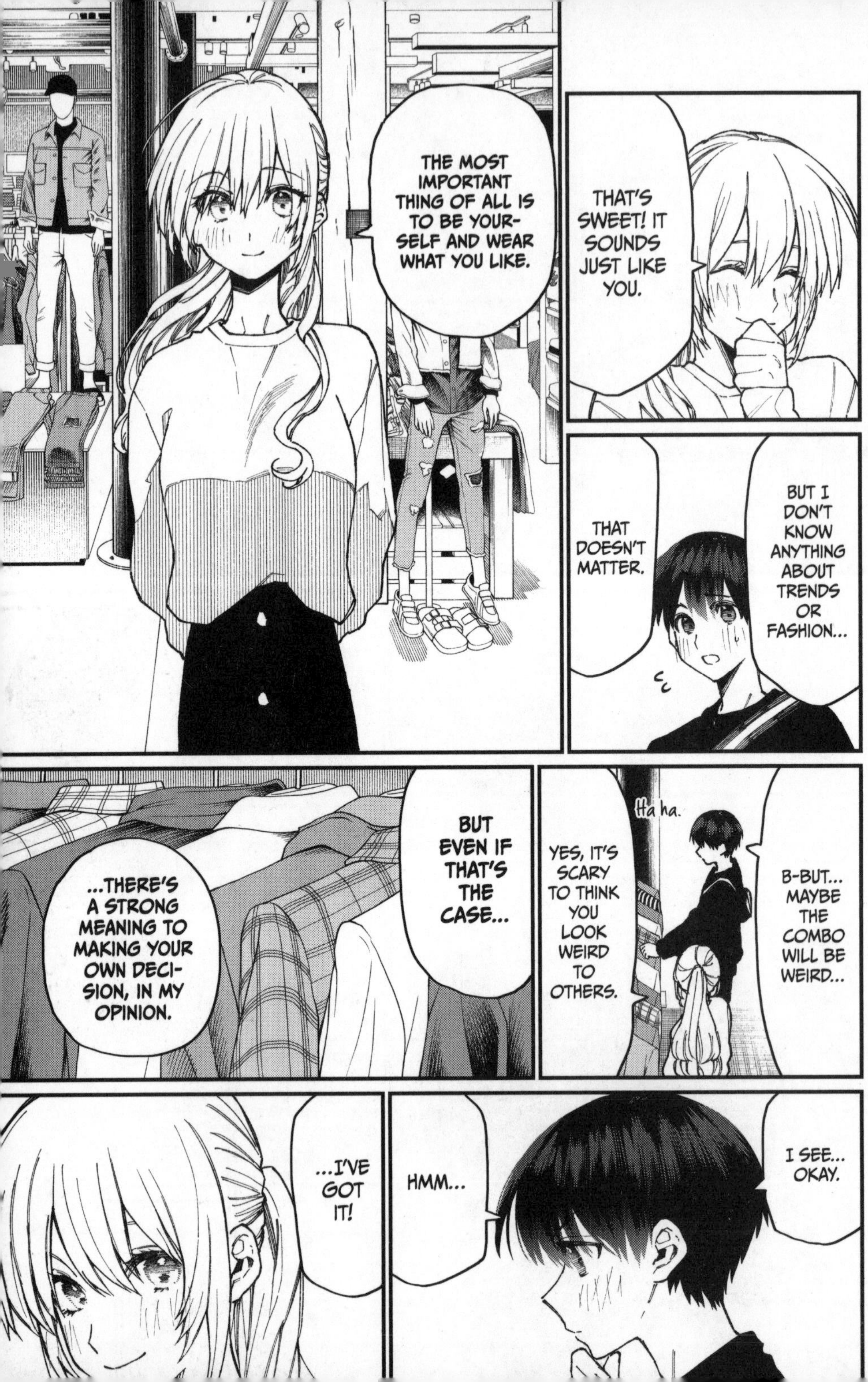
THAT'S SWEET! IT SOUNDS JUST LIKE YOU.
BUT I DON'T KNOW ANYTHING ABOUT TRENDS OR FASHION...
THAT DOESN'T MATTER.
THE MOST IMPORTANT THING OF ALL IS TO BE YOURSELF AND WEAR WHAT YOU LIKE.
B-BUT... MAYBE THE COMBO WILL BE WEIRD...
Ha ha.
YES, IT'S SCARY TO THINK YOU LOOK WEIRD TO OTHERS.
BUT EVEN IF THAT'S THE CASE...
...THERE'S A STRONG MEANING TO MAKING YOUR OWN DECISION, IN MY OPINION.
I SEE... OKAY.
HMM...
...I'VE GOT IT!

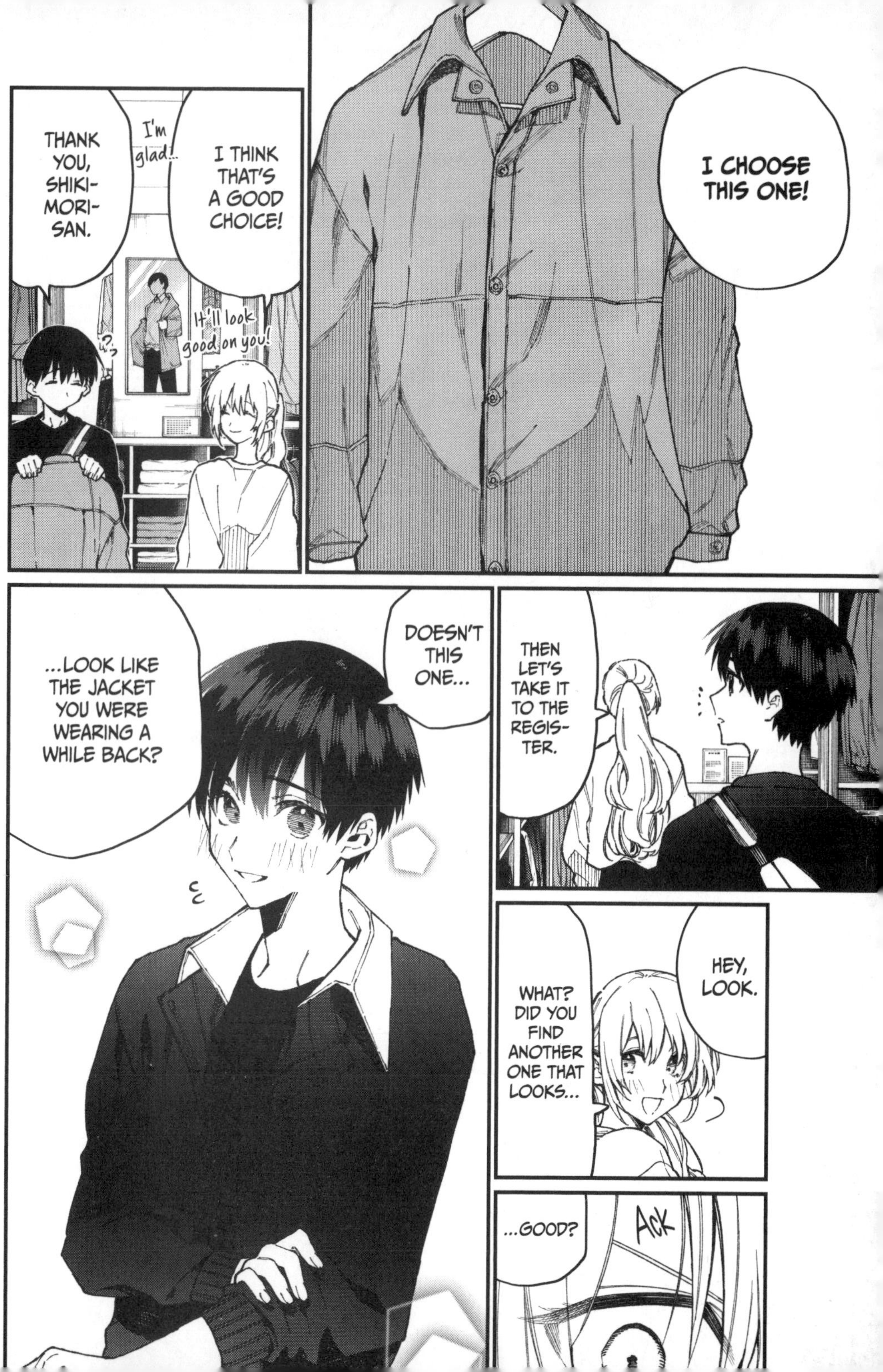
I CHOOSE THIS ONE!
I THINK THAT'S A GOOD CHOICE!
I'm glad...
THANK YOU, SHIKIMORI-SAN.
It'll look good on you!
THEN LET'S TAKE IT TO THE REGISTER.
...
HEY, LOOK.
WHAT? DID YOU FIND ANOTHER ONE THAT LOOKS...
...GOOD?
Ack
DOESN'T THIS ONE...
...LOOK LIKE THE JACKET YOU WERE WEARING A WHILE BACK?

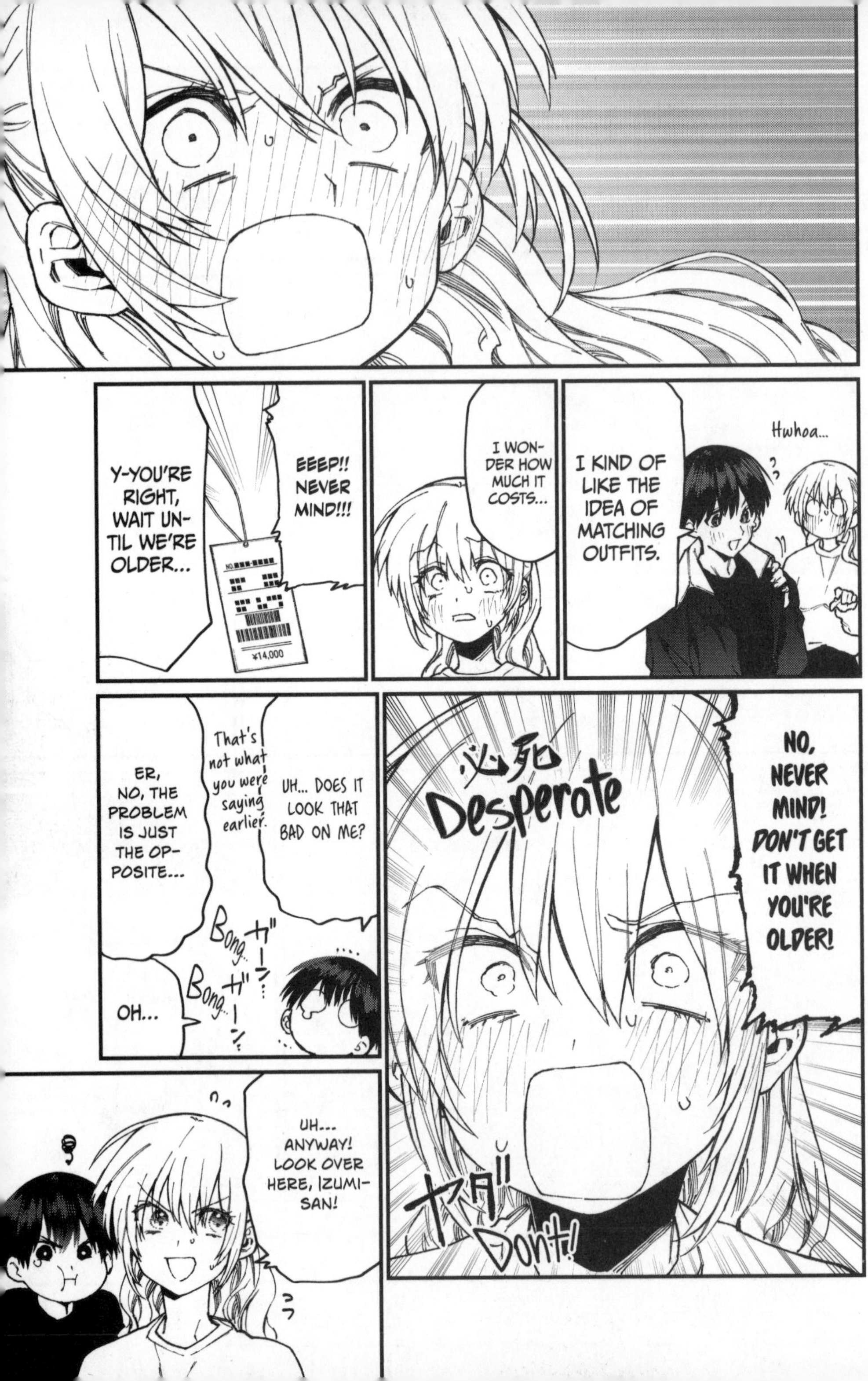
Hwhoa...
I KIND OF LIKE THE IDEA OF MATCHING OUTFITS.
I WONDER HOW MUCH IT COSTS...
EEEP!! NEVER MIND!!!
¥14,000
Y-YOU'RE RIGHT, WAIT UNTIL WE'RE OLDER...
NO, NEVER MIND! DON'T GET IT WHEN YOU'RE OLDER!
必死
Desperate
ヤダ!!
Don't!
UH... DOES IT LOOK THAT BAD ON ME?
That's not what you were saying earlier.
ER, NO, THE PROBLEM IS JUST THE OPPOSITE...
OH...
ガーン
Bong...
ガーン
Bong...
UH... ANYWAY! LOOK OVER HERE, IZUMI-SAN!

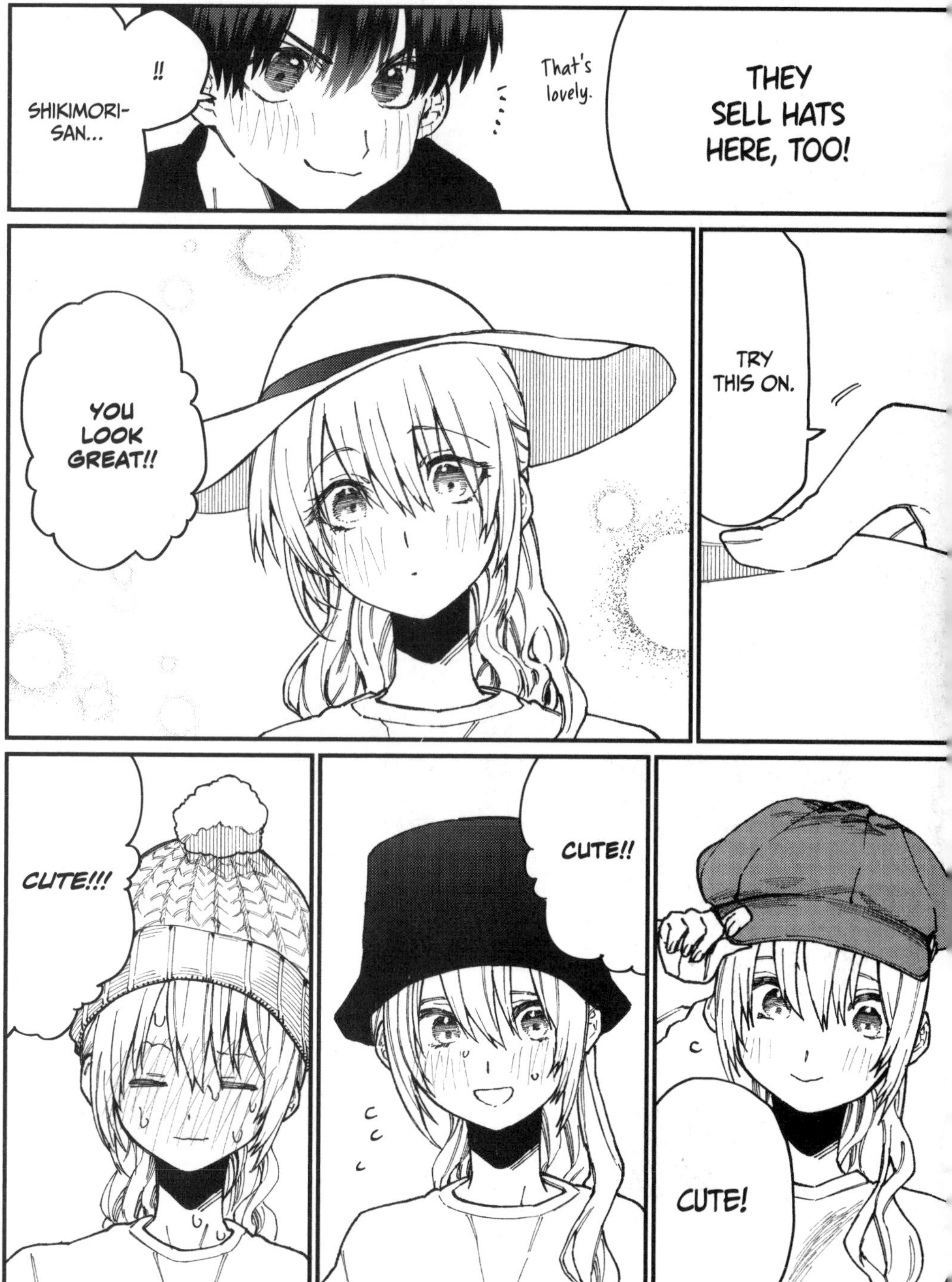
THEY SELL HATS HERE, TOO!
That's lovely.
......
!!
SHIKIMORI-SAN...
TRY THIS ON.
YOU LOOK GREAT!!
CUTE!
CUTE!!
CUTE!!!

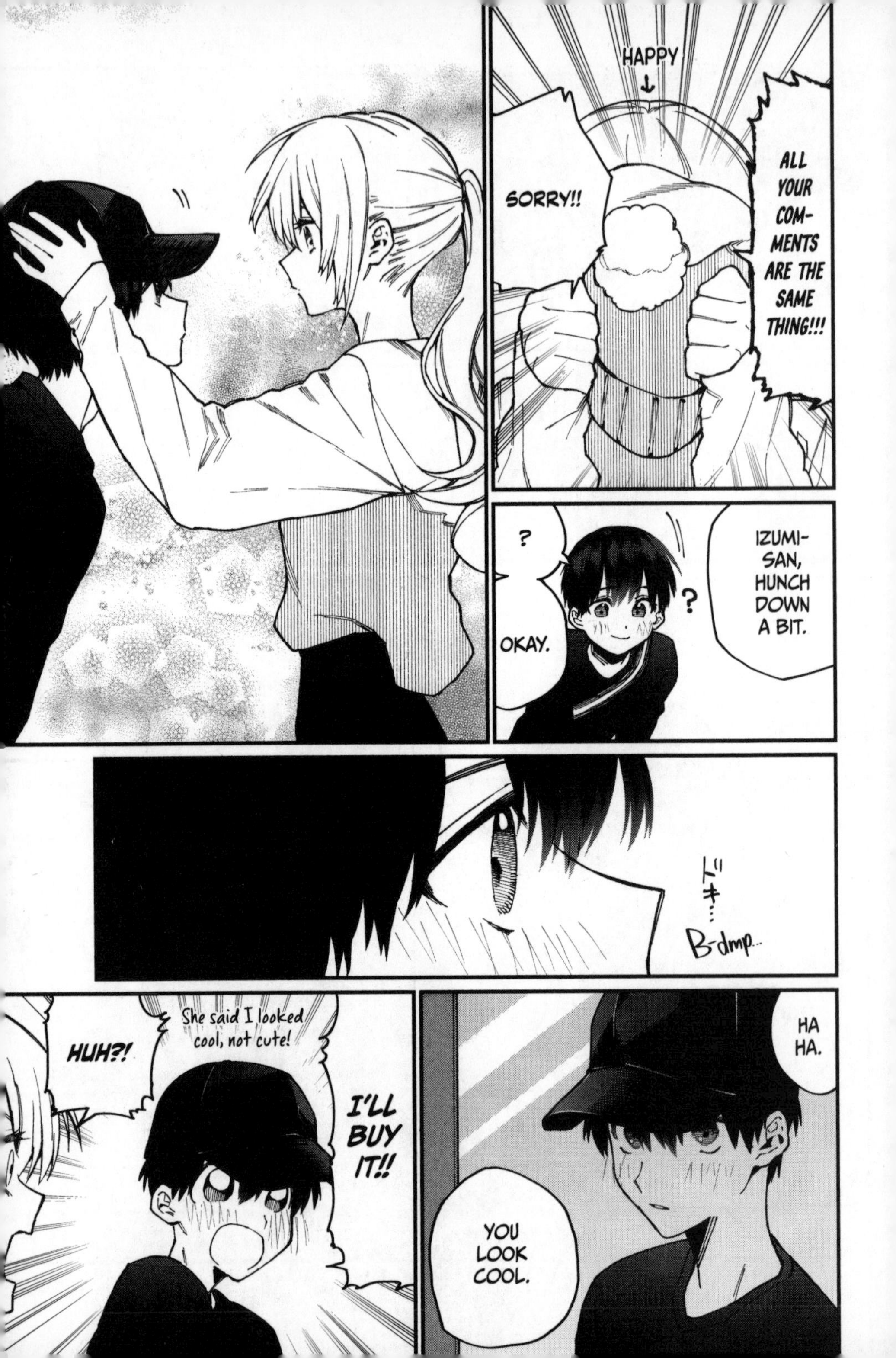

HAPPY
ALL YOUR COM-MENTS ARE THE SAME THING!!!
SORRY!!
IZUMI-SAN, HUNCH DOWN A BIT.
?
?
OKAY.
ドキ…
B-dmp...
HA HA.
YOU LOOK COOL.
She said I looked cool, not cute!
I'LL BUY IT!!
HUH?!

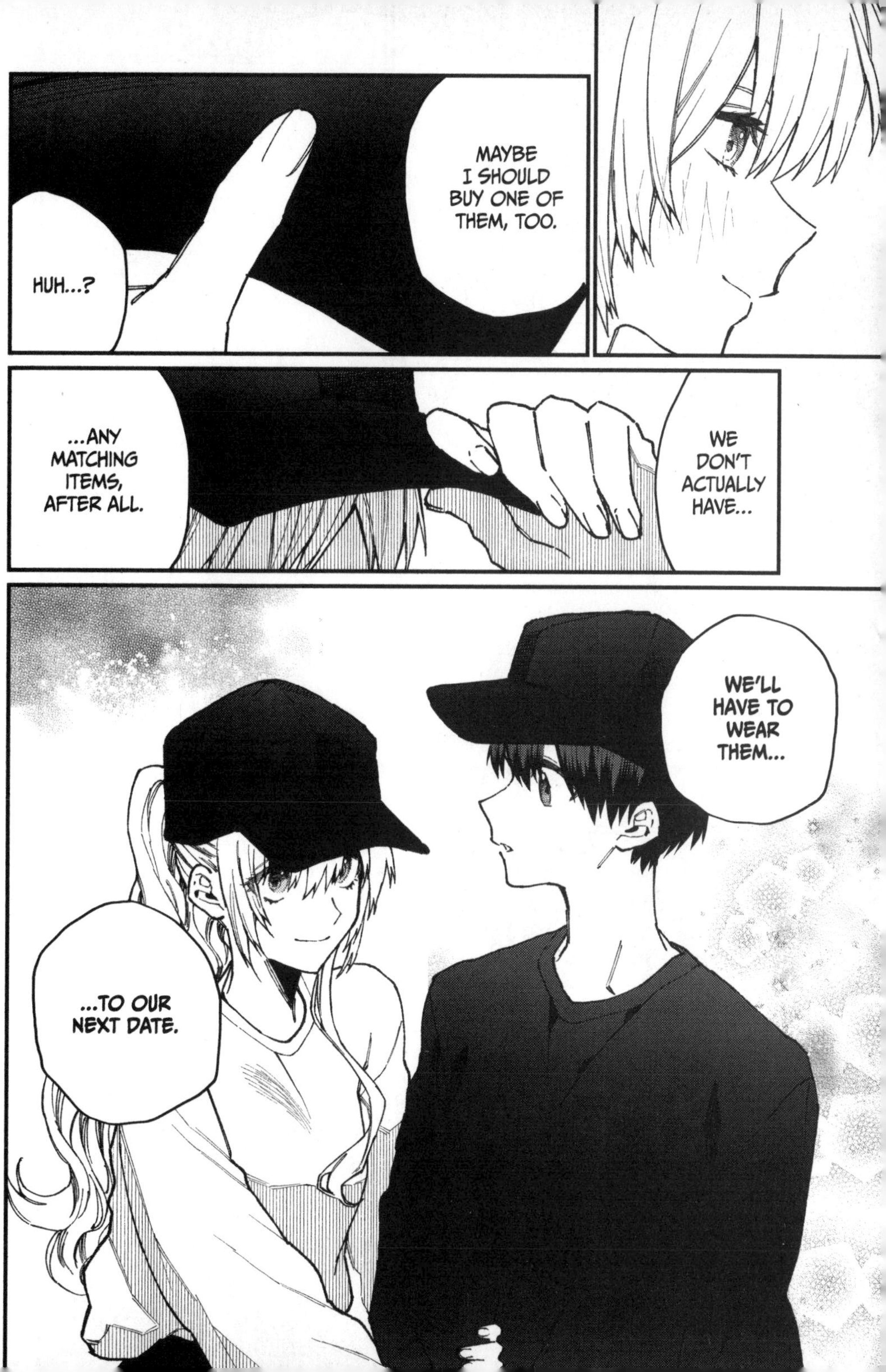
MAYBE I SHOULD BUY ONE OF THEM, TOO.
HUH...?
WE DON'T ACTUALLY HAVE...
...ANY MATCHING ITEMS, AFTER ALL.
WE'LL HAVE TO WEAR THEM...
...TO OUR NEXT DATE.

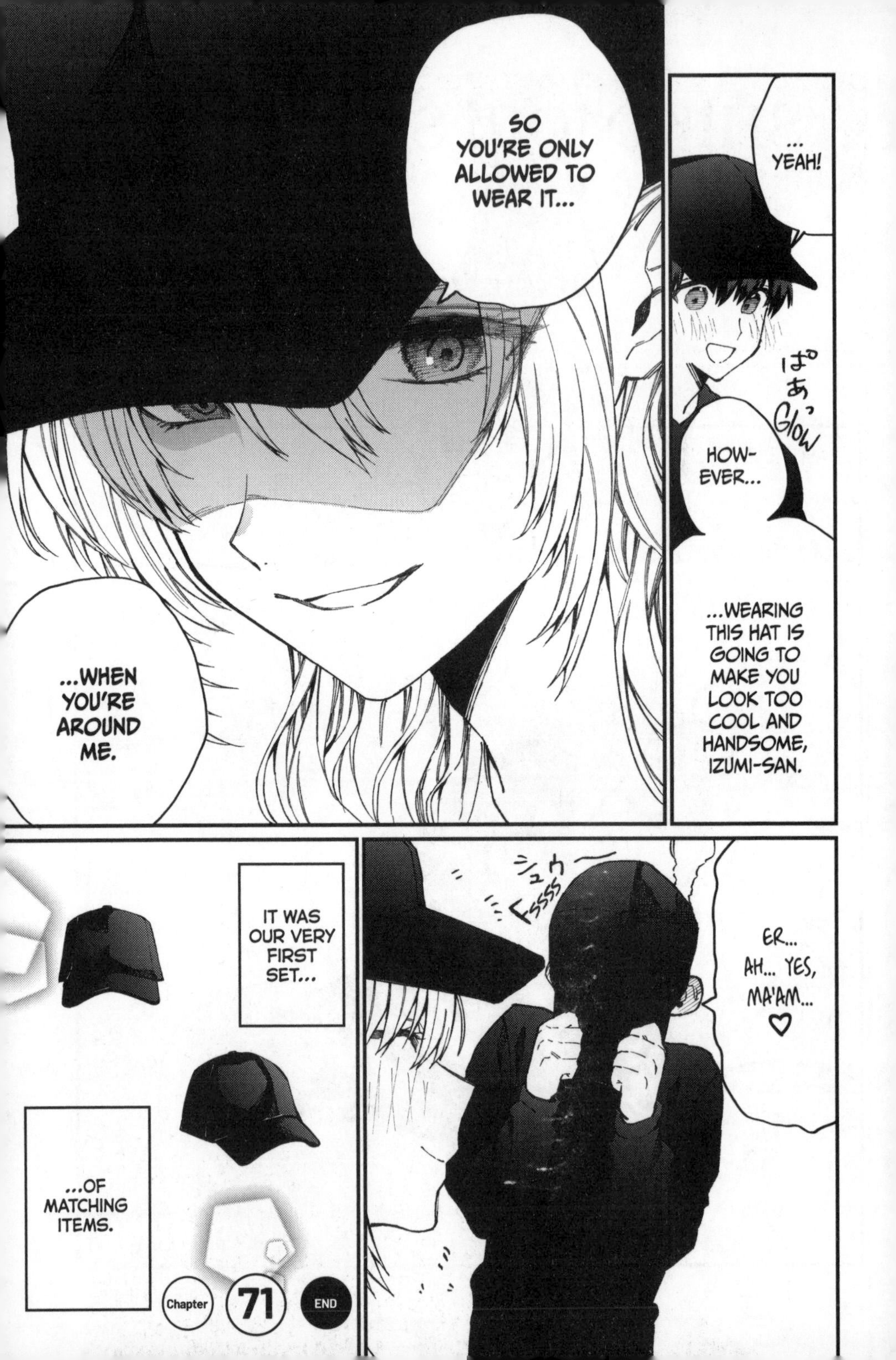
...YEAH!
ぱあっ
GLOW
HOW-EVER...
...WEARING THIS HAT IS GOING TO MAKE YOU LOOK TOO COOL AND HANDSOME, IZUMI-SAN.
SO YOU'RE ONLY ALLOWED TO WEAR IT...
...WHEN YOU'RE AROUND ME.
シュウ〜
FSSSS
ER... AH... YES, MA'AM... ♡
IT WAS OUR VERY FIRST SET...
...OF MATCHING ITEMS.
Chapter 71 END

SHIKIMORI'S not just a cutie

I just can't decide!!

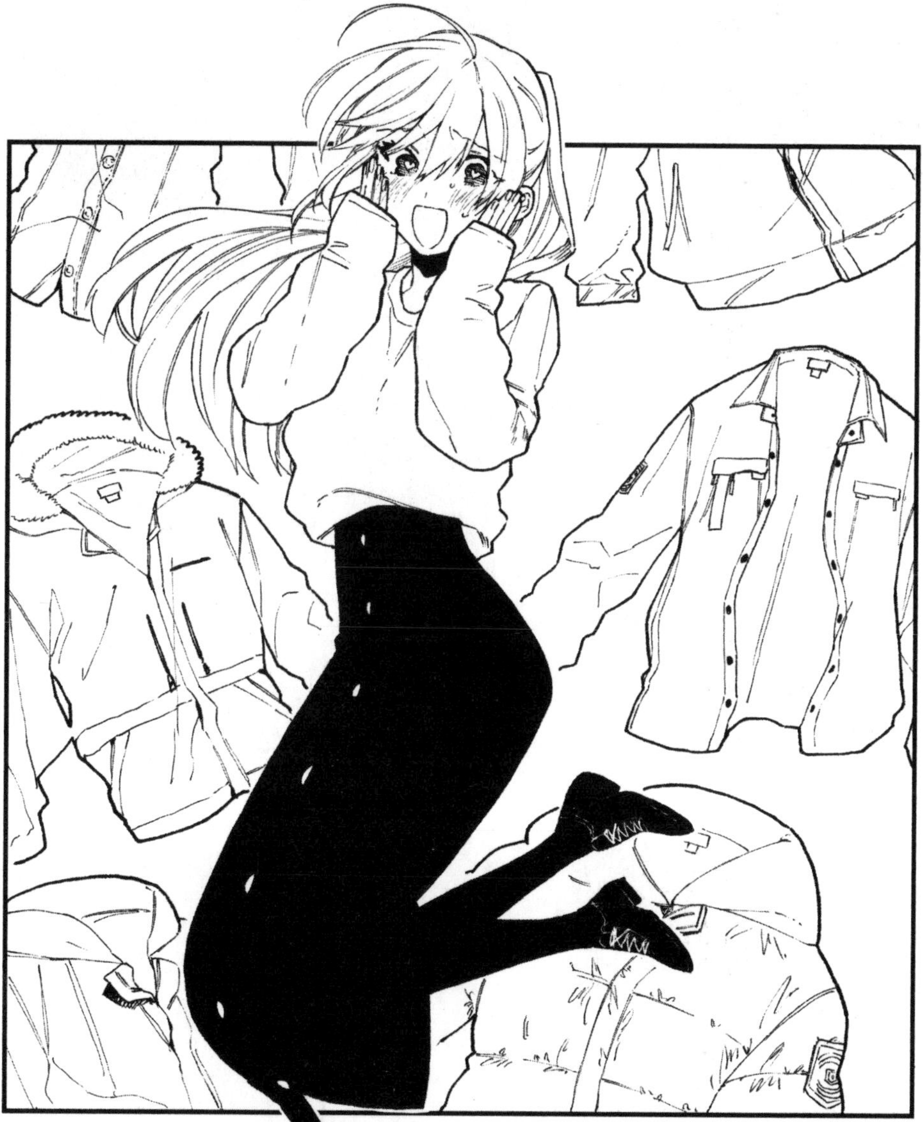

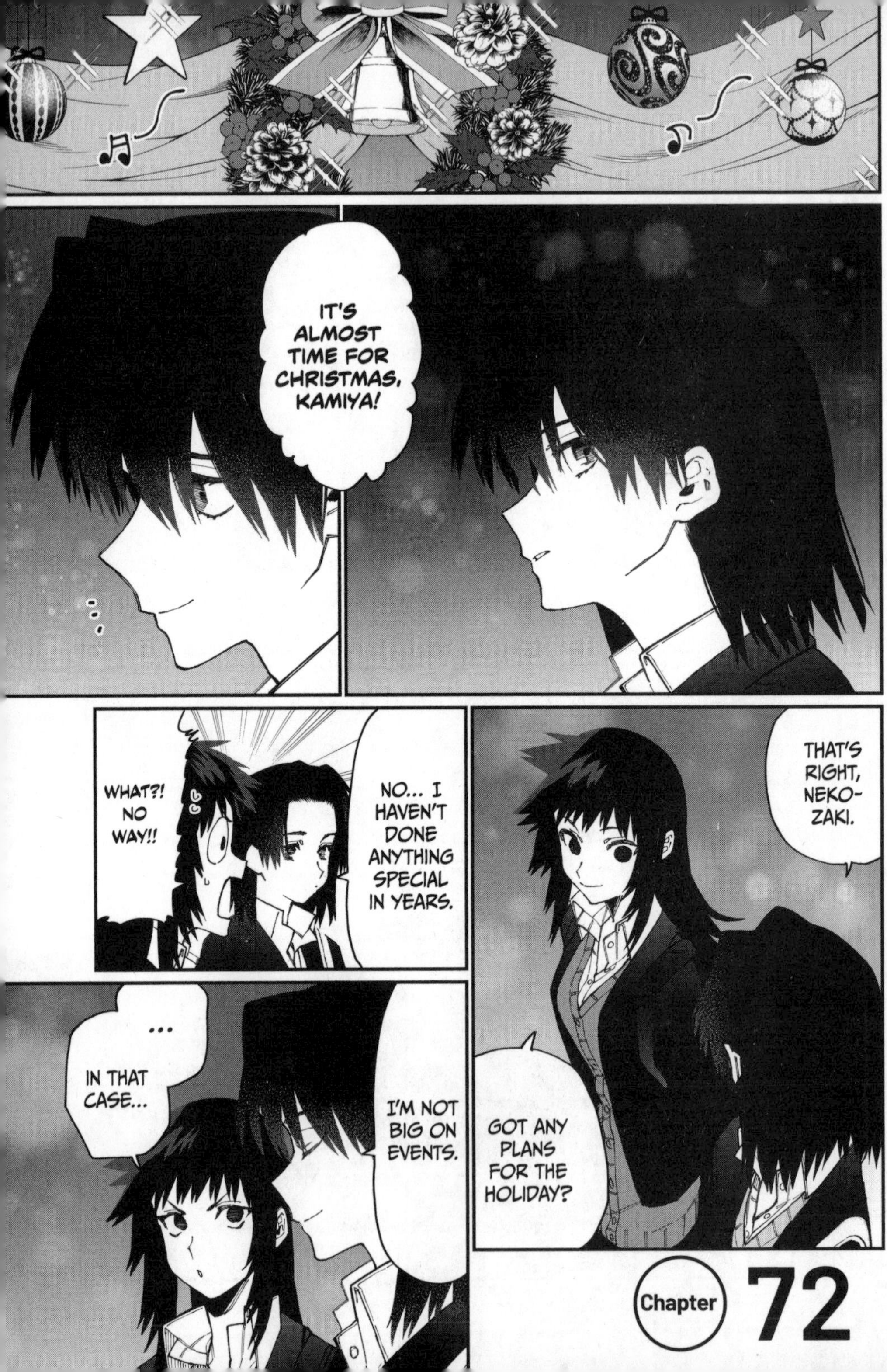
IT'S ALMOST TIME FOR CHRISTMAS, KAMIYA!
THAT'S RIGHT, NEKO-ZAKI.
GOT ANY PLANS FOR THE HOLIDAY?
NO... I HAVEN'T DONE ANYTHING SPECIAL IN YEARS.
WHAT?! NO WAY!!
I'M NOT BIG ON EVENTS.
...
IN THAT CASE...

Chapter 72

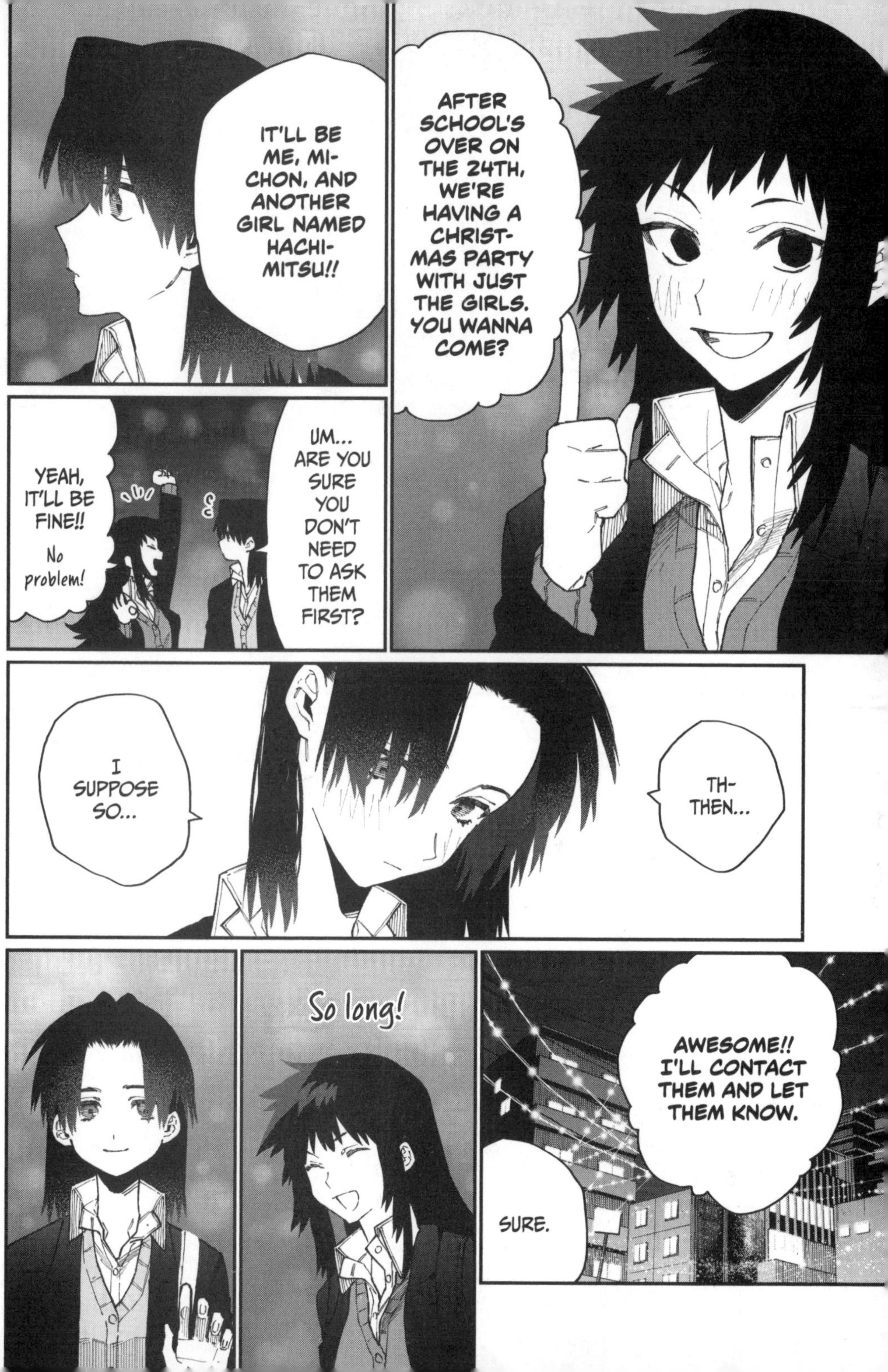
AFTER SCHOOL'S OVER ON THE 24TH, WE'RE HAVING A CHRIST-MAS PARTY WITH JUST THE GIRLS. YOU WANNA COME?
IT'LL BE ME, MI-CHON, AND ANOTHER GIRL NAMED HACHI-MITSU!!
UM... ARE YOU SURE YOU DON'T NEED TO ASK THEM FIRST?
YEAH, IT'LL BE FINE!!
No problem!
TH-THEN...
I SUPPOSE SO...
AWESOME!! I'LL CONTACT THEM AND LET THEM KNOW.
SURE.
So long!

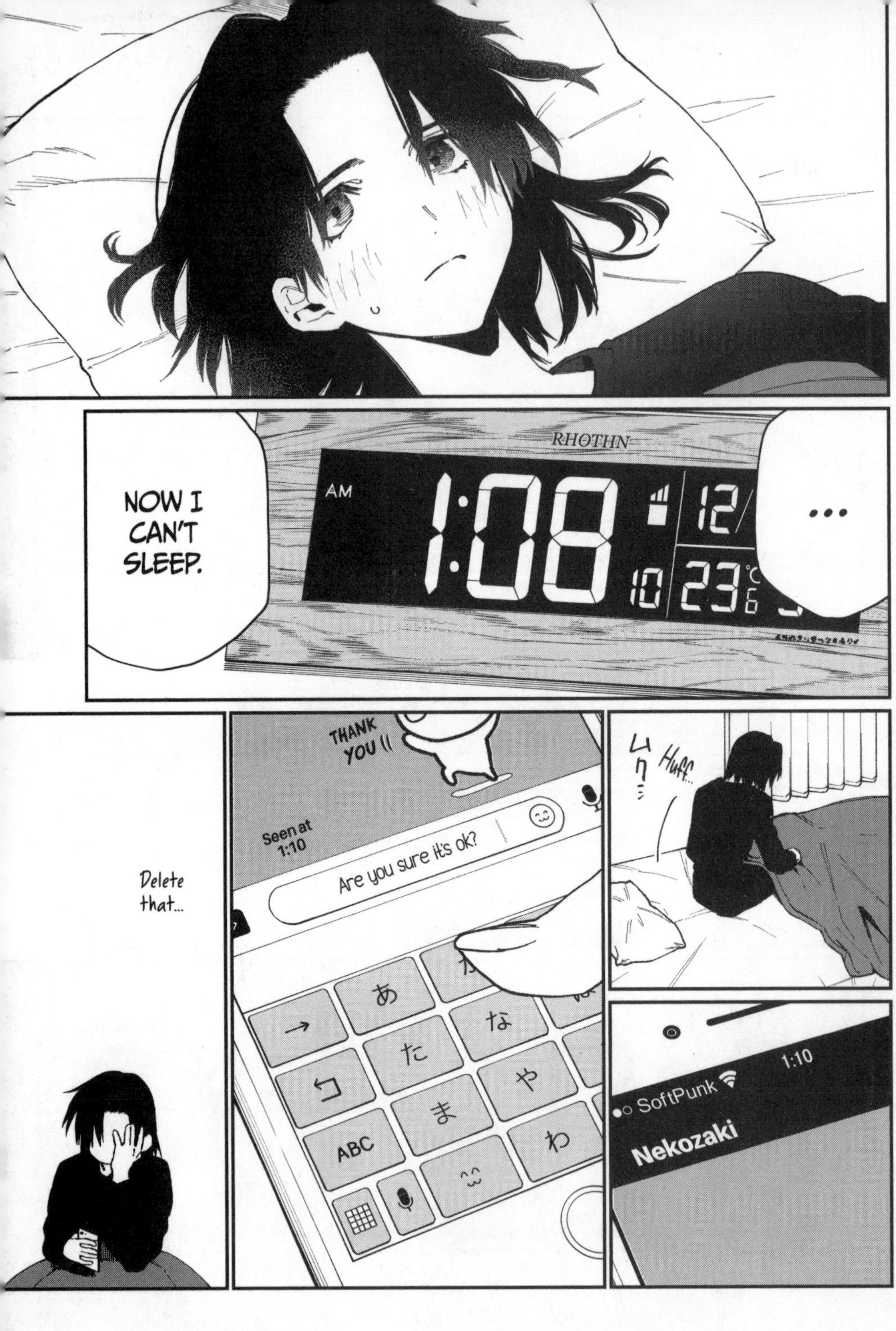

...
NOW I CAN'T SLEEP.
RHOTHN
AM
1:08
ムク
Huff...
1:10
SoftPunk
Nekozaki
THANK YOU
Seen at 1:10
Are you sure it's ok?
あ
→
な
た
や
ま
ABC
わ
Delete that...

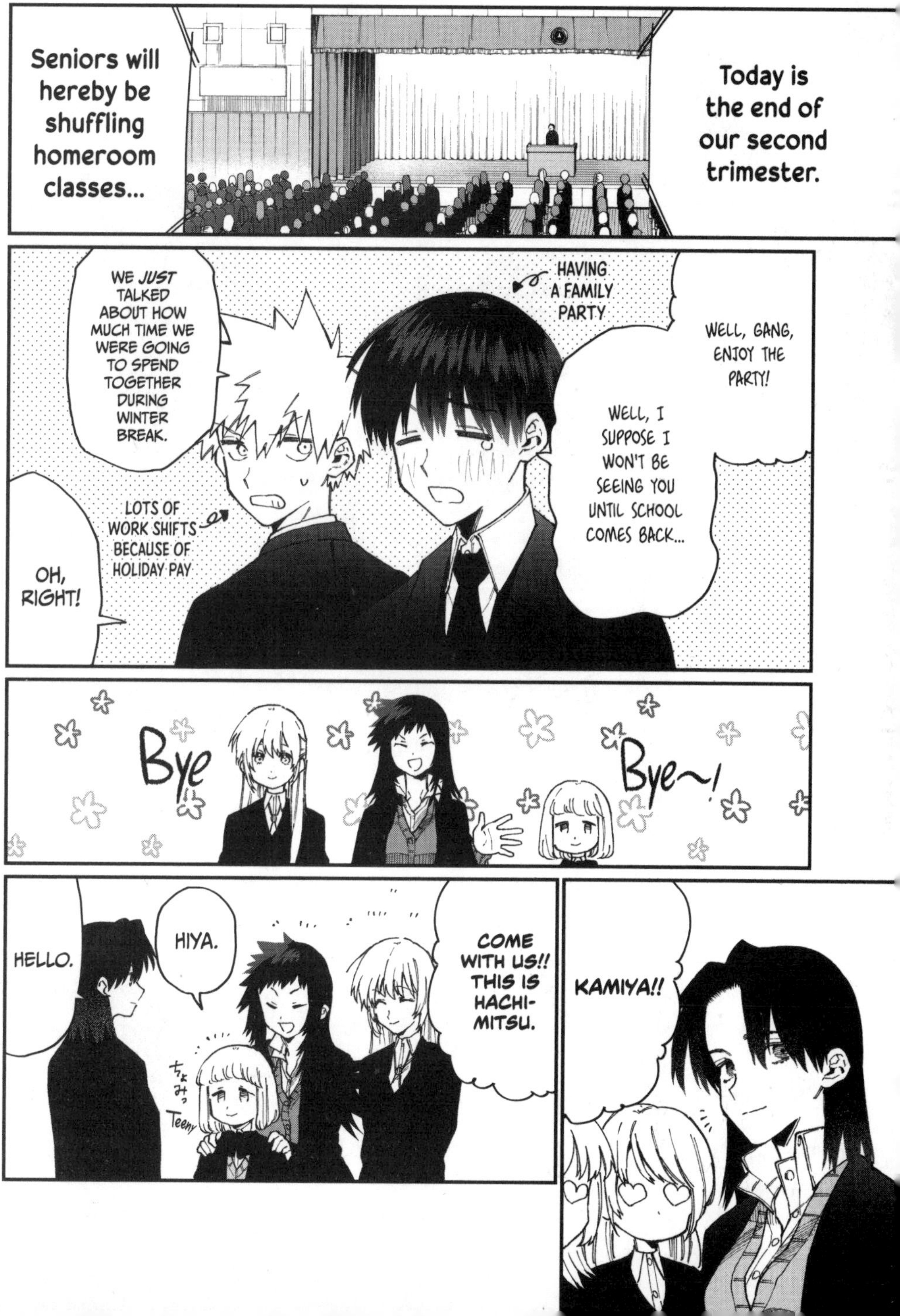
Today is the end of our second trimester.
Seniors will hereby be shuffling homeroom classes...
WELL, GANG, ENJOY THE PARTY!
HAVING A FAMILY PARTY
WELL, I SUPPOSE I WON'T BE SEEING YOU UNTIL SCHOOL COMES BACK...
WE JUST TALKED ABOUT HOW MUCH TIME WE WERE GOING TO SPEND TOGETHER DURING WINTER BREAK.
LOTS OF WORK SHIFTS BECAUSE OF HOLIDAY PAY
OH, RIGHT!
Bye~!
Bye
KAMIYA!!
COME WITH US!! THIS IS HACHI-MITSU.
HIYA.
HELLO.
ちょみっ
Teeny

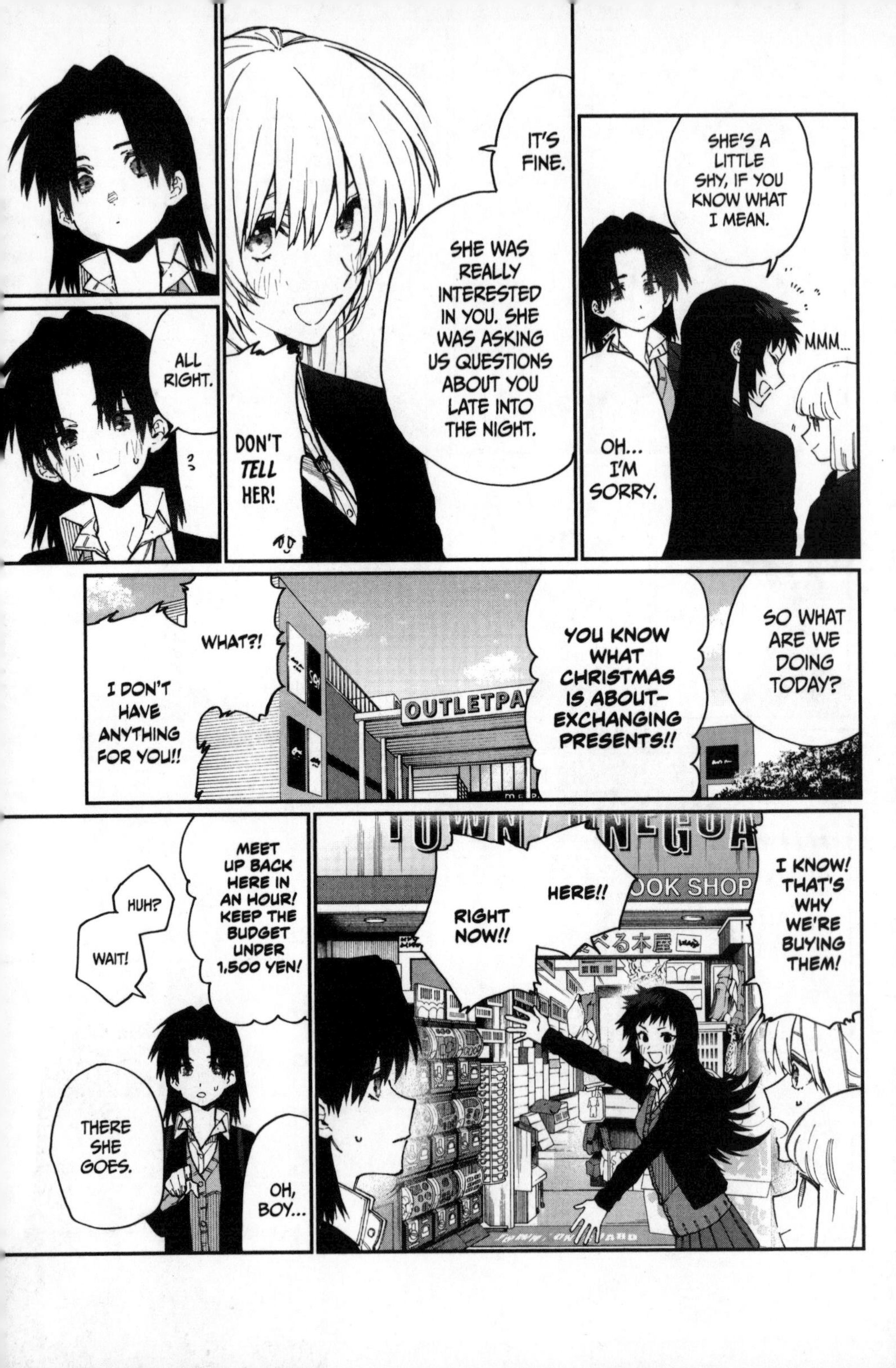
SHE'S A LITTLE SHY, IF YOU KNOW WHAT I MEAN.
MMM...
OH... I'M SORRY.
IT'S FINE.
SHE WAS REALLY INTERESTED IN YOU. SHE WAS ASKING US QUESTIONS ABOUT YOU LATE INTO THE NIGHT.
DON'T *TELL* HER!
ALL RIGHT.
SO WHAT ARE WE DOING TODAY?
YOU KNOW WHAT CHRISTMAS IS ABOUT—EXCHANGING PRESENTS!!
WHAT?!
I DON'T HAVE ANYTHING FOR YOU!!
I KNOW! THAT'S WHY WE'RE BUYING THEM!
HERE!!
RIGHT NOW!!
MEET UP BACK HERE IN AN HOUR! KEEP THE BUDGET UNDER 1,500 YEN!
HUH?
WAIT!
OH, BOY...
THERE SHE GOES.

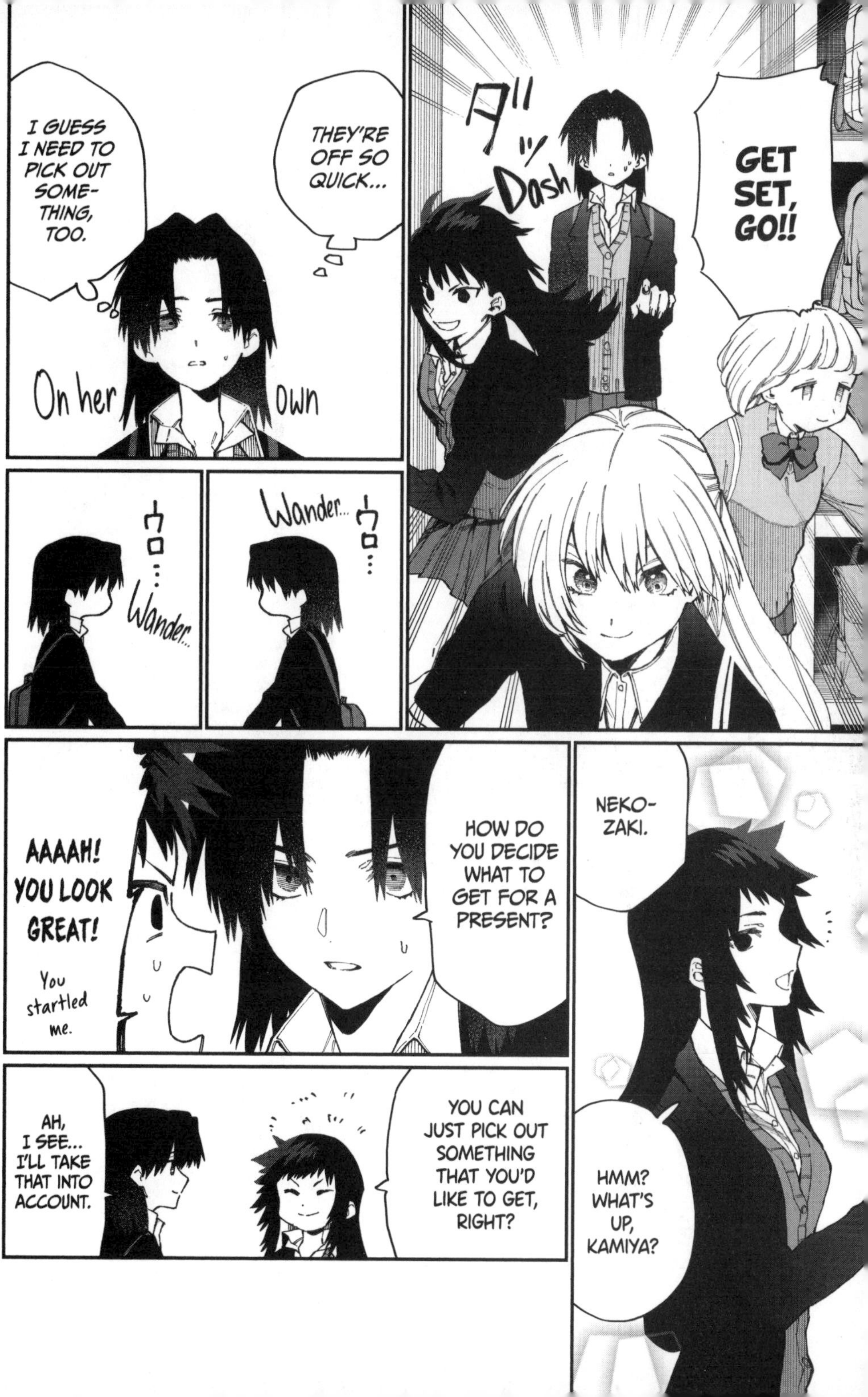
GET SET, GO!!
ダッ
Dash
THEY'RE OFF SO QUICK...
I GUESS I NEED TO PICK OUT SOME-THING, TOO.
On her own
ウロ
Wander...
ウロ...
Wander...
NEKO-ZAKI.
HMM? WHAT'S UP, KAMIYA?
HOW DO YOU DECIDE WHAT TO GET FOR A PRESENT?
AAAAH! YOU LOOK GREAT!
You startled me.
YOU CAN JUST PICK OUT SOMETHING THAT YOU'D LIKE TO GET, RIGHT?
AH, I SEE... I'LL TAKE THAT INTO ACCOUNT.

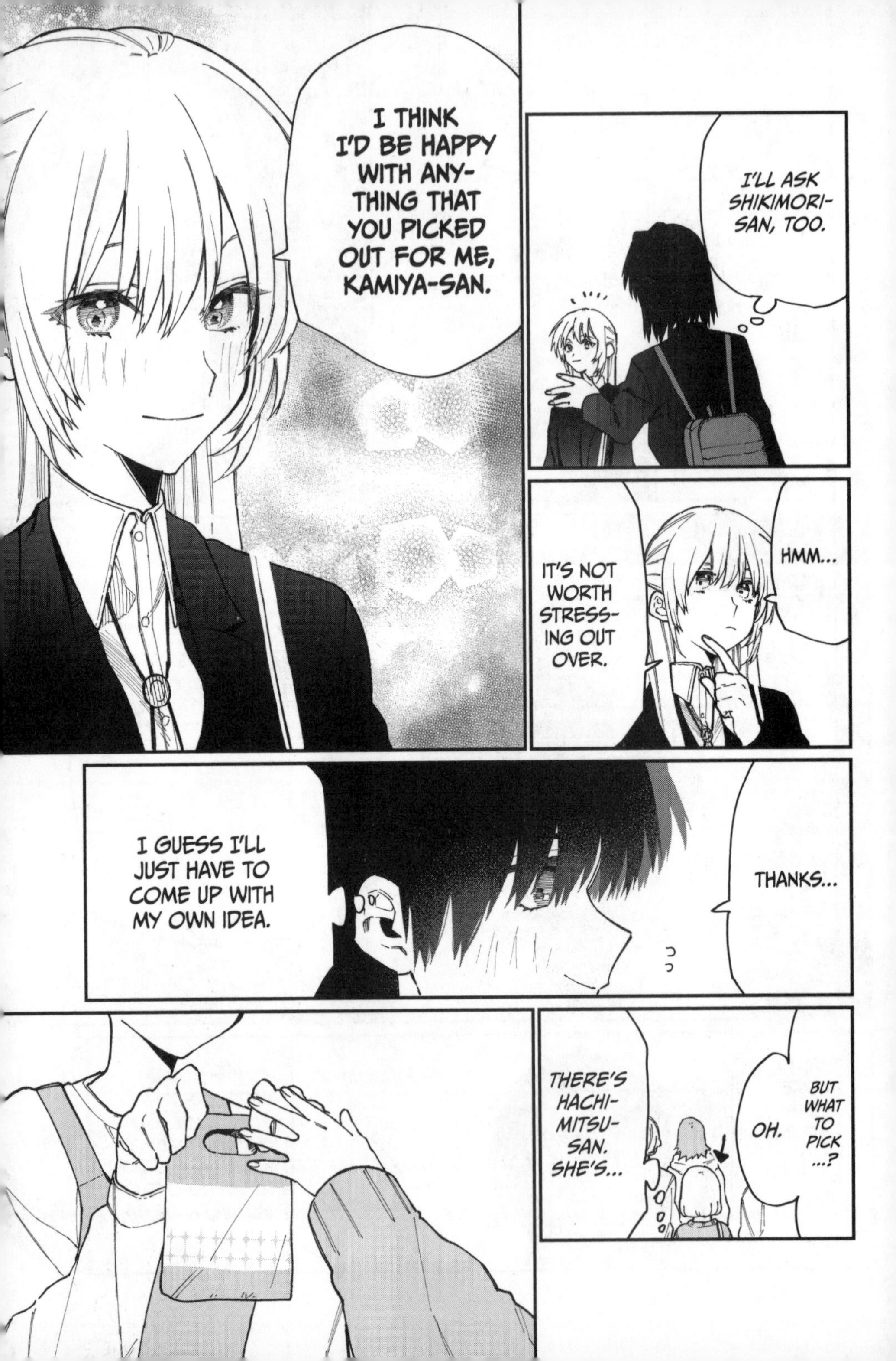
I'LL ASK SHIKIMORI-SAN, TOO.
HMM...
IT'S NOT WORTH STRESSING OUT OVER.
I THINK I'D BE HAPPY WITH ANYTHING THAT YOU PICKED OUT FOR ME, KAMIYA-SAN.
THANKS...
I GUESS I'LL JUST HAVE TO COME UP WITH MY OWN IDEA.
BUT WHAT TO PICK ...?
OH.
THERE'S HACHIMITSU-SAN. SHE'S...

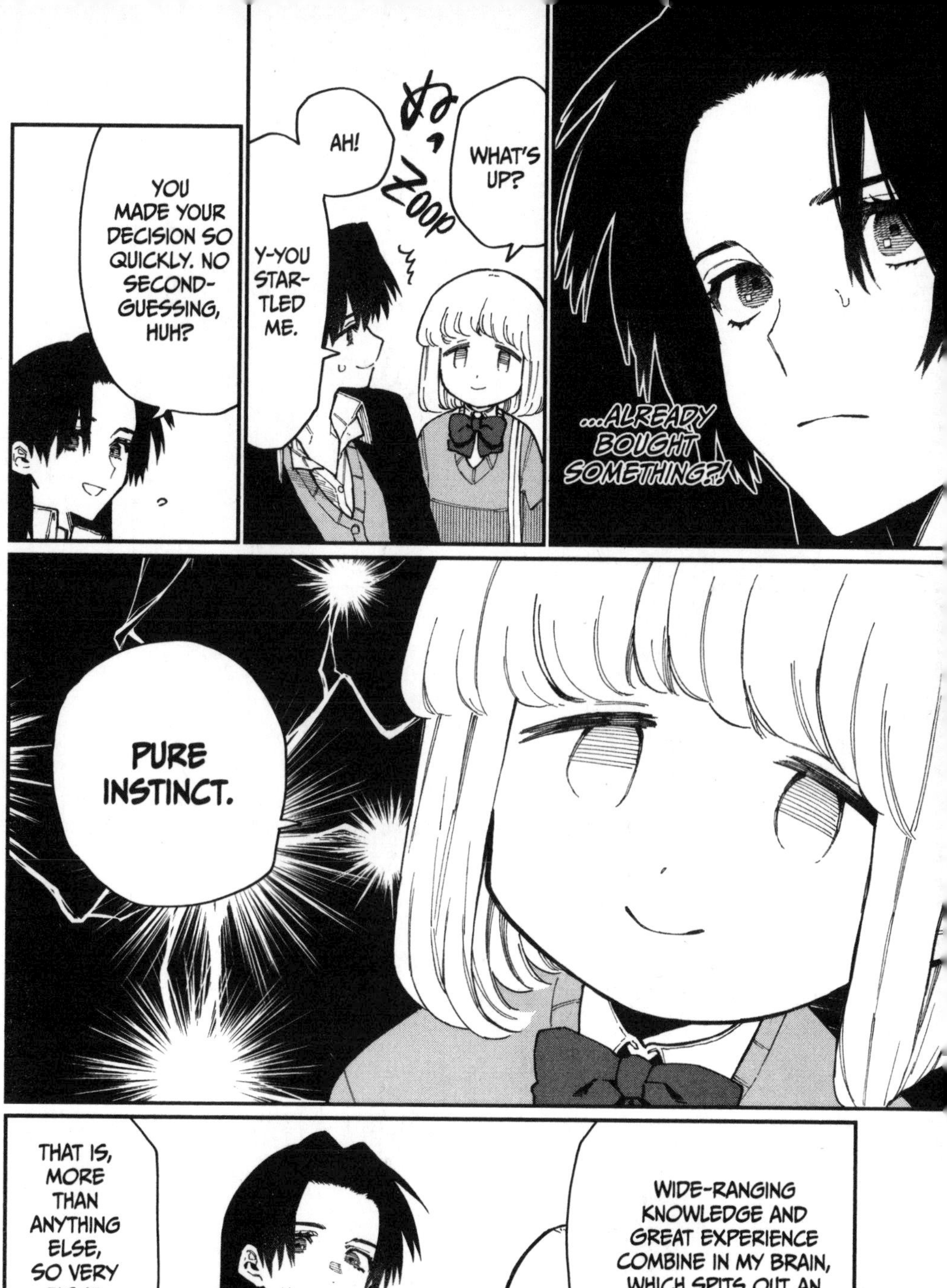
...ALREADY BOUGHT SOMETHING?!
ぬっ
ZOOP
AH!
Y-YOU STARTLED ME.
WHAT'S UP?
YOU MADE YOUR DECISION SO QUICKLY. NO SECOND-GUESSING, HUH?
PURE INSTINCT.
WIDE-RANGING KNOWLEDGE AND GREAT EXPERIENCE COMBINE IN MY BRAIN, WHICH SPITS OUT AN INSTINCTUAL ANSWER...
THAT IS, MORE THAN ANYTHING ELSE, SO VERY RIGHT.

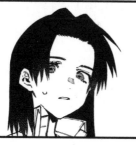

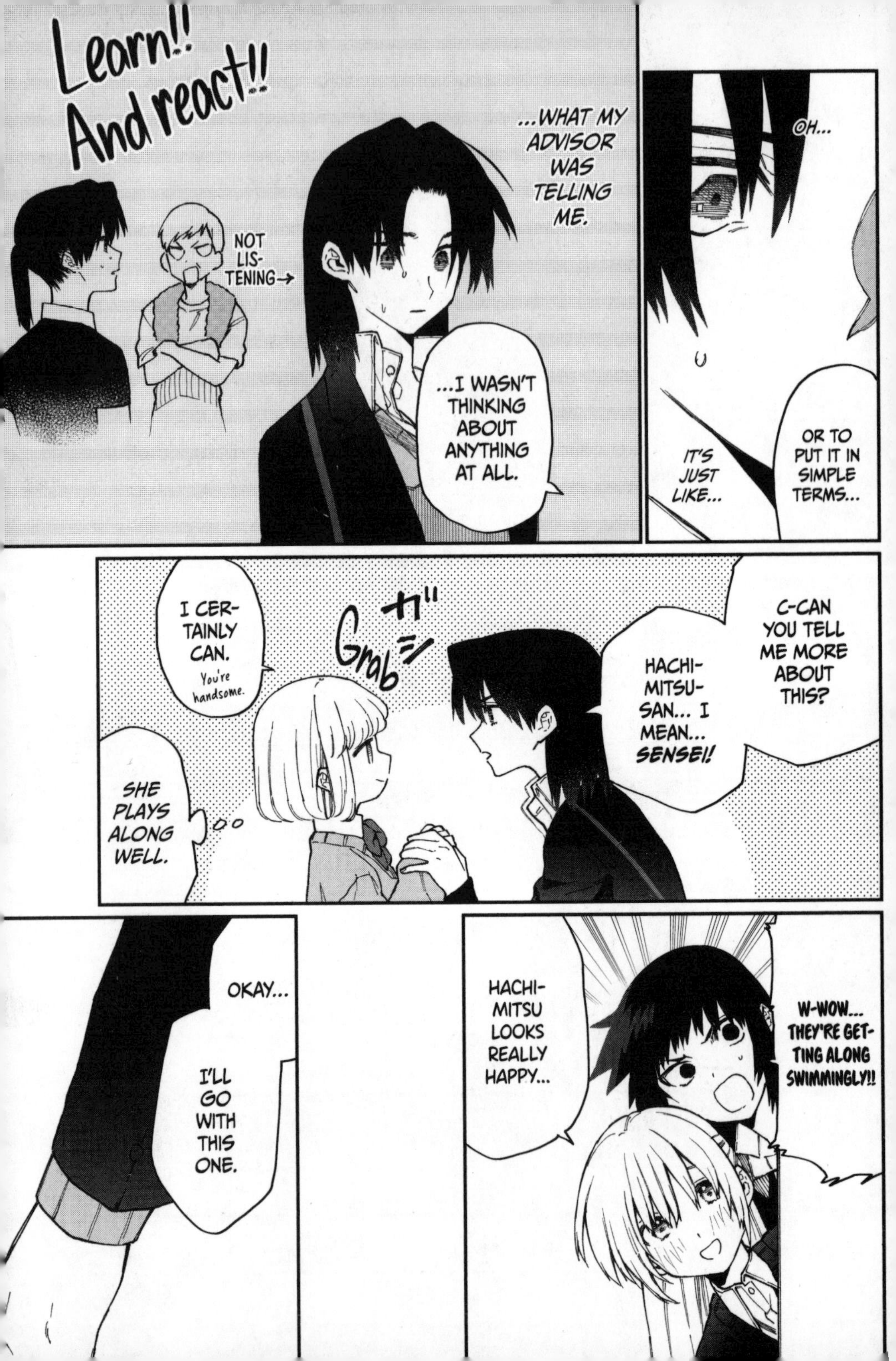
OH...
OR TO PUT IT IN SIMPLE TERMS...
IT'S JUST LIKE...
...WHAT MY ADVISOR WAS TELLING ME.
Learn!! And react!!
NOT LISTENING→
...I WASN'T THINKING ABOUT ANYTHING AT ALL.
C-CAN YOU TELL ME MORE ABOUT THIS?
HACHIMITSU-SAN... I MEAN... SENSEI!
Grab
I CERTAINLY CAN.
You're handsome.
SHE PLAYS ALONG WELL.
W-WOW... THEY'RE GETTING ALONG SWIMMINGLY!!
HACHIMITSU LOOKS REALLY HAPPY...
OKAY...
I'LL GO WITH THIS ONE.

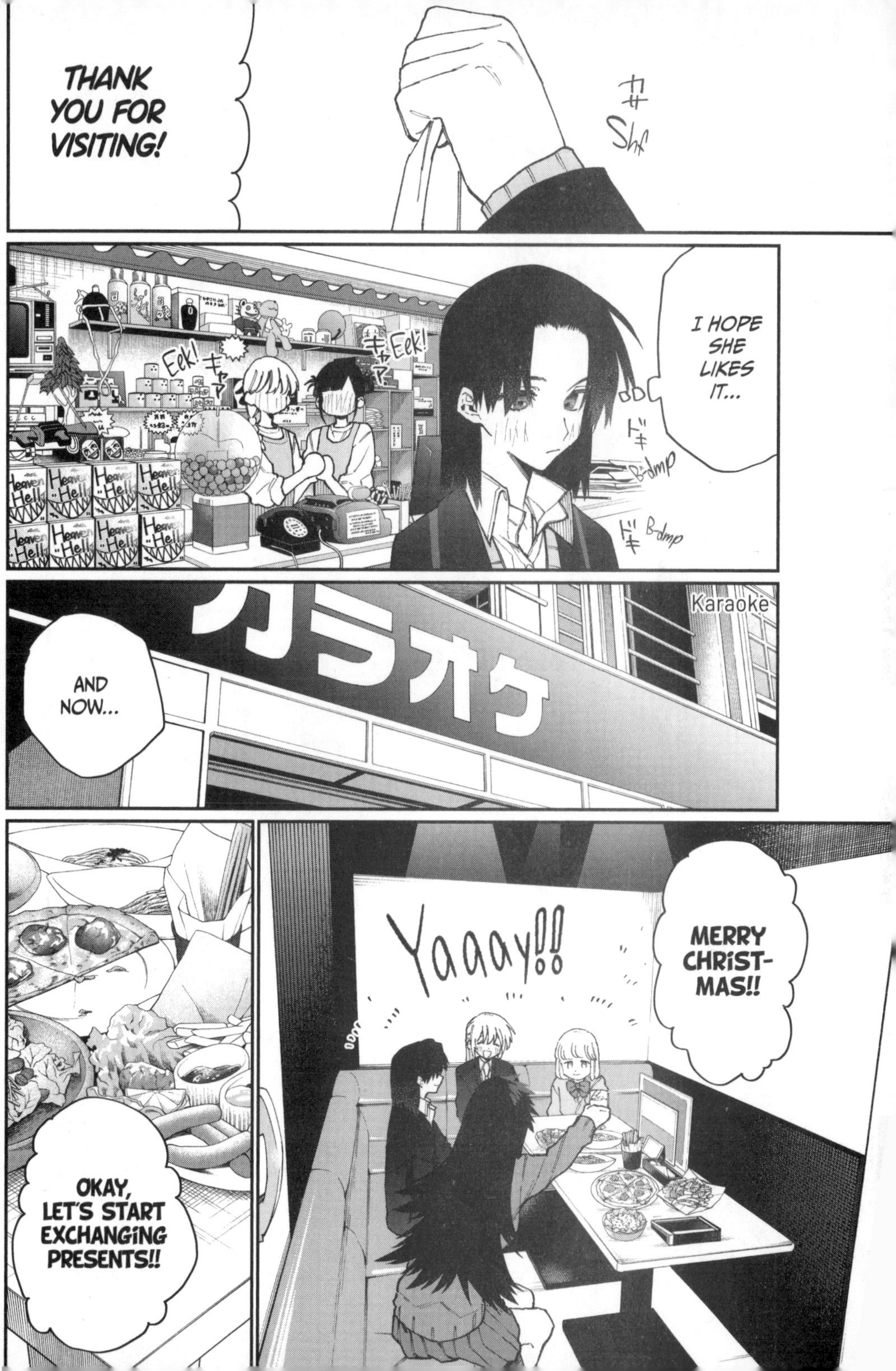
カサ
Shf
THANK YOU FOR VISITING!
I HOPE SHE LIKES IT...
ドキ
B-dmp
ドキ
B-dmp
キャア
Eek!
キャア
Eek!
Heaven Hell
Karaoke
AND NOW...
MERRY CHRISTMAS!!
Yaaay!!
OKAY, LET'S START EXCHANGING PRESENTS!!

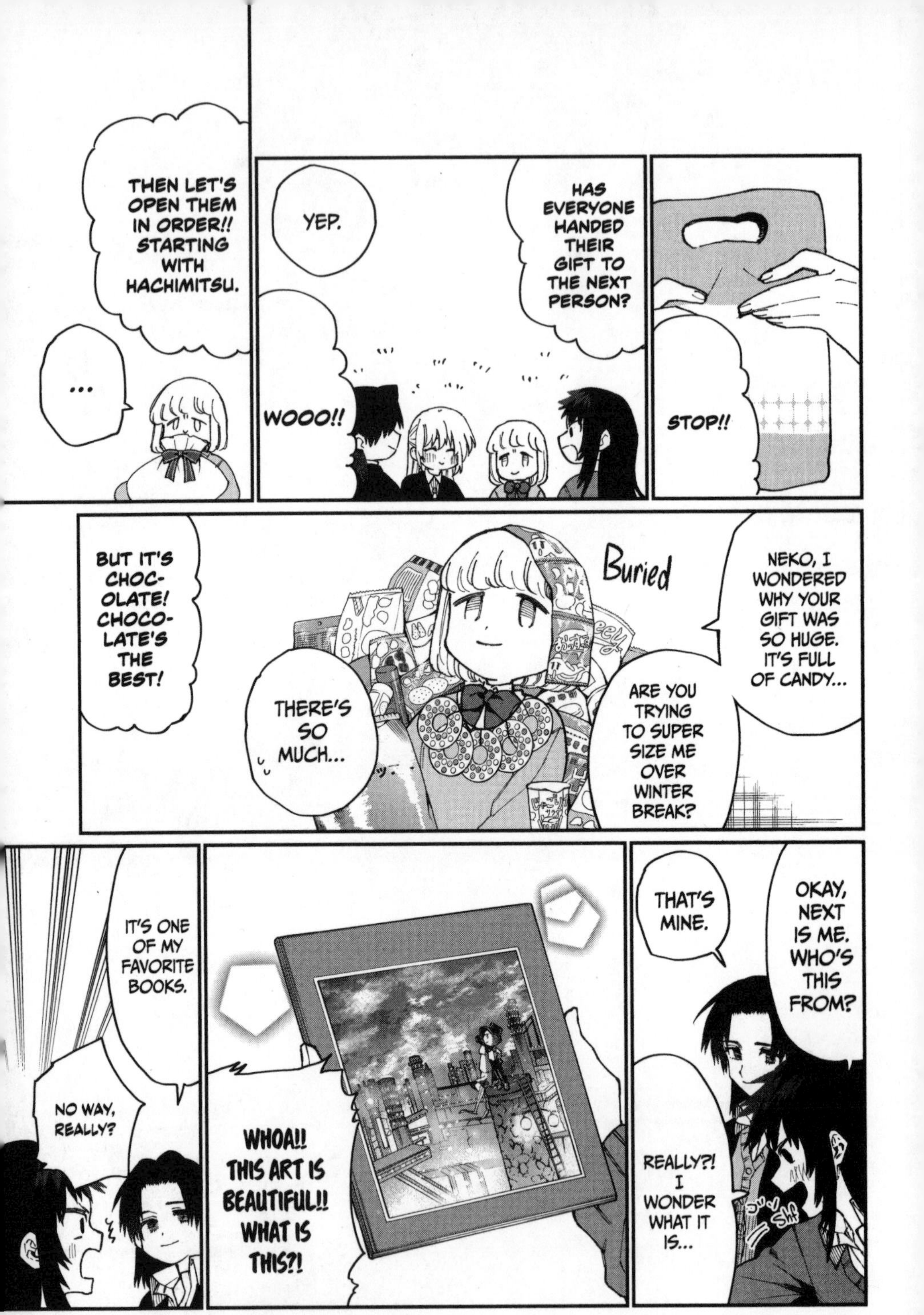
STOP!!
HAS EVERYONE HANDED THEIR GIFT TO THE NEXT PERSON?
YEP.
WOOO!!
THEN LET'S OPEN THEM IN ORDER!! STARTING WITH HACHIMITSU.
...
NEKO, I WONDERED WHY YOUR GIFT WAS SO HUGE. IT'S FULL OF CANDY...
ARE YOU TRYING TO SUPER SIZE ME OVER WINTER BREAK?
Buried
THERE'S SO MUCH...
BUT IT'S CHOCO-LATE! CHOCO-LATE'S THE BEST!
OKAY, NEXT IS ME. WHO'S THIS FROM?
THAT'S MINE.
REALLY?! I WONDER WHAT IT IS...
WHOA!! THIS ART IS BEAUTIFUL!! WHAT IS THIS?!
IT'S ONE OF MY FAVORITE BOOKS.
NO WAY, REALLY?

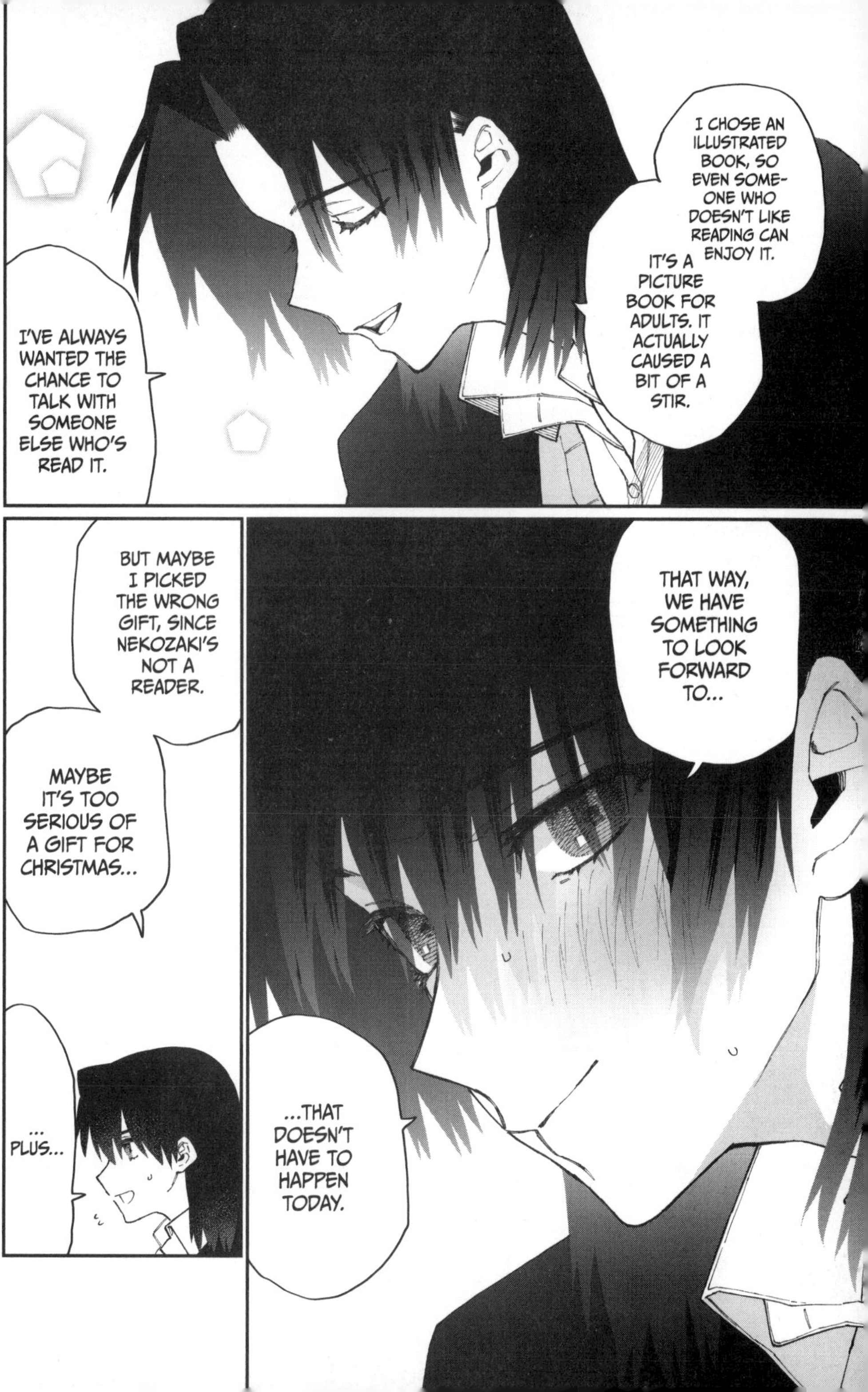
I CHOSE AN ILLUSTRATED BOOK, SO EVEN SOME-ONE WHO DOESN'T LIKE READING CAN ENJOY IT.
IT'S A PICTURE BOOK FOR ADULTS. IT ACTUALLY CAUSED A BIT OF A STIR.
I'VE ALWAYS WANTED THE CHANCE TO TALK WITH SOMEONE ELSE WHO'S READ IT.
BUT MAYBE I PICKED THE WRONG GIFT, SINCE NEKOZAKI'S NOT A READER.
MAYBE IT'S TOO SERIOUS OF A GIFT FOR CHRISTMAS...
... PLUS...
THAT WAY, WE HAVE SOMETHING TO LOOK FORWARD TO...
...THAT DOESN'T HAVE TO HAPPEN TODAY.

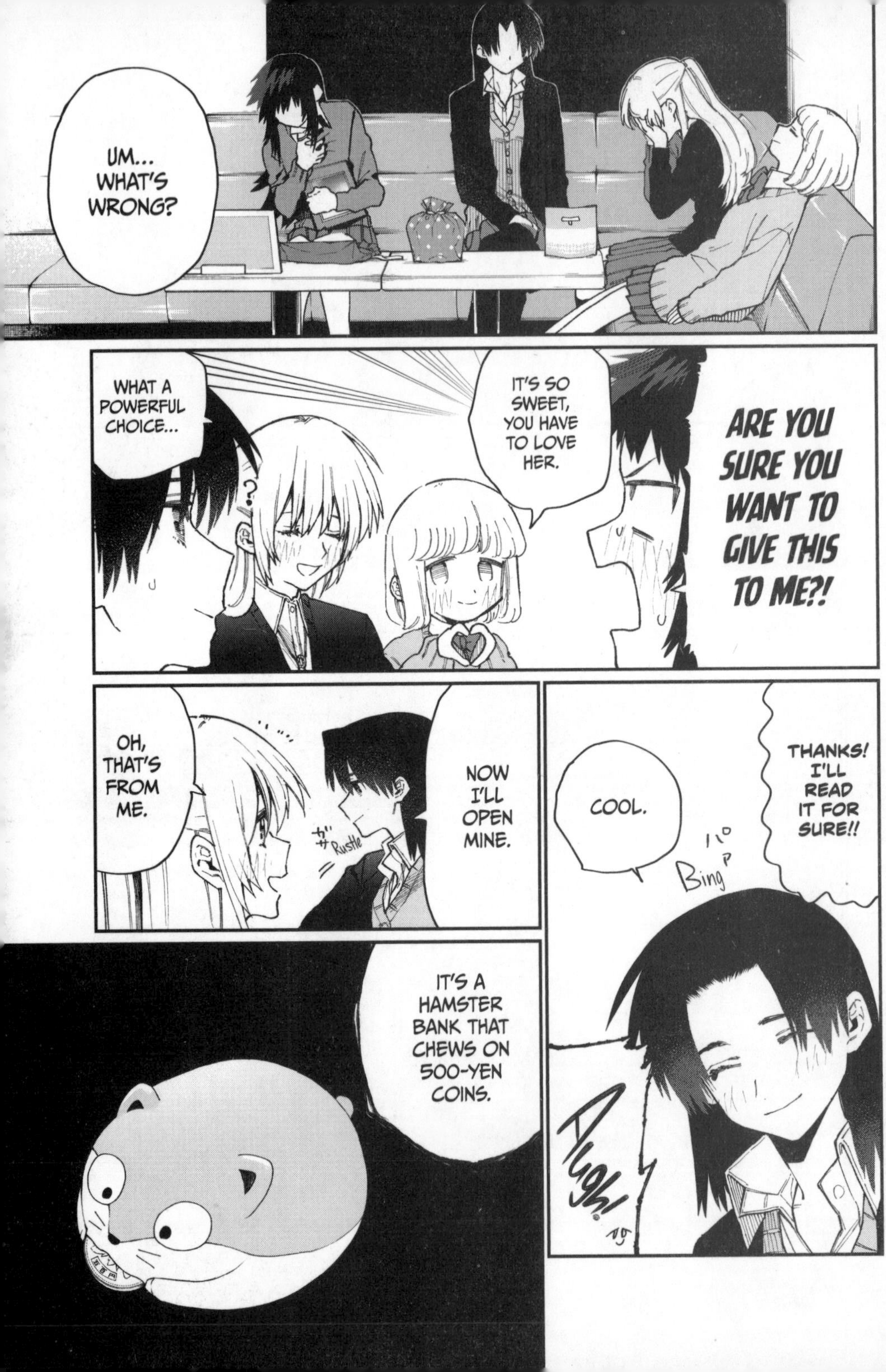
UM... WHAT'S WRONG?
ARE YOU SURE YOU WANT TO GIVE THIS TO ME?!
IT'S SO SWEET, YOU HAVE TO LOVE HER.
WHAT A POWERFUL CHOICE...
?
THANKS! I'LL READ IT FOR SURE!!
COOL.
Bing
Augh!
NOW I'LL OPEN MINE.
Rustle
OH, THAT'S FROM ME.
IT'S A HAMSTER BANK THAT CHEWS ON 500-YEN COINS.

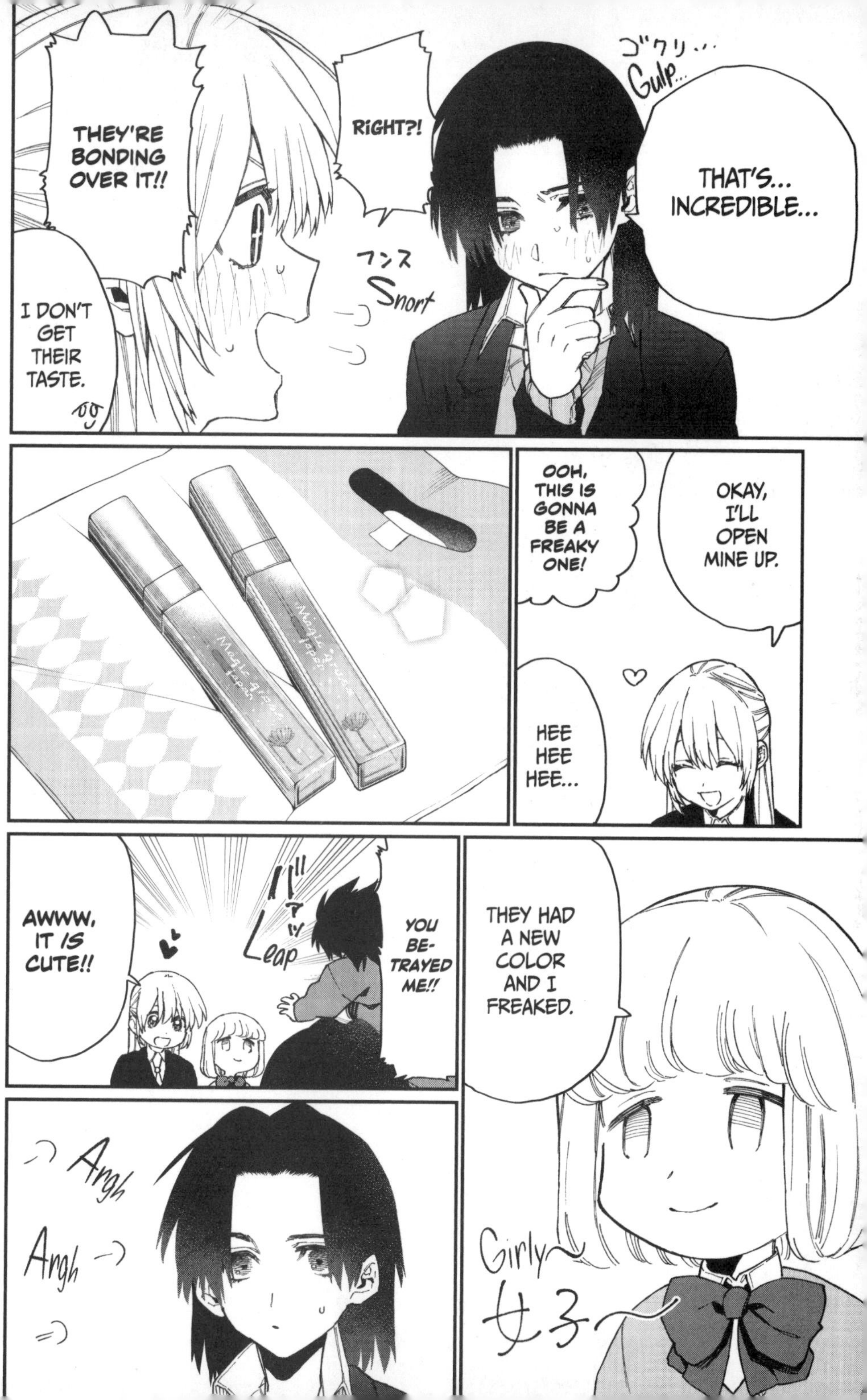

ゴクリ…
Gulp...
THAT'S... INCREDIBLE...
RIGHT?!
フンス
Snort
THEY'RE BONDING OVER IT!!
I DON'T GET THEIR TASTE.
OKAY, I'LL OPEN MINE UP.
OOH, THIS IS GONNA BE A FREAKY ONE!
HEE HEE HEE...
THEY HAD A NEW COLOR AND I FREAKED.
Girly~
女子~
バッ
Leap
YOU BE-TRAYED ME!!
AWWW, IT IS CUTE!!
Argh
Argh

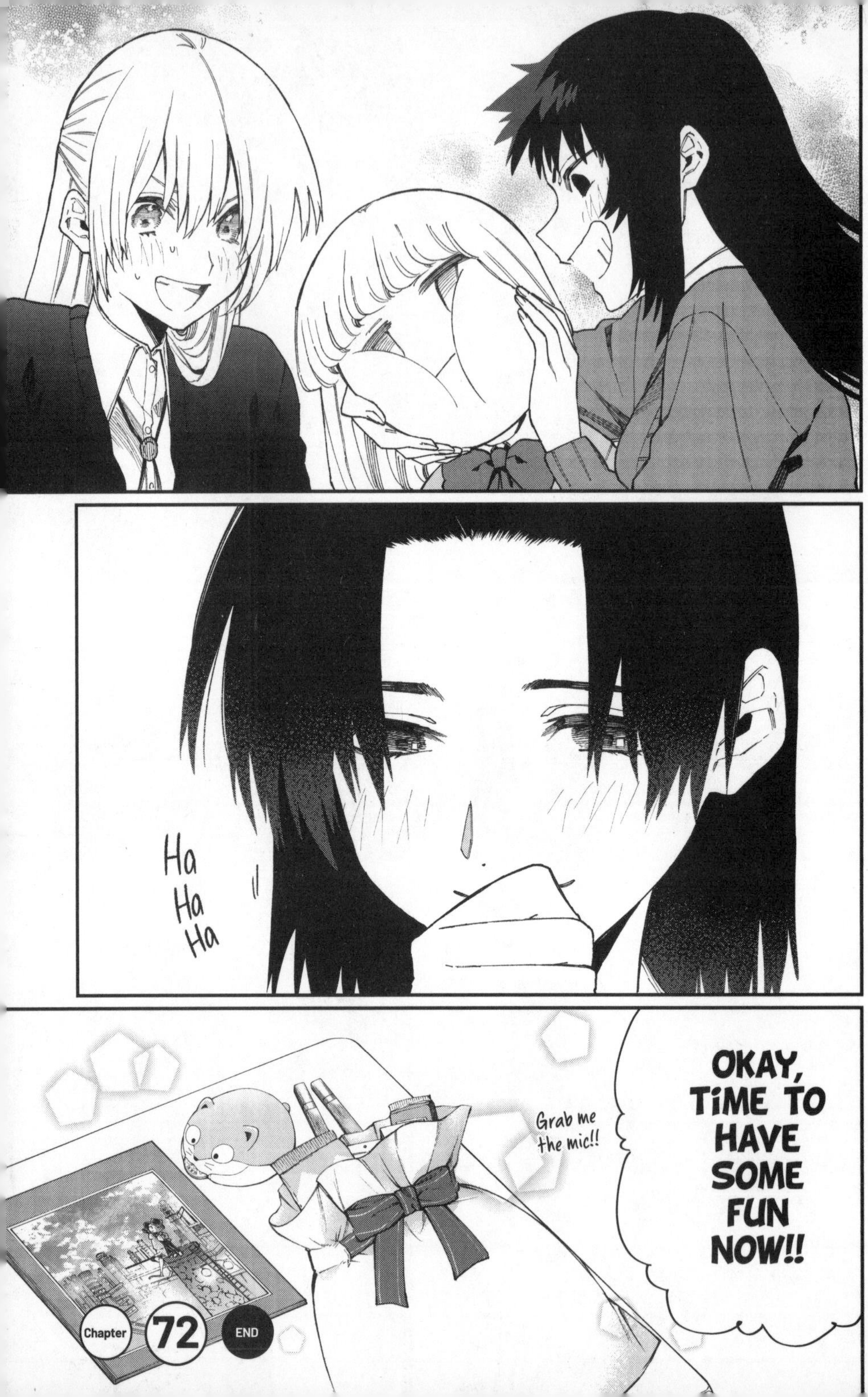
Ha Ha Ha
OKAY, TIME TO HAVE SOME FUN NOW!!
Grab me the mic!!
Chapter 72 END

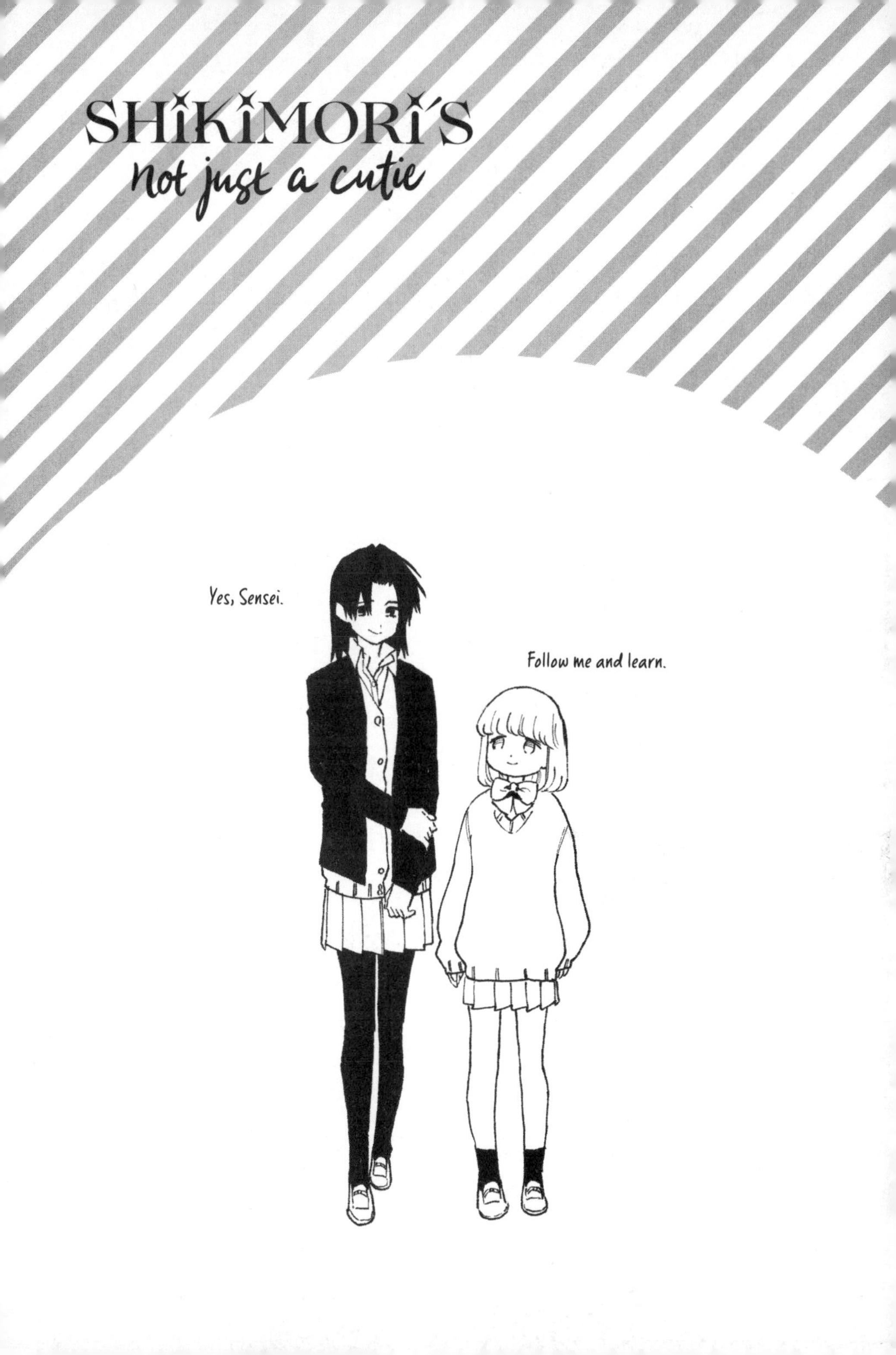
SHIKIMORI'S
not just a cutie
Follow me and learn.
Yes, Sensei.

Chapter 73

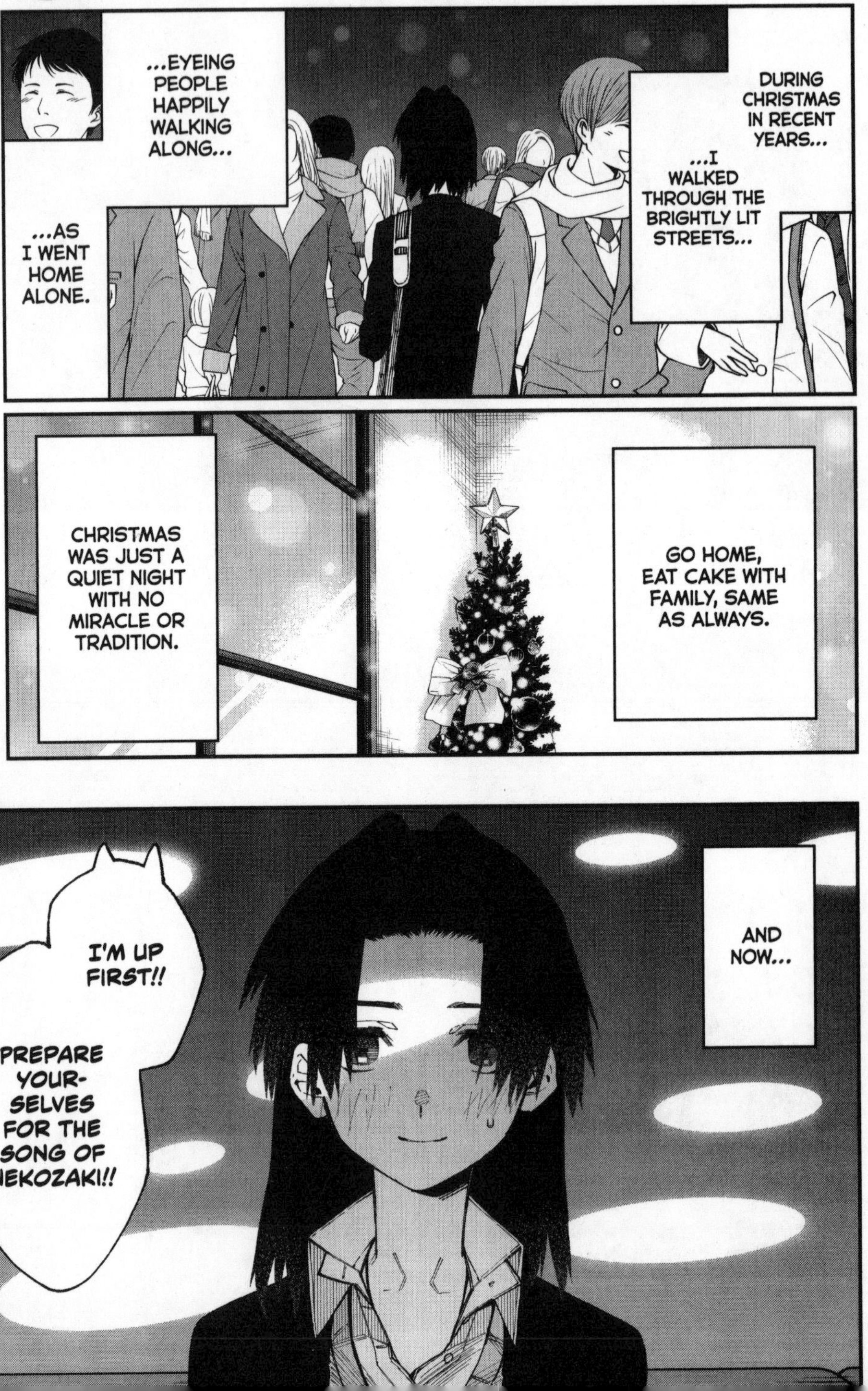
DURING CHRISTMAS IN RECENT YEARS...
...I WALKED THROUGH THE BRIGHTLY LIT STREETS...
...EYEING PEOPLE HAPPILY WALKING ALONG...
...AS I WENT HOME ALONE.
GO HOME, EAT CAKE WITH FAMILY, SAME AS ALWAYS.
CHRISTMAS WAS JUST A QUIET NIGHT WITH NO MIRACLE OR TRADITION.
AND NOW...
I'M UP FIRST!!
PREPARE YOUR-SELVES FOR THE SONG OF NEKOZAKI!!

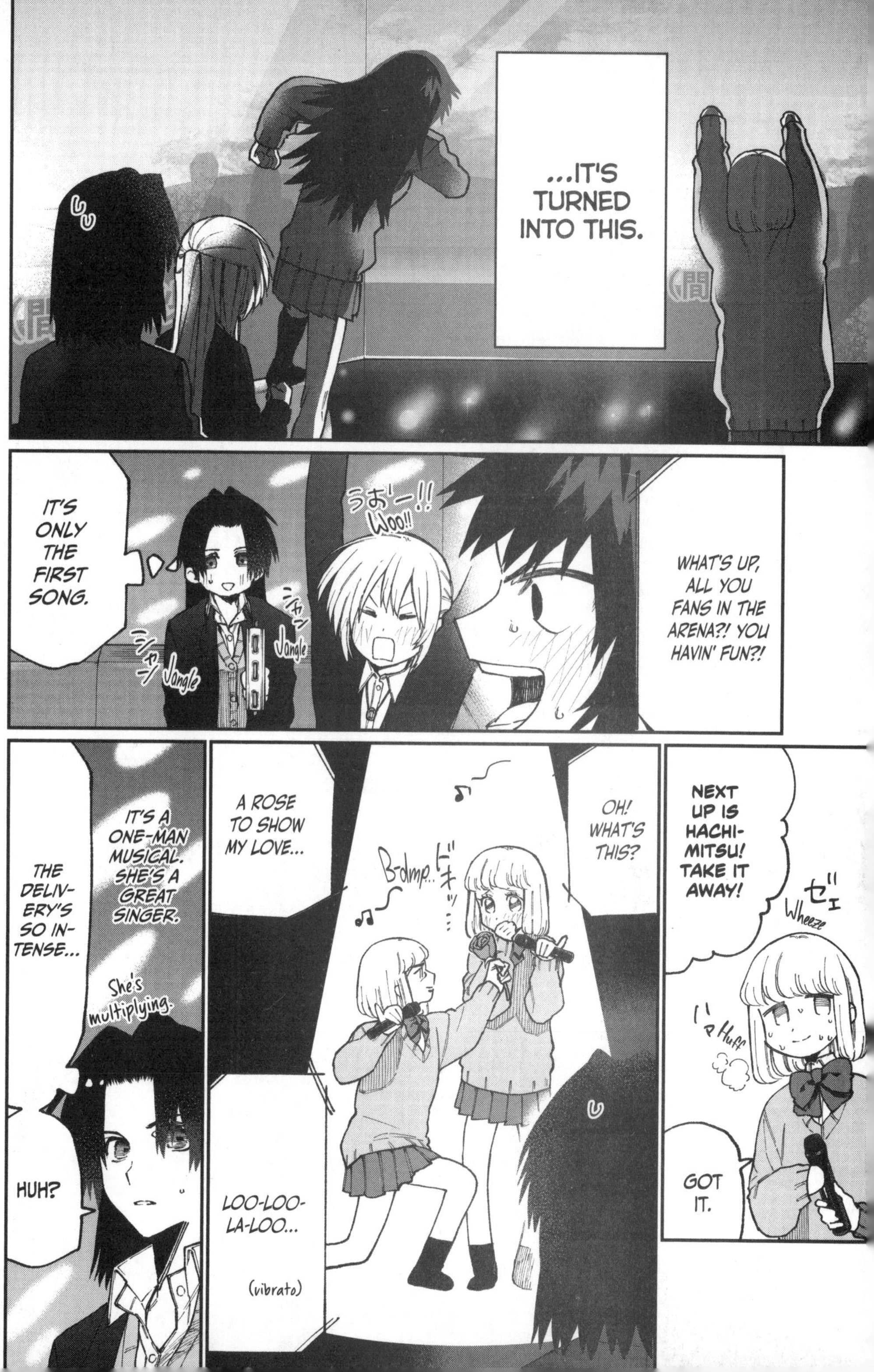

...IT'S TURNED INTO THIS.
WHAT'S UP, ALL YOU FANS IN THE ARENA?! YOU HAVIN' FUN?!
うおー!! Woo!!
シャン Jangle
シャン Jangle
IT'S ONLY THE FIRST SONG.
NEXT UP IS HACHI-MITSU! TAKE IT AWAY!
ゼェ Wheeze
ハァ Huff
GOT IT.
OH! WHAT'S THIS?
A ROSE TO SHOW MY LOVE...
ドキッ B-dmp...
LOO-LOO-LA-LOO...
(vibrato)
IT'S A ONE-MAN MUSICAL. SHE'S A GREAT SINGER.
THE DELIV-ERY'S SO IN-TENSE...
She's multiplying.
HUH?

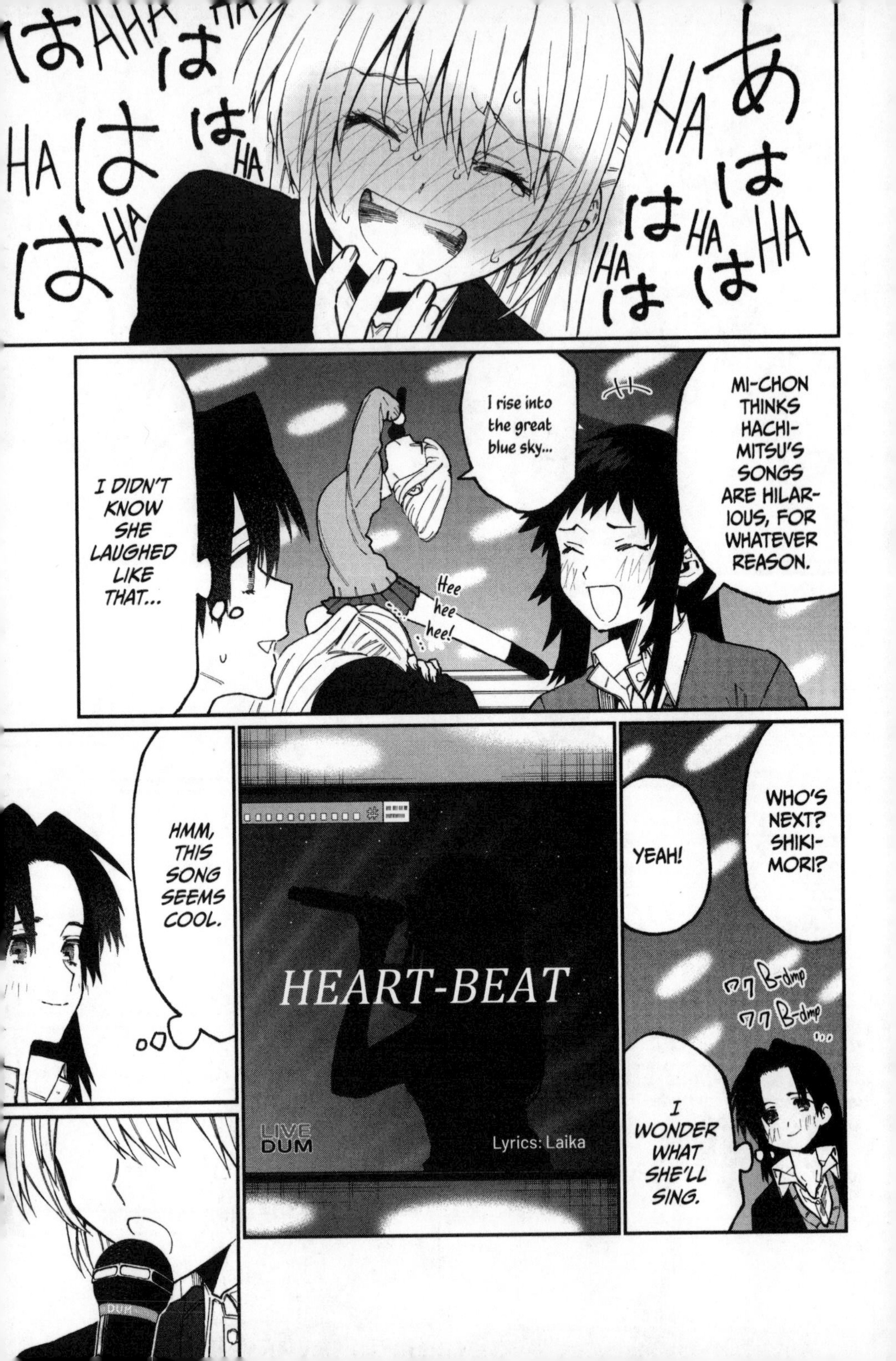
あはははは
HA HA HA HA
はAHAははははは
HA HA HA
MI-CHON THINKS HACHI-MITSU'S SONGS ARE HILARIOUS, FOR WHATEVER REASON.
I rise into the great blue sky...
Hee hee hee!
I DIDN'T KNOW SHE LAUGHED LIKE THAT...
WHO'S NEXT? SHIKI-MORI?
YEAH!
B-dmp B-dmp
...
I WONDER WHAT SHE'LL SING.
HEART-BEAT
LIVE DUM
Lyrics: Laika
HMM, THIS SONG SEEMS COOL.
DUM

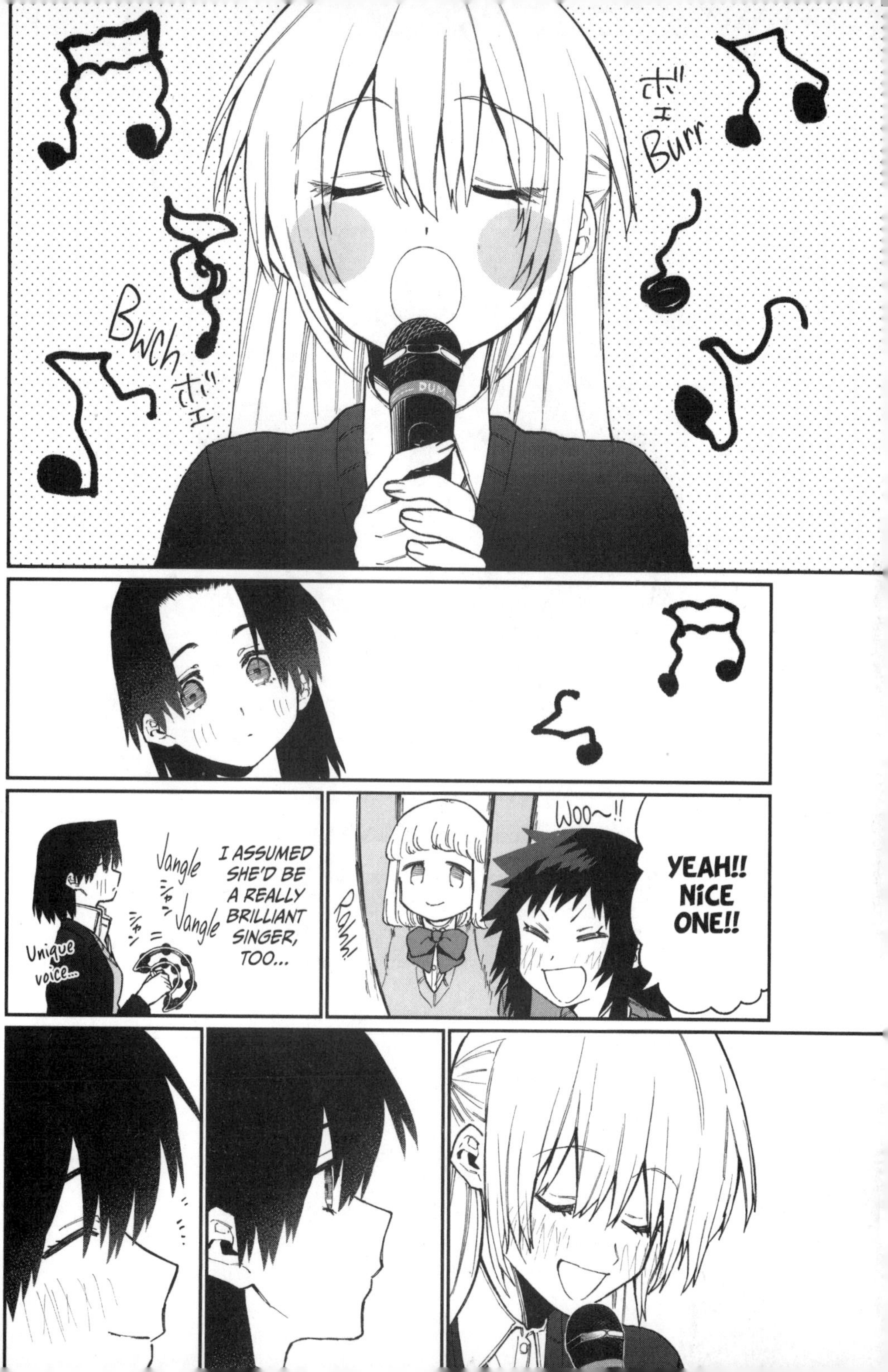

ボエ
Burr
Bwch
ボエ
Woo~!!
YEAH!! NiCE ONE!!
Rahh!
I ASSUMED SHE'D BE A REALLY BRILLIANT SINGER, TOO...
Jangle
Jangle
Unique voice...

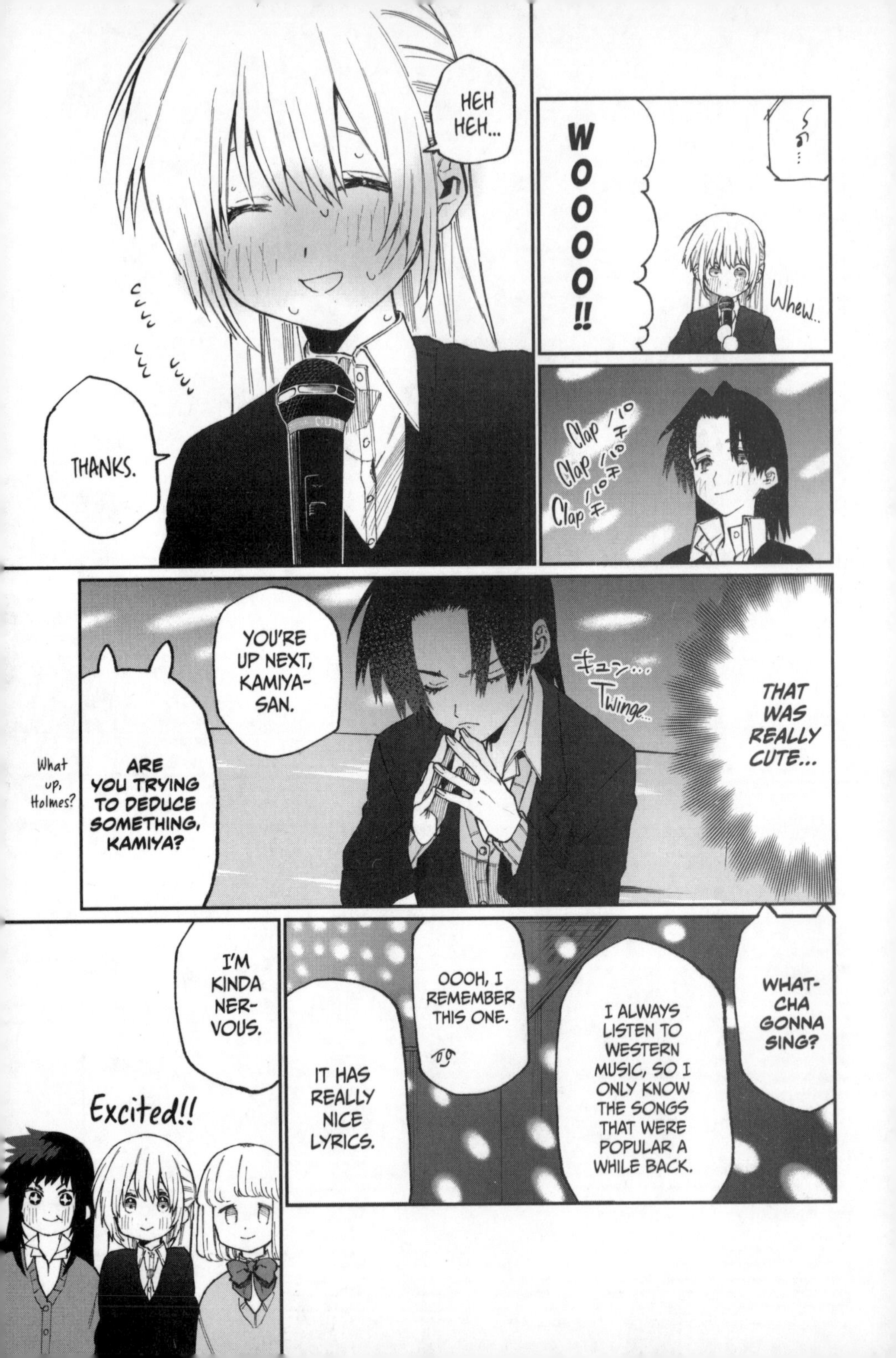

WOOOOO!!
Whew...
Clap パチ
Clap パチ
Clap パチ
HEH HEH...
THANKS.
THAT WAS REALLY CUTE...
キュン... Twinge...
YOU'RE UP NEXT, KAMIYA-SAN.
ARE YOU TRYING TO DEDUCE SOMETHING, KAMIYA?
What up, Holmes?
WHAT-CHA GONNA SING?
I ALWAYS LISTEN TO WESTERN MUSIC, SO I ONLY KNOW THE SONGS THAT WERE POPULAR A WHILE BACK.
OOOH, I REMEMBER THIS ONE.
IT HAS REALLY NICE LYRICS.
I'M KINDA NER-VOUS.
Excited!!

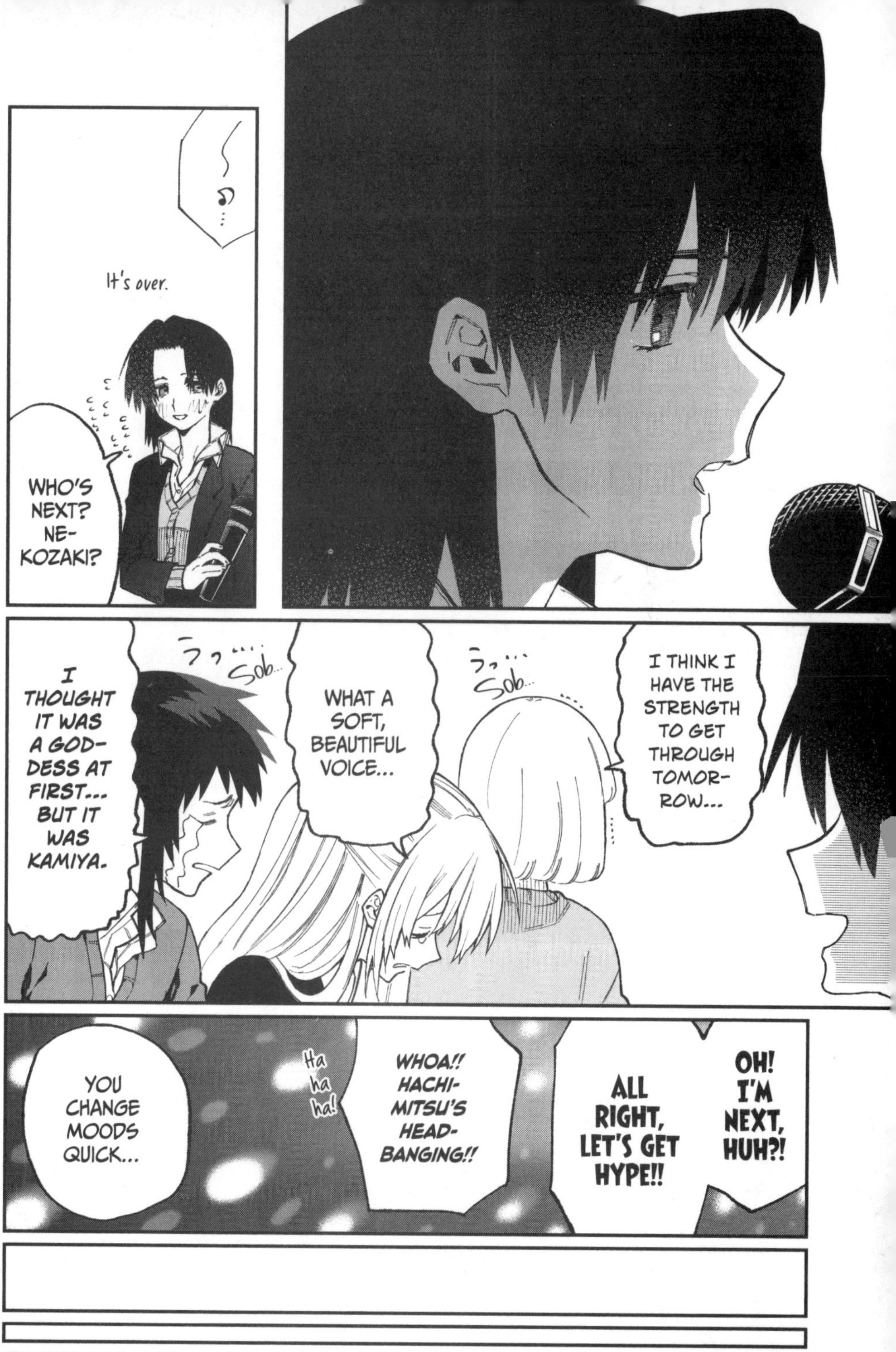
♪...
It's over.
WHO'S NEXT? NE-KOZAKI?
I THINK I HAVE THE STRENGTH TO GET THROUGH TOMORROW...
うっ... Sob...
WHAT A SOFT, BEAUTIFUL VOICE...
うっ.... Sob...
I THOUGHT IT WAS A GODDESS AT FIRST... BUT IT WAS KAMIYA.
OH! I'M NEXT, HUH?!
ALL RIGHT, LET'S GET HYPE!!
WHOA!! HACHIMITSU'S HEADBANGING!!
Ha ha ha!
YOU CHANGE MOODS QUICK...

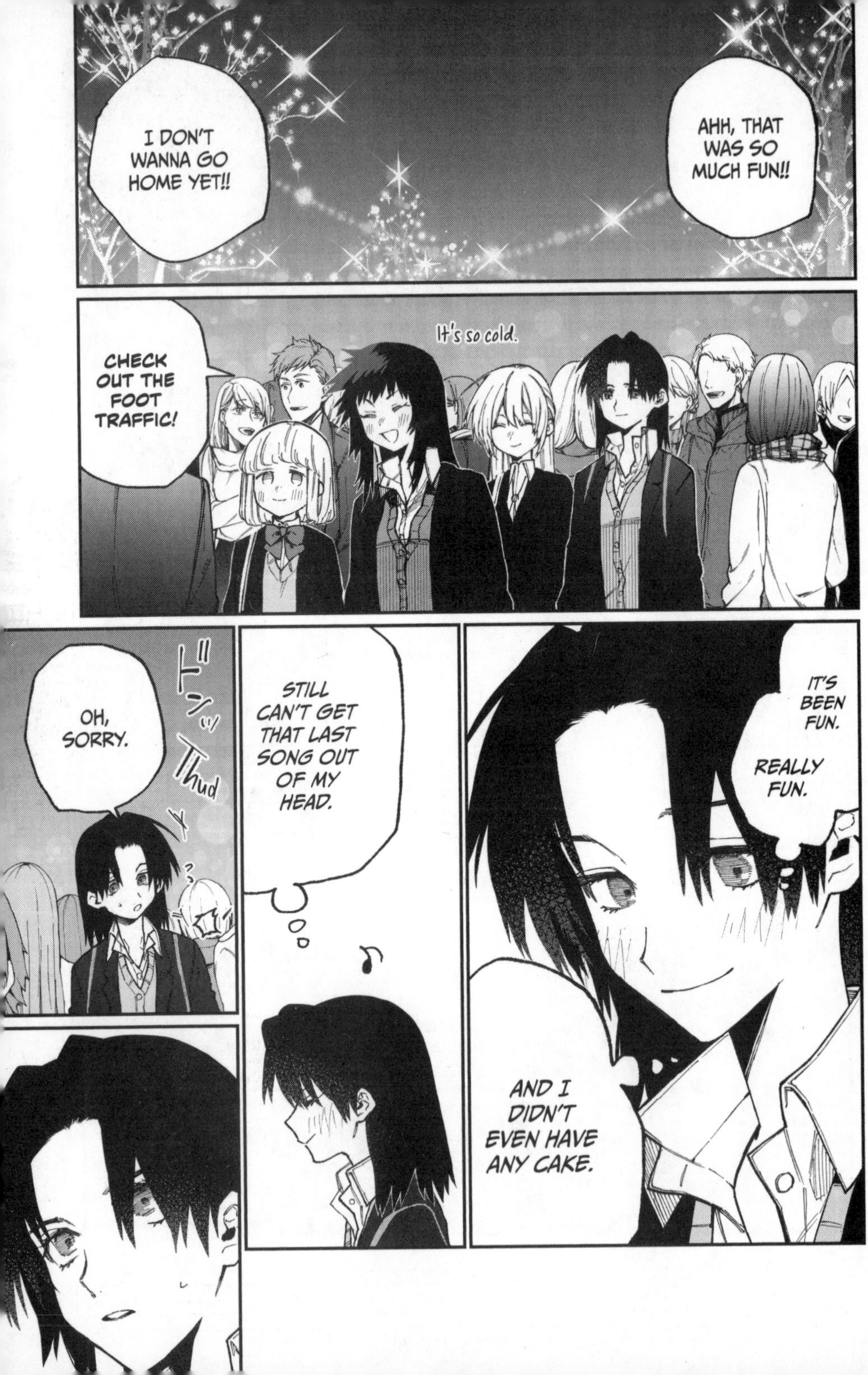
AHH, THAT WAS SO MUCH FUN!!
I DON'T WANNA GO HOME YET!!
It's so cold.
CHECK OUT THE FOOT TRAFFIC!
IT'S BEEN FUN.
REALLY FUN.
AND I DIDN'T EVEN HAVE ANY CAKE.
STILL CAN'T GET THAT LAST SONG OUT OF MY HEAD.
ドッ
Thud
OH, SORRY.

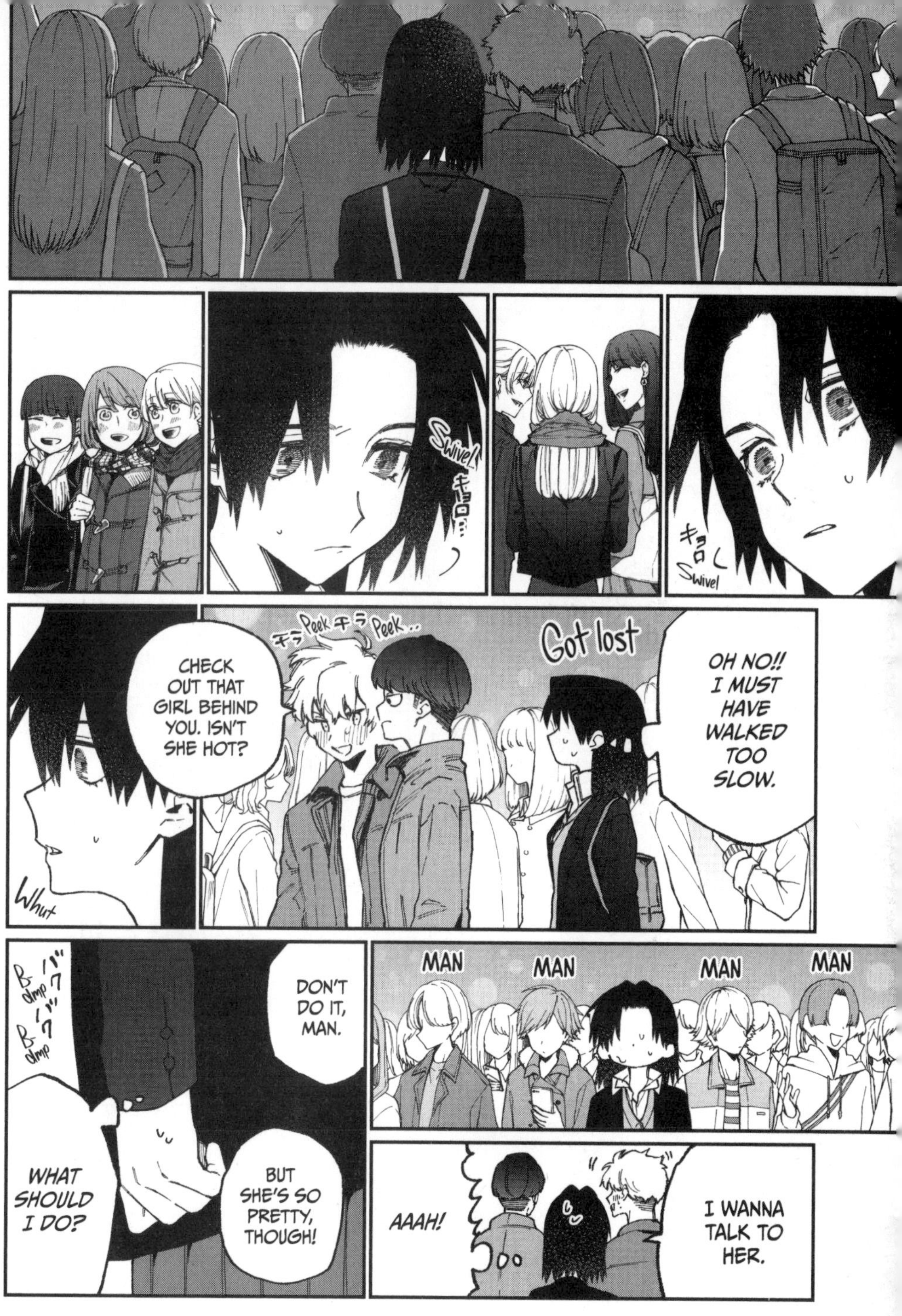

Swivel キョロ
Swivel キョロ…
OH NO!! I MUST HAVE WALKED TOO SLOW.
Got lost
チラ Peek チラ Peek..
CHECK OUT THAT GIRL BEHIND YOU. ISN'T SHE HOT?
Whut
MAN MAN MAN MAN
I WANNA TALK TO HER.
AAAH!
DON'T DO IT, MAN.
B- dmp
B- dmp
BUT SHE'S SO PRETTY, THOUGH!
WHAT SHOULD I DO?

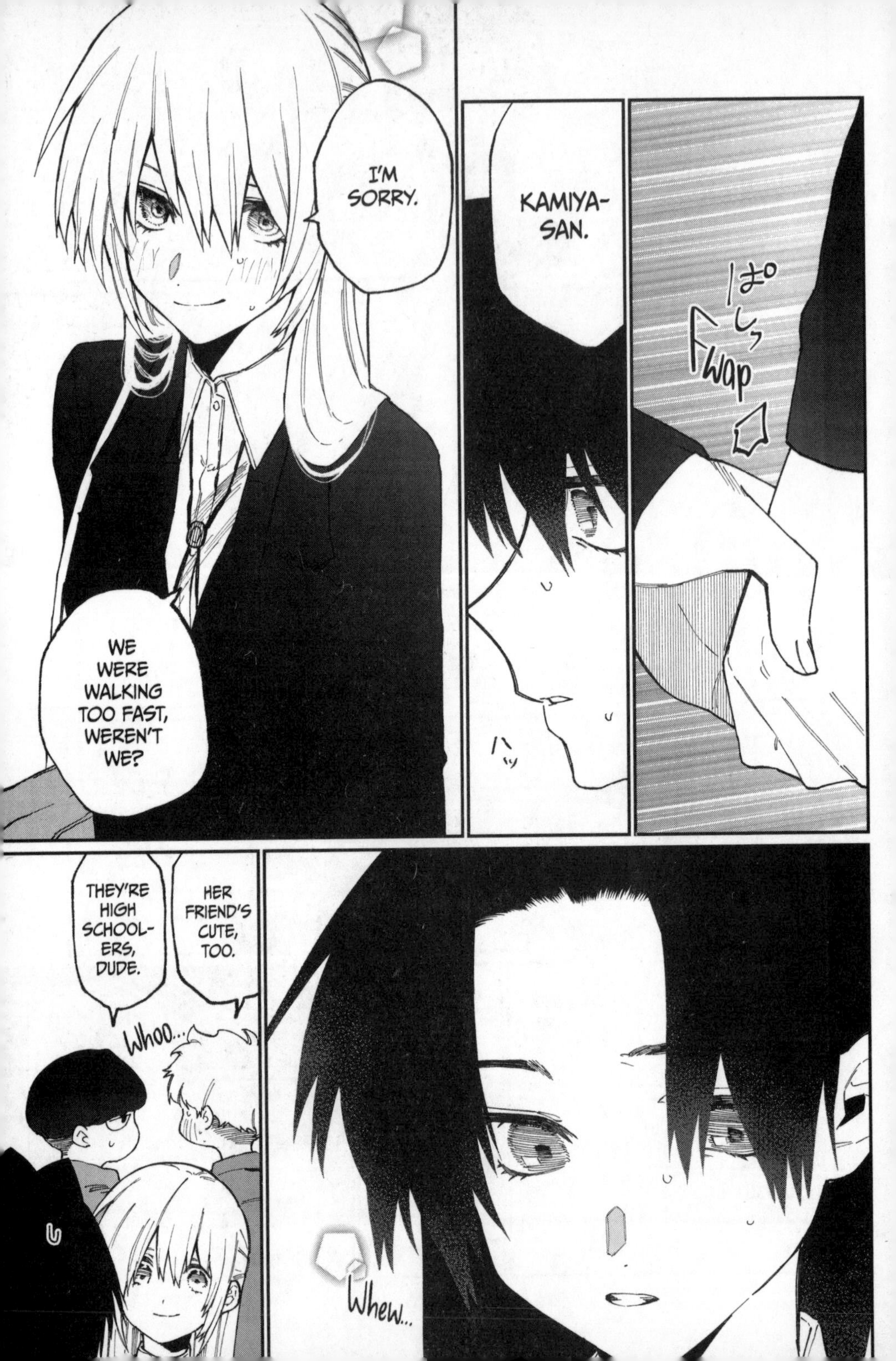
ぱしっ
Fwap
KAMIYA-SAN.
ハッ
I'M SORRY.
WE WERE WALKING TOO FAST, WEREN'T WE?
Whew...
HER FRIEND'S CUTE, TOO.
THEY'RE HIGH SCHOOL-ERS, DUDE.
Whoo...

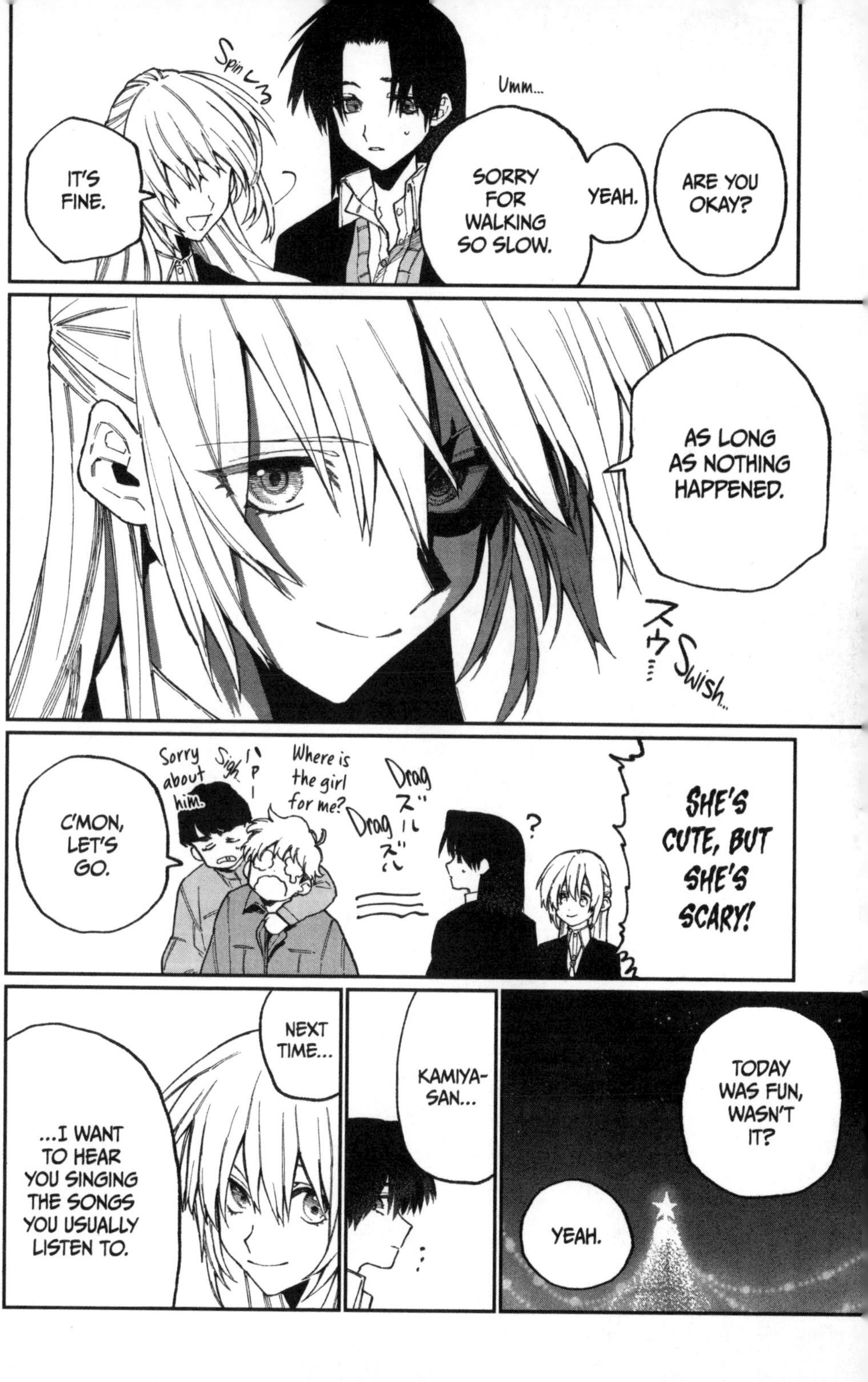
ARE YOU OKAY?
YEAH.
Umm...
SORRY FOR WALKING SO SLOW.
Spin くる
IT'S FINE.
AS LONG AS NOTHING HAPPENED.
スウ… Swish...
SHE'S CUTE, BUT SHE'S SCARY!
?
Drag ズル
Drag ズル
Where is the girl for me?
Sigh
Sorry about him.
C'MON, LET'S GO.
TODAY WAS FUN, WASN'T IT?
YEAH.
KAMIYA-SAN...
NEXT TIME...
...I WANT TO HEAR YOU SINGING THE SONGS YOU USUALLY LISTEN TO.

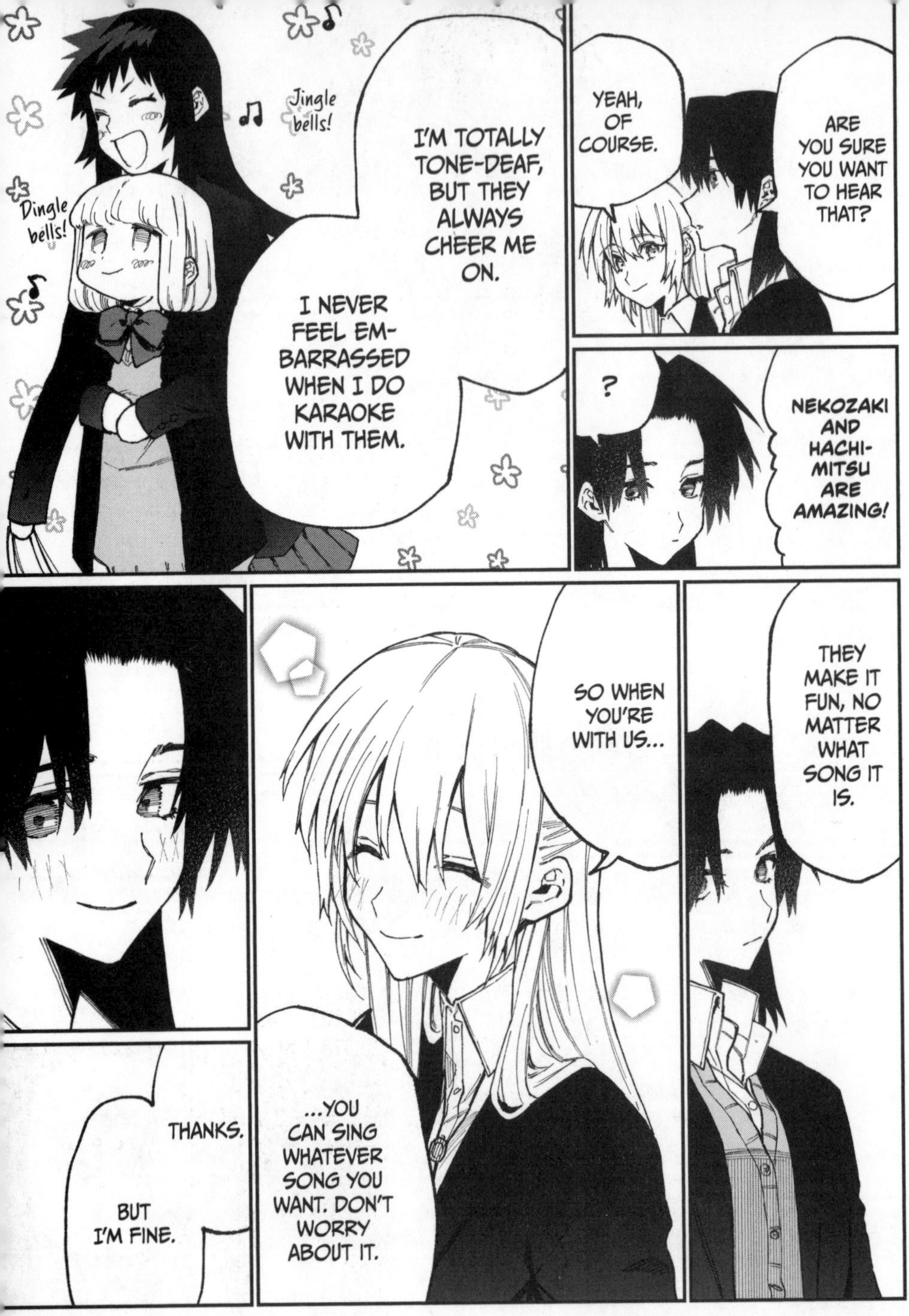
ARE YOU SURE YOU WANT TO HEAR THAT?
YEAH, OF COURSE.
NEKOZAKI AND HACHIMITSU ARE AMAZING!
?
I'M TOTALLY TONE-DEAF, BUT THEY ALWAYS CHEER ME ON.
I NEVER FEEL EM-BARRASSED WHEN I DO KARAOKE WITH THEM.
Jingle bells!
Dingle bells!
THEY MAKE IT FUN, NO MATTER WHAT SONG IT IS.
SO WHEN YOU'RE WITH US...
...YOU CAN SING WHATEVER SONG YOU WANT. DON'T WORRY ABOUT IT.
THANKS.
BUT I'M FINE.

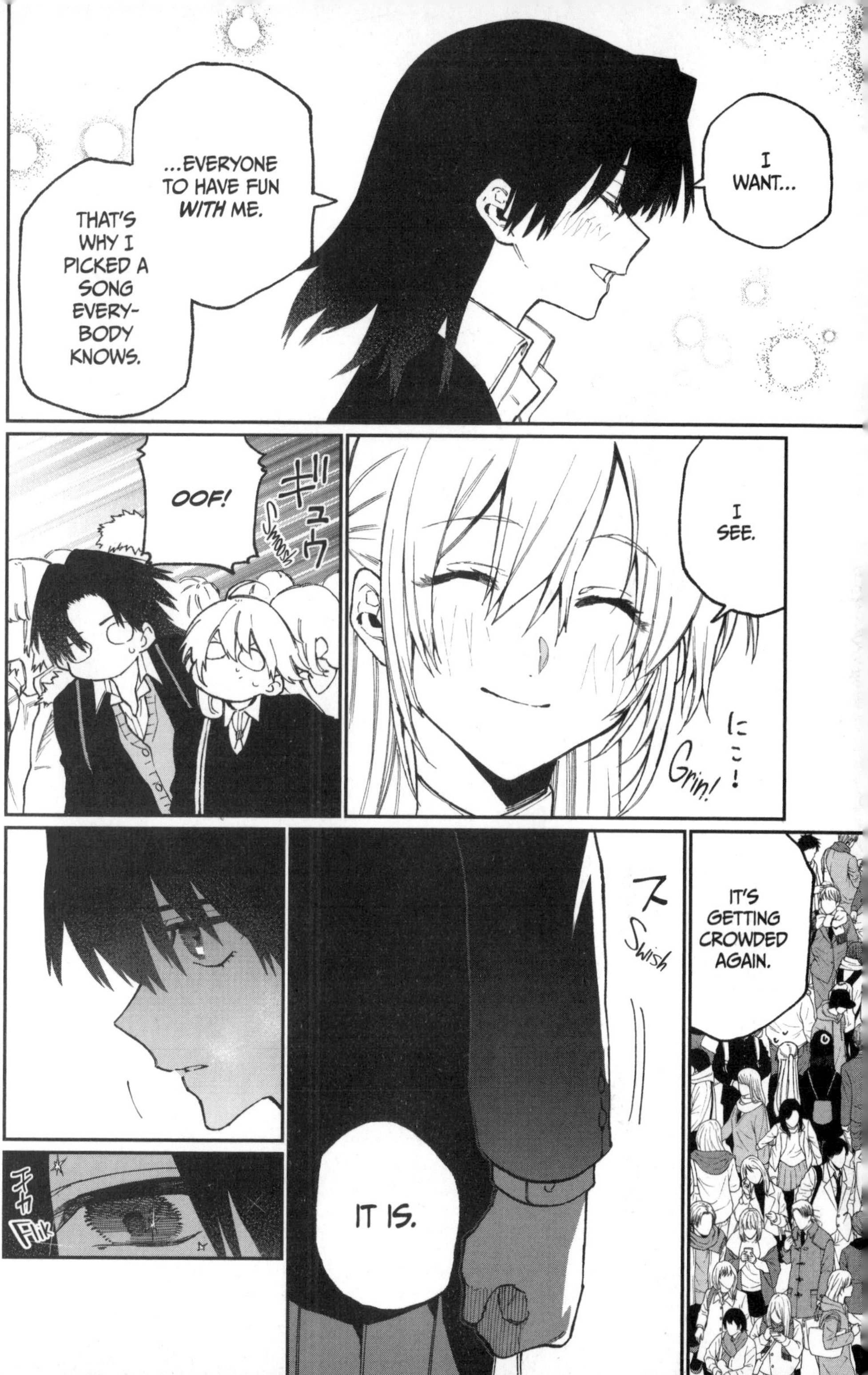
I WANT...
...EVERYONE TO HAVE FUN WITH ME.
THAT'S WHY I PICKED A SONG EVERY-BODY KNOWS.
I SEE.
にこ！
Grin!
OOF!
ギュウ
Smoosh
IT'S GETTING CROWDED AGAIN.
ス
Swish
IT IS.
チカ
Flik

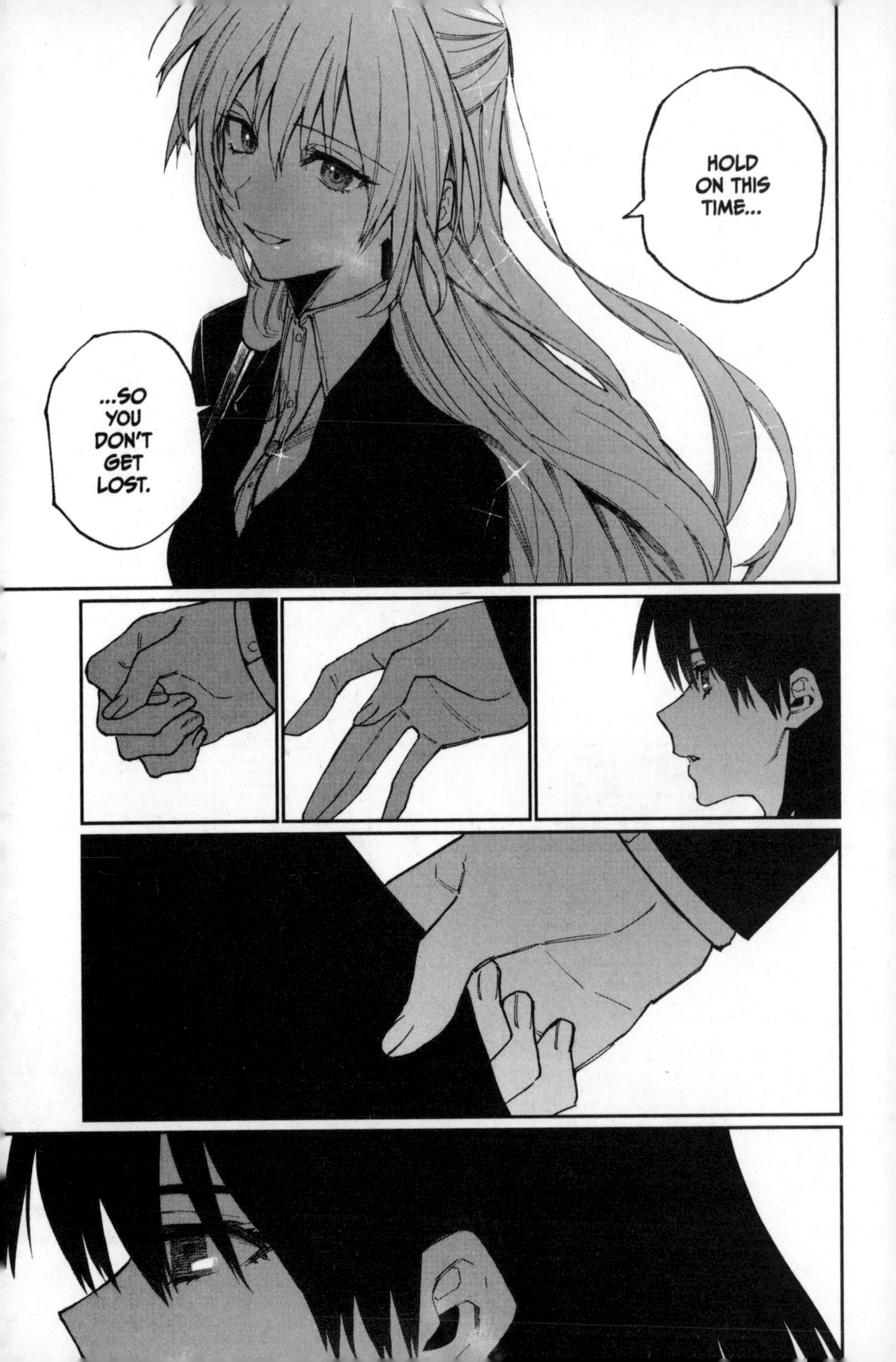
HOLD ON THIS TIME...
...SO YOU DON'T GET LOST.

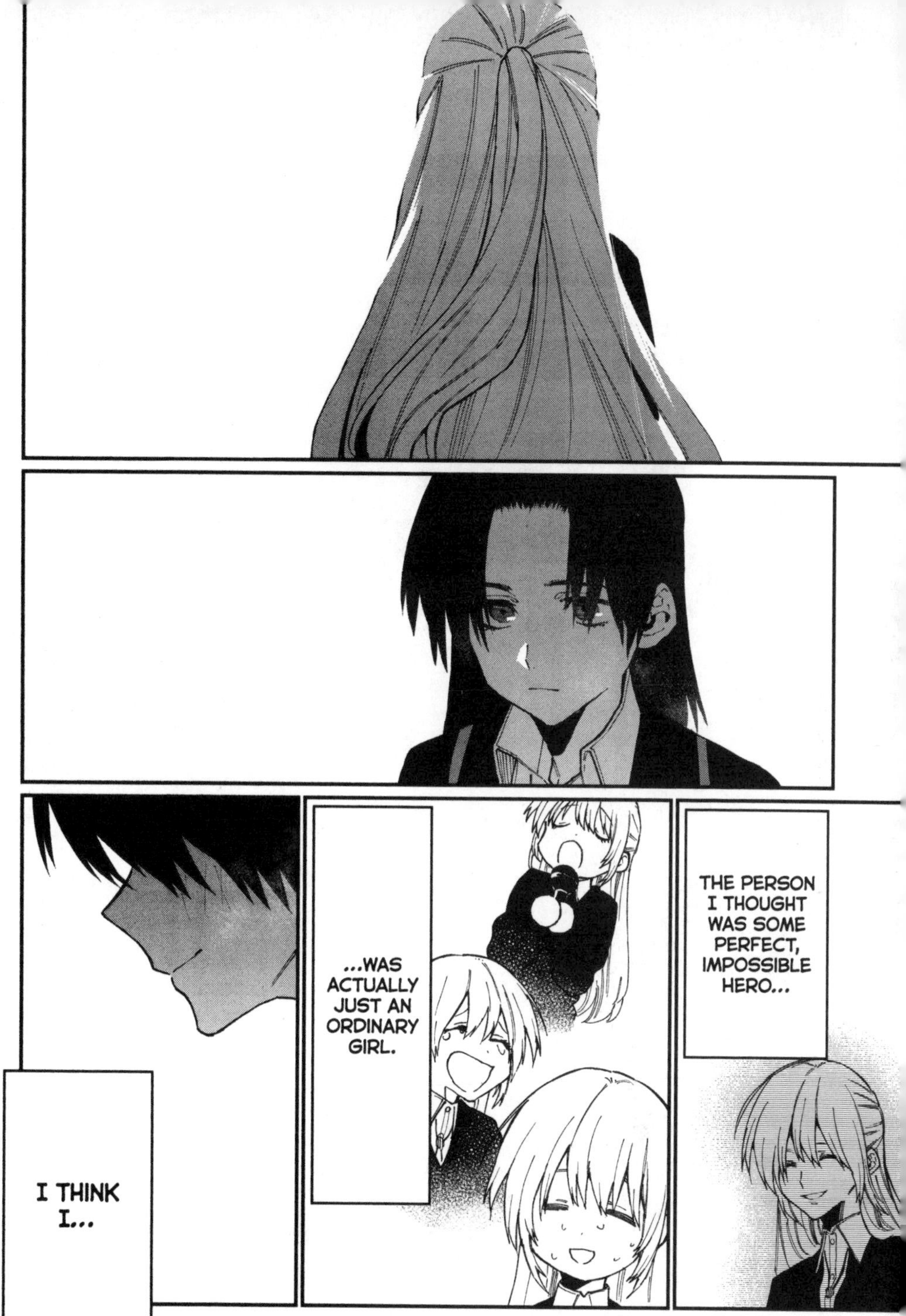
THE PERSON I THOUGHT WAS SOME PERFECT, IMPOSSIBLE HERO...
...WAS ACTUALLY JUST AN ORDINARY GIRL.
I THINK I...

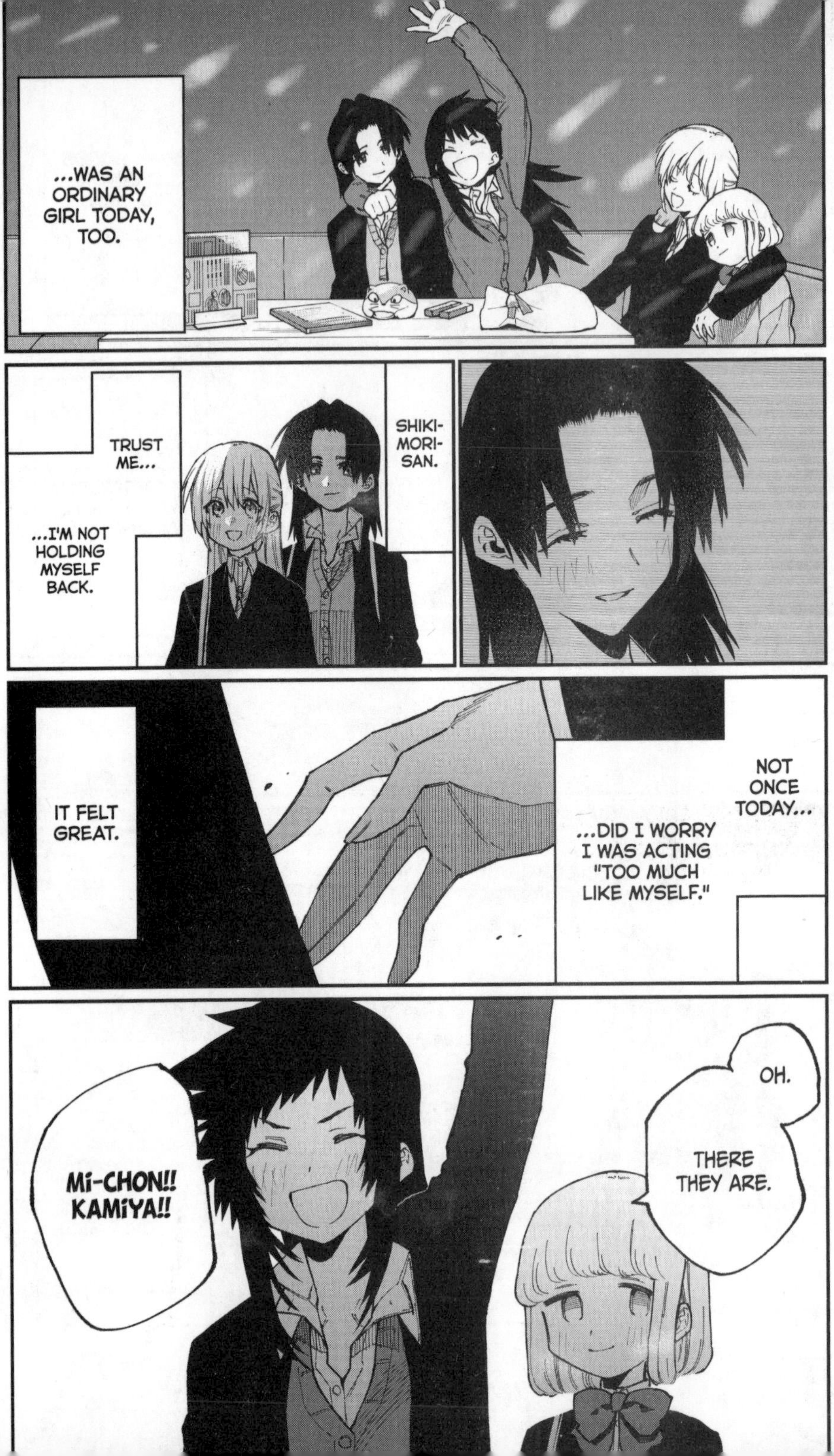
...WAS AN ORDINARY GIRL TODAY, TOO.
SHIKI-MORI-SAN.
TRUST ME...
...I'M NOT HOLDING MYSELF BACK.
NOT ONCE TODAY...
...DID I WORRY I WAS ACTING "TOO MUCH LIKE MYSELF."
IT FELT GREAT.
OH.
THERE THEY ARE.
Mi-CHON!! KAMiYA!!

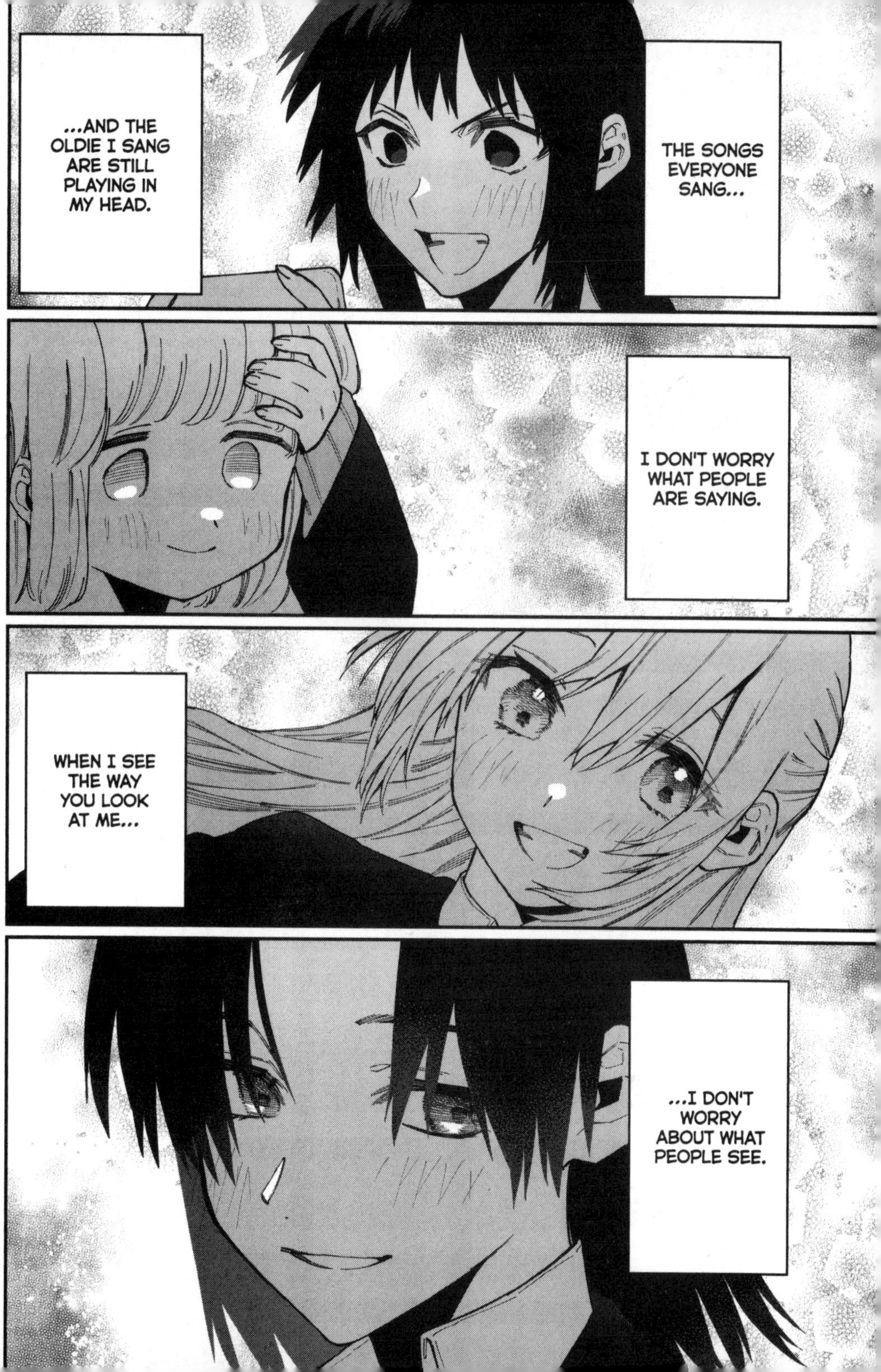
THE SONGS EVERYONE SANG...
...AND THE OLDIE I SANG ARE STILL PLAYING IN MY HEAD.
I DON'T WORRY WHAT PEOPLE ARE SAYING.
WHEN I SEE THE WAY YOU LOOK AT ME...
...I DON'T WORRY ABOUT WHAT PEOPLE SEE.

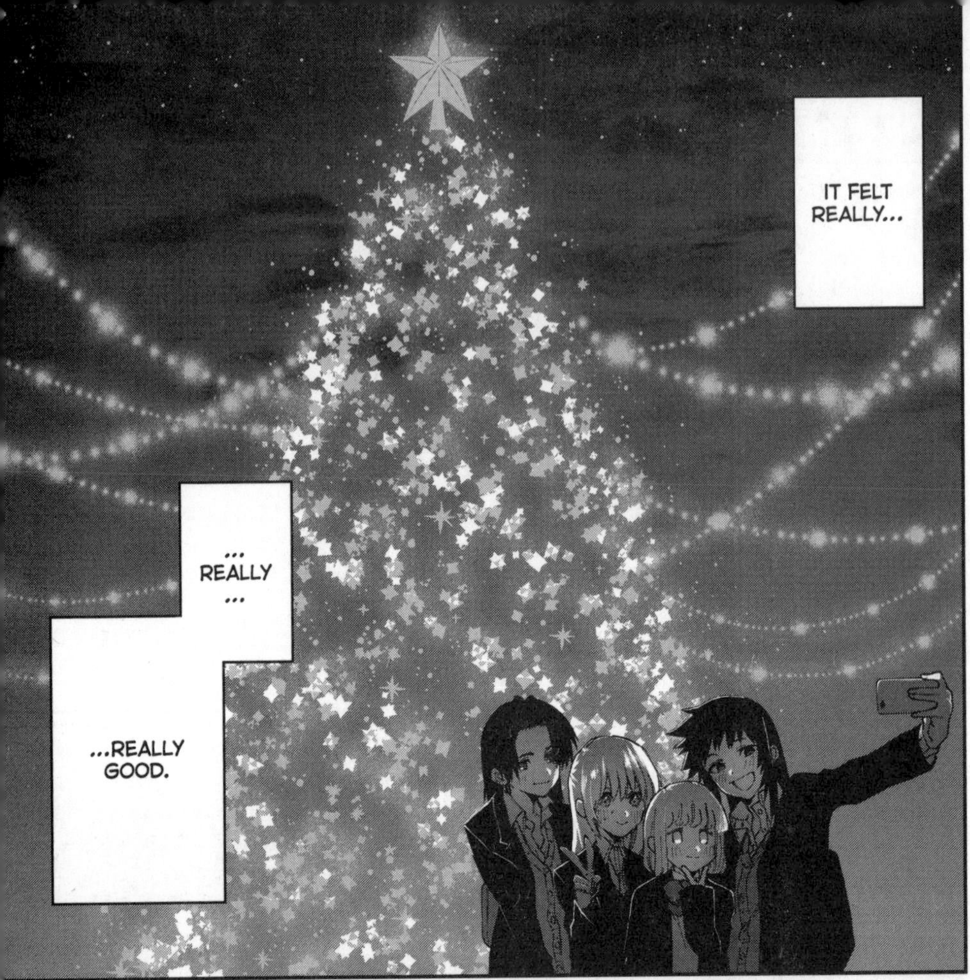
IT FELT REALLY...
... REALLY ...
...REALLY GOOD.

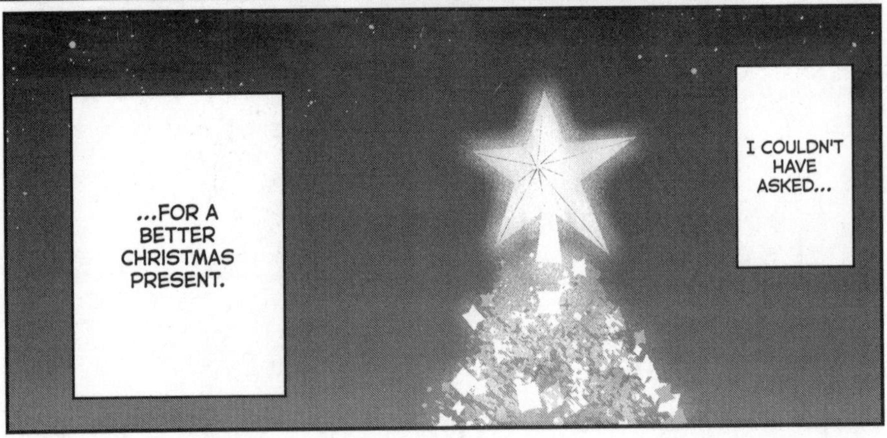
I COULDN'T HAVE ASKED...
...FOR A BETTER CHRISTMAS PRESENT.

Chapter 73 END

SHIKIMORI'S not just a cutie

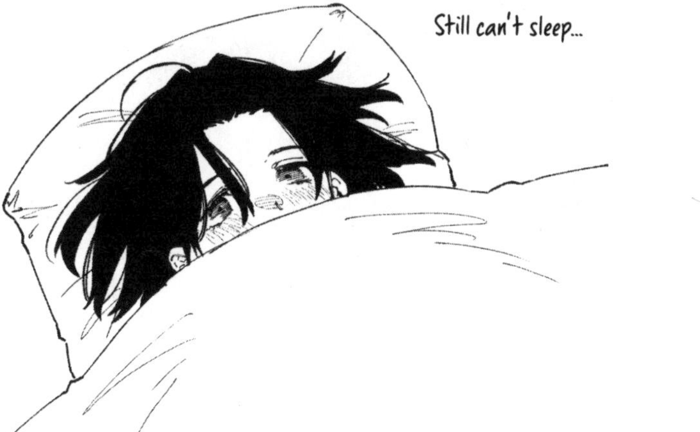
Still can't sleep...

SHIKIMORI'S not just a cutie

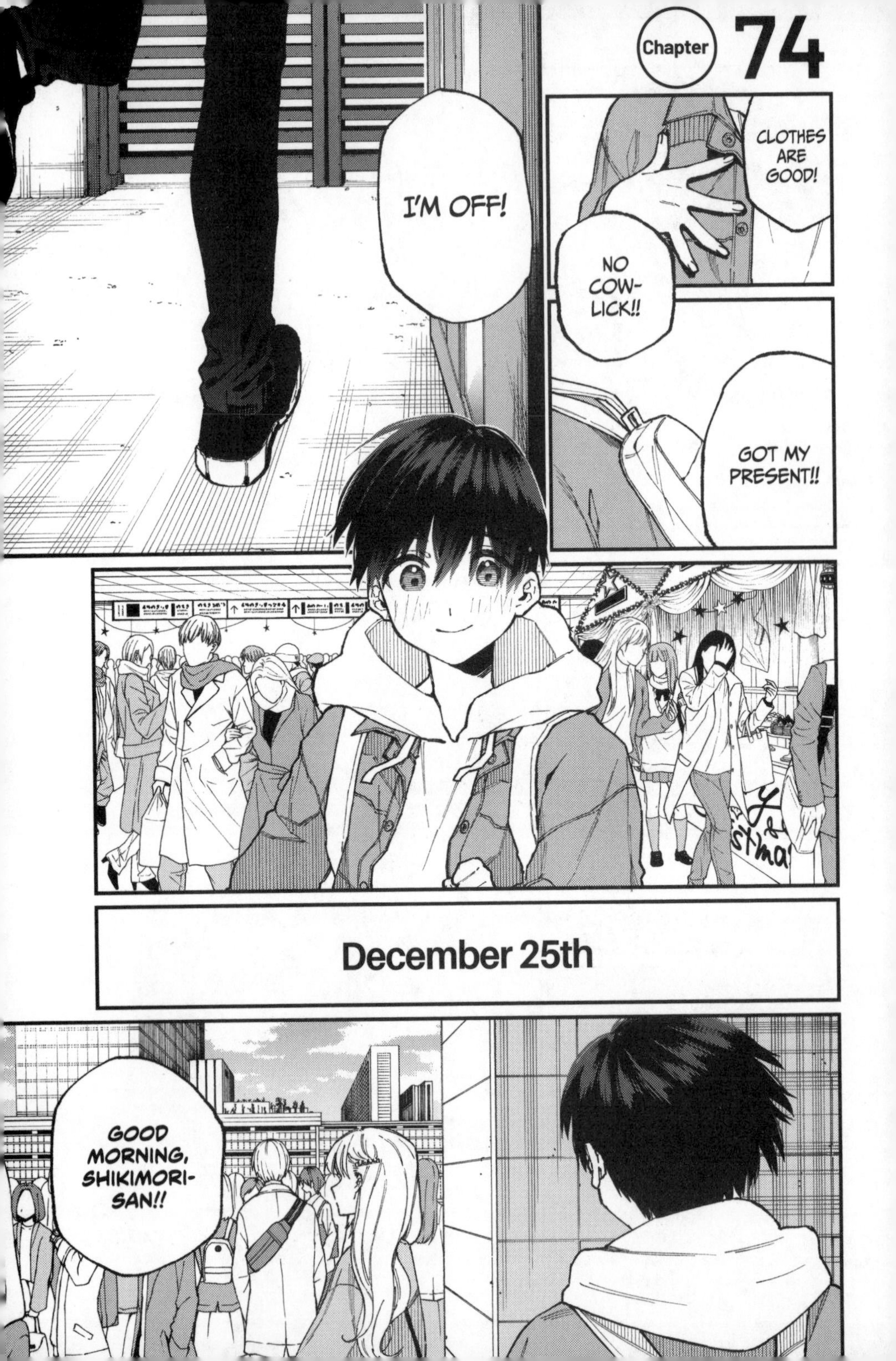
Chapter 74
CLOTHES ARE GOOD!
NO COW-LICK!!
GOT MY PRESENT!!
I'M OFF!
December 25th
GOOD MORNING, SHIKIMORI-SAN!!

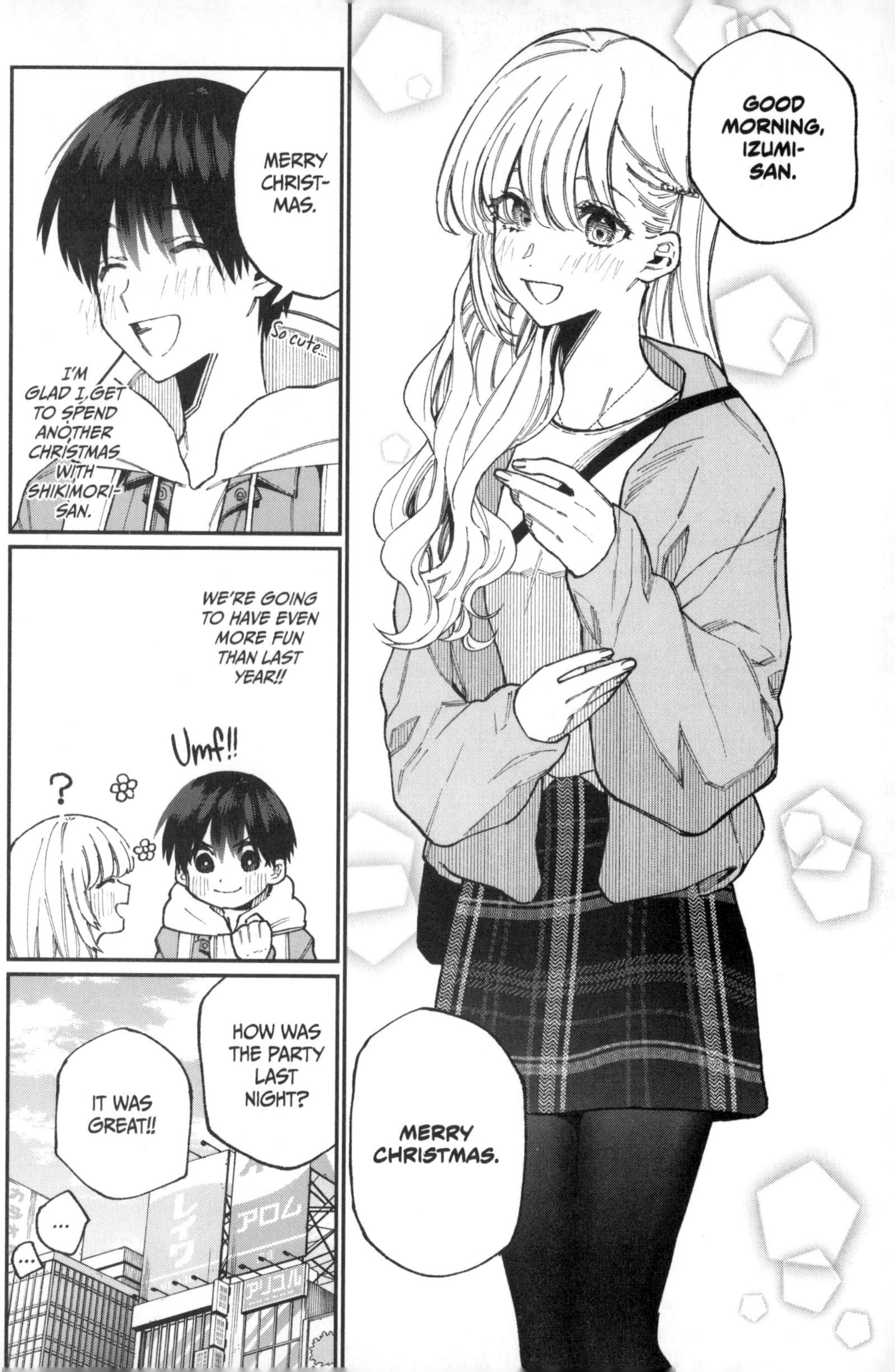
GOOD MORNING, IZUMI-SAN.
MERRY CHRISTMAS.
MERRY CHRIST-MAS.
So cute...
I'M GLAD I GET TO SPEND ANOTHER CHRISTMAS WITH SHIKIMORI-SAN.
WE'RE GOING TO HAVE EVEN MORE FUN THAN LAST YEAR!!
Umf!!
?
HOW WAS THE PARTY LAST NIGHT?
IT WAS GREAT!!
...
...

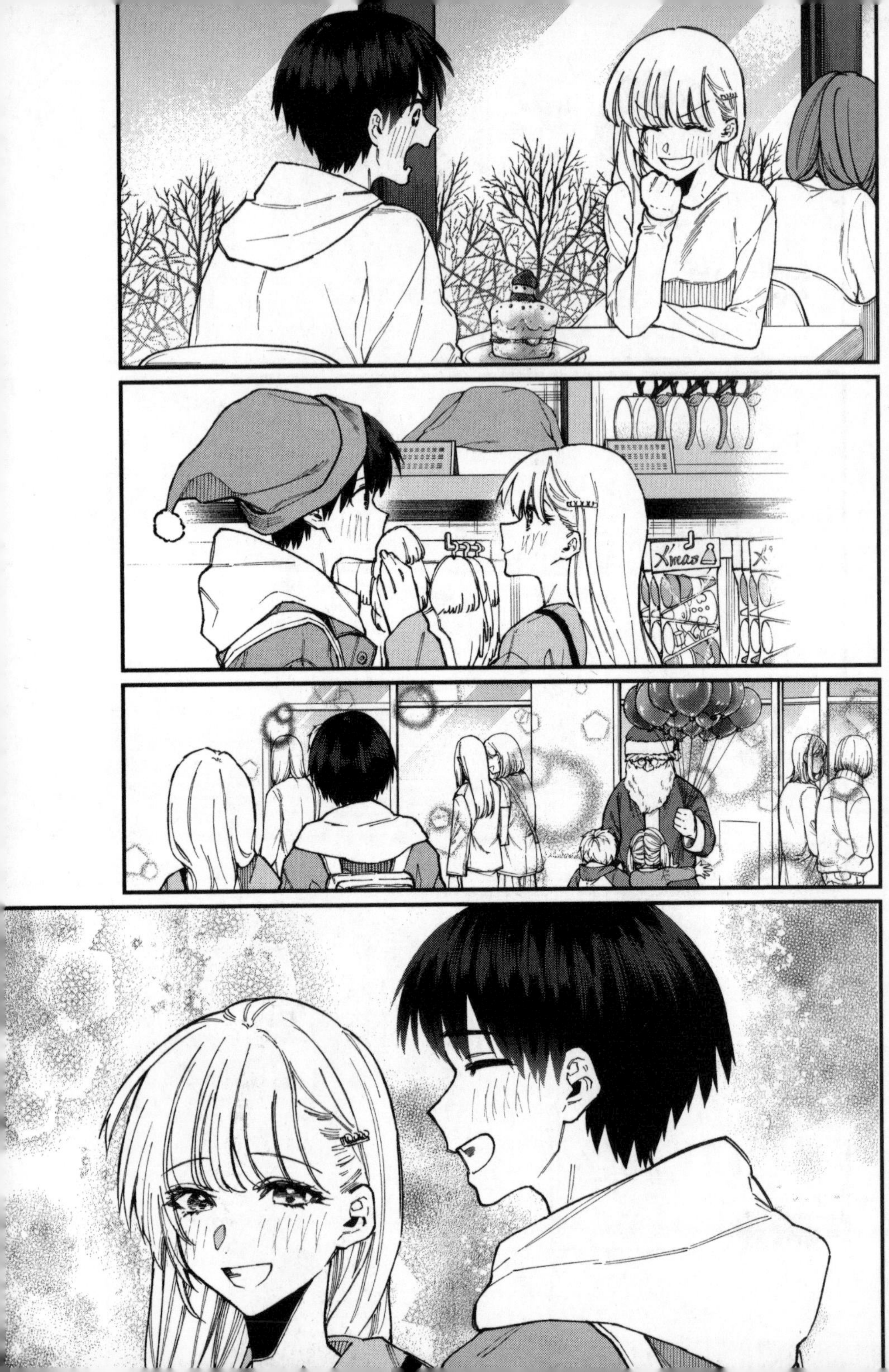
X'mas

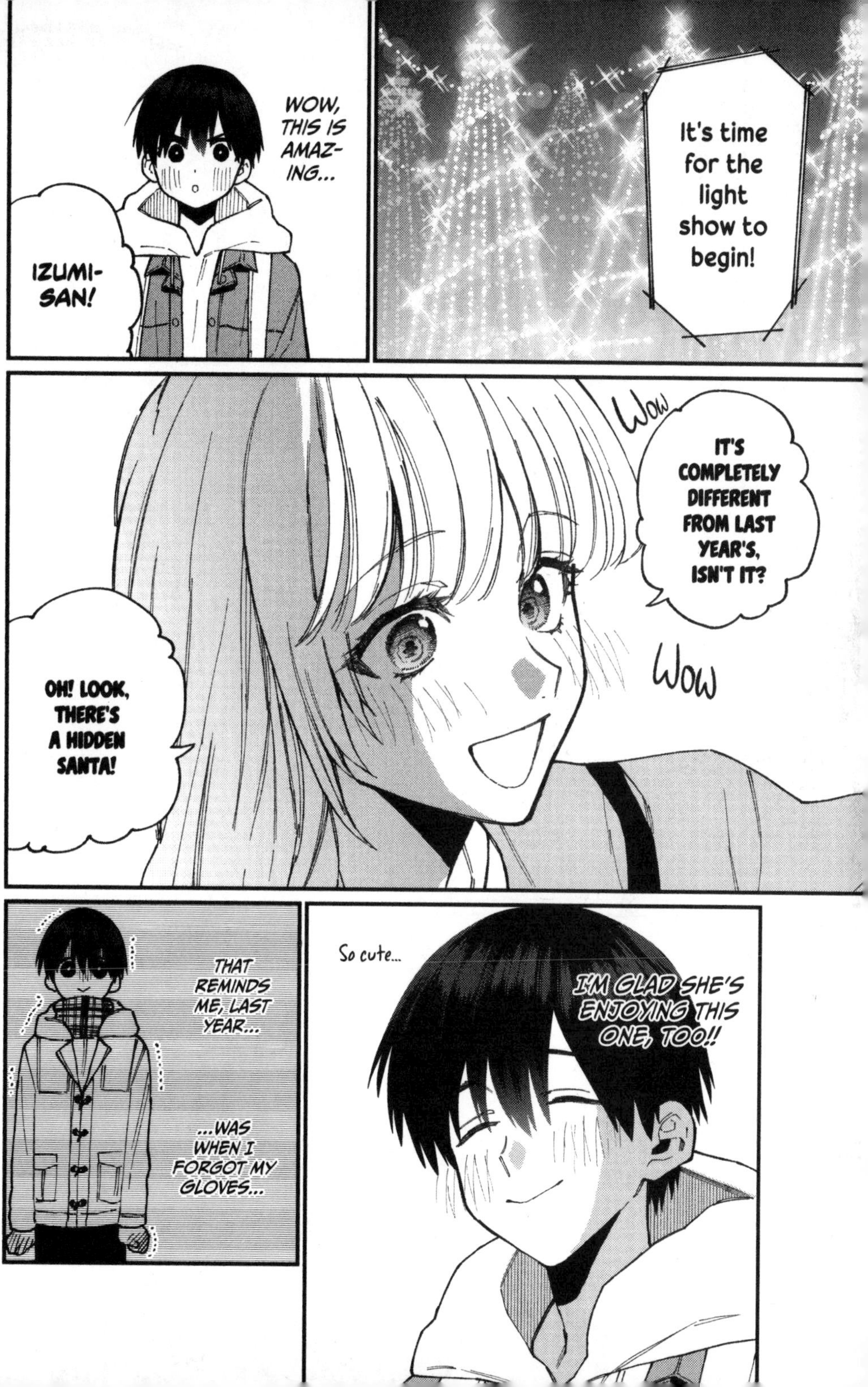
It's time for the light show to begin!
WOW, THIS IS AMAZ-ING...
IZUMI-SAN!
Wow
IT'S COMPLETELY DIFFERENT FROM LAST YEAR'S, ISN'T IT?
Wow
OH! LOOK, THERE'S A HIDDEN SANTA!
So cute...
I'M GLAD SHE'S ENJOYING THIS ONE, TOO!!
THAT REMINDS ME, LAST YEAR...
...WAS WHEN I FORGOT MY GLOVES...

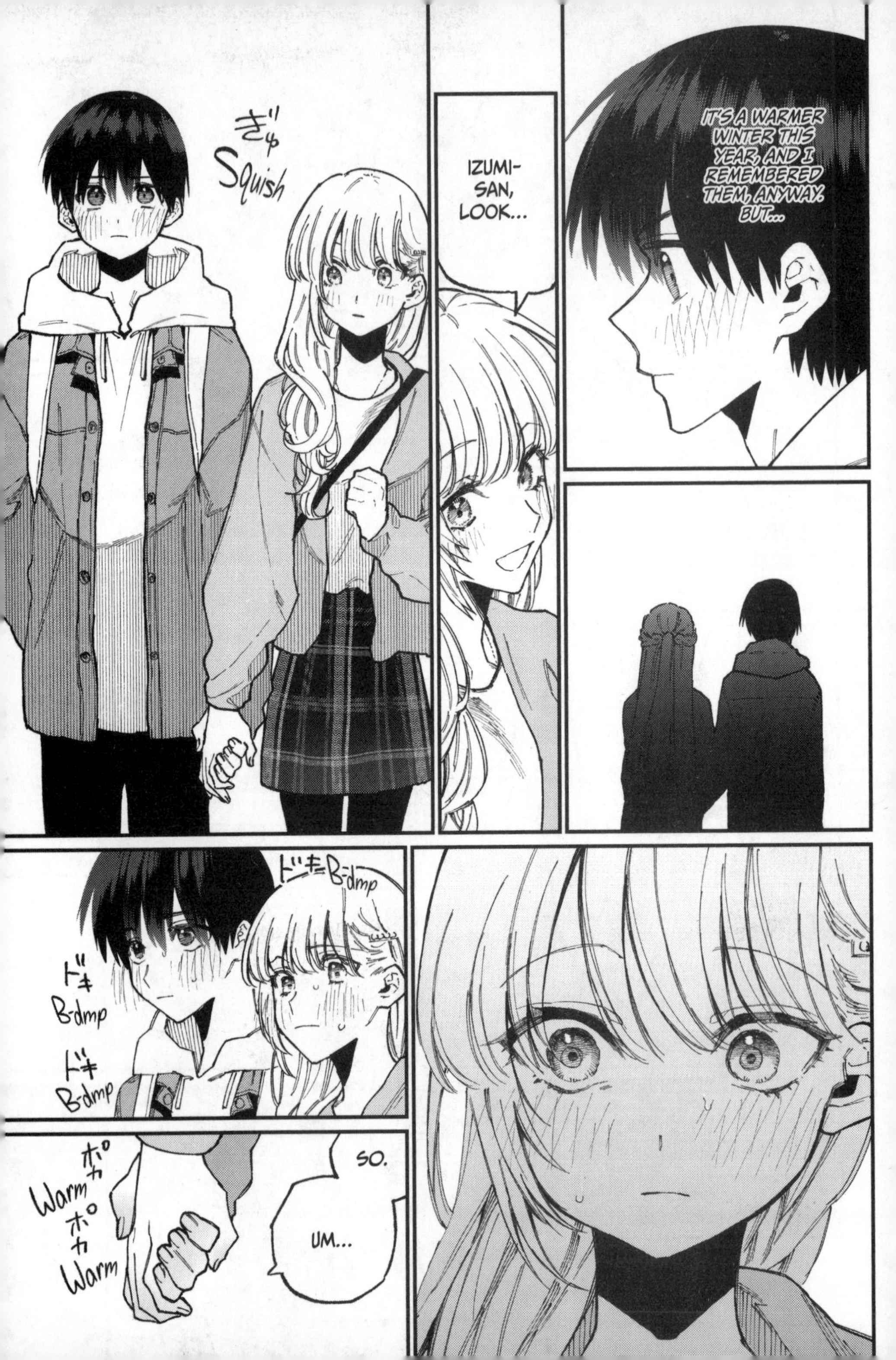
IT'S A WARMER WINTER THIS YEAR, AND I REMEMBERED THEM, ANYWAY. BUT...
IZUMI-SAN, LOOK...
ぎゅ Squish
ドキ B-dmp
ドキ B-dmp
ドキ B-dmp
SO.
UM...
ポカ Warm
ポカ Warm

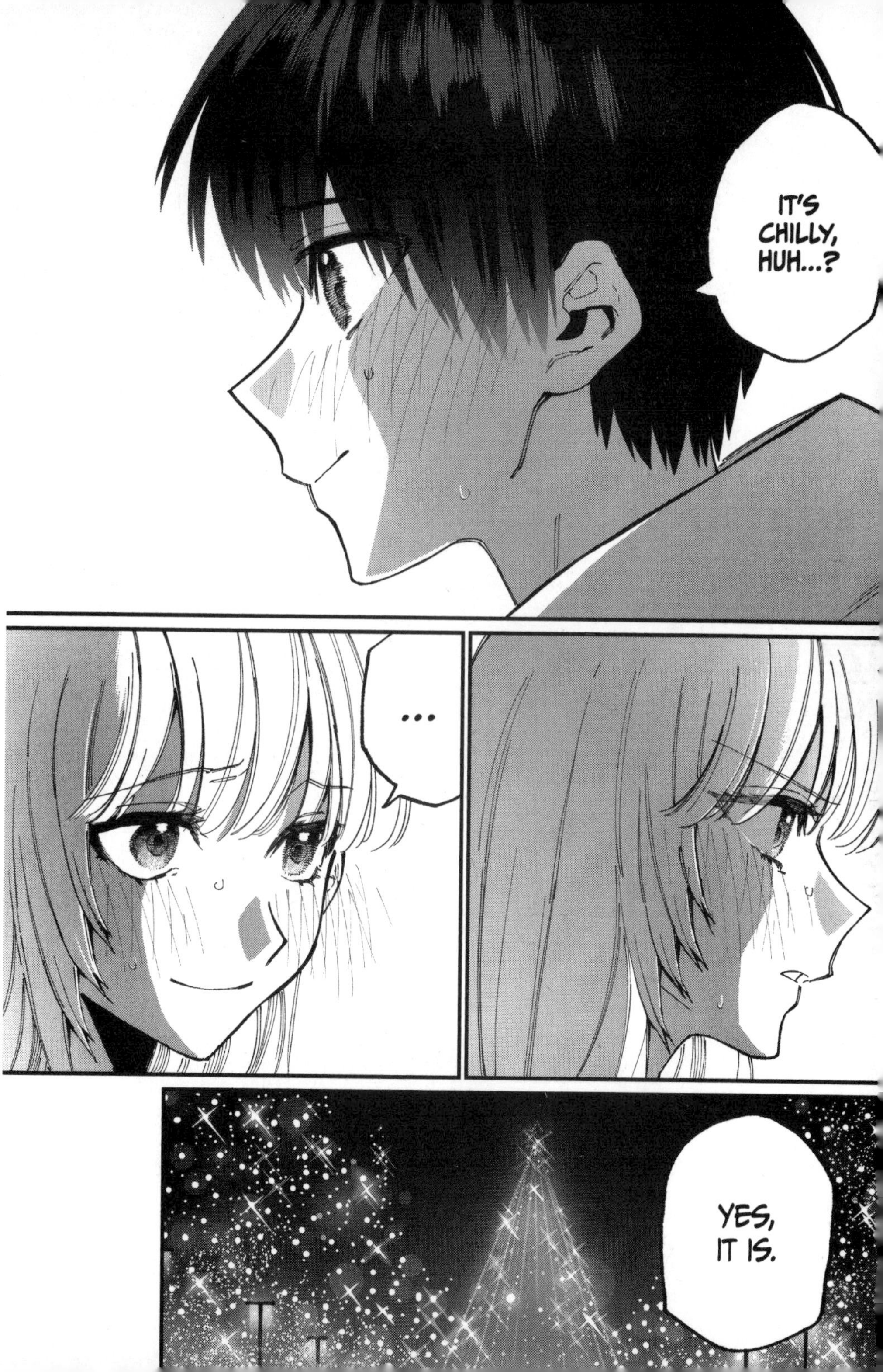
IT'S CHILLY, HUH...?
...
YES, IT IS.

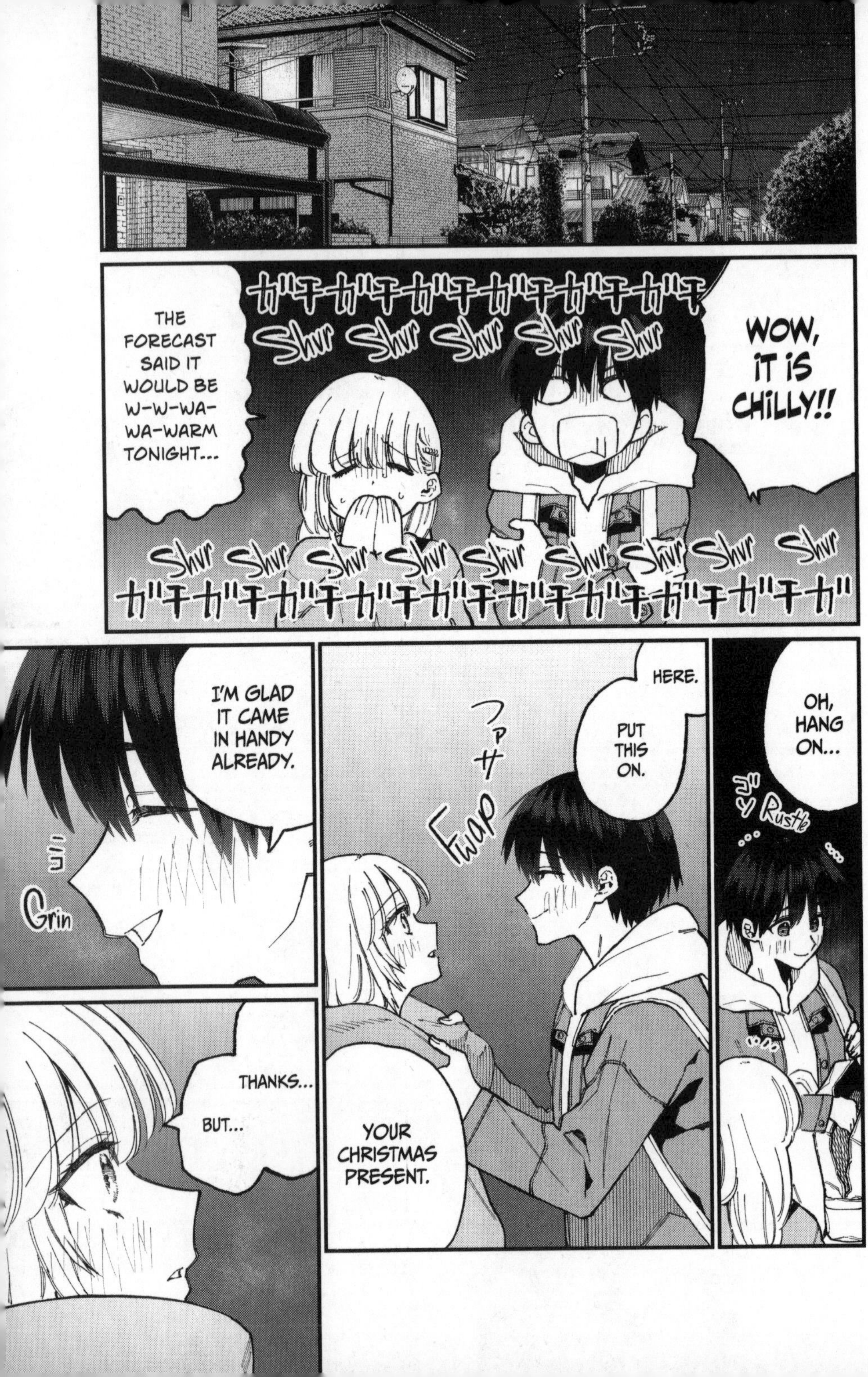
WOW, IT IS CHILLY!!
ガチガチガチガチガチガチ
Shvr Shvr Shvr Shvr Shvr
Shvr Shvr Shvr Shvr Shvr Shvr Shvr Shvr Shvr
ガチガチガチガチガチガチガチガチガチガ
THE FORECAST SAID IT WOULD BE W-W-WA-WA-WARM TONIGHT...
OH, HANG ON...
ゴソ Rustle
...
HERE.
PUT THIS ON.
ファサ
Fwap
YOUR CHRISTMAS PRESENT.
I'M GLAD IT CAME IN HANDY ALREADY.
ニコ
Grin
THANKS...
BUT...

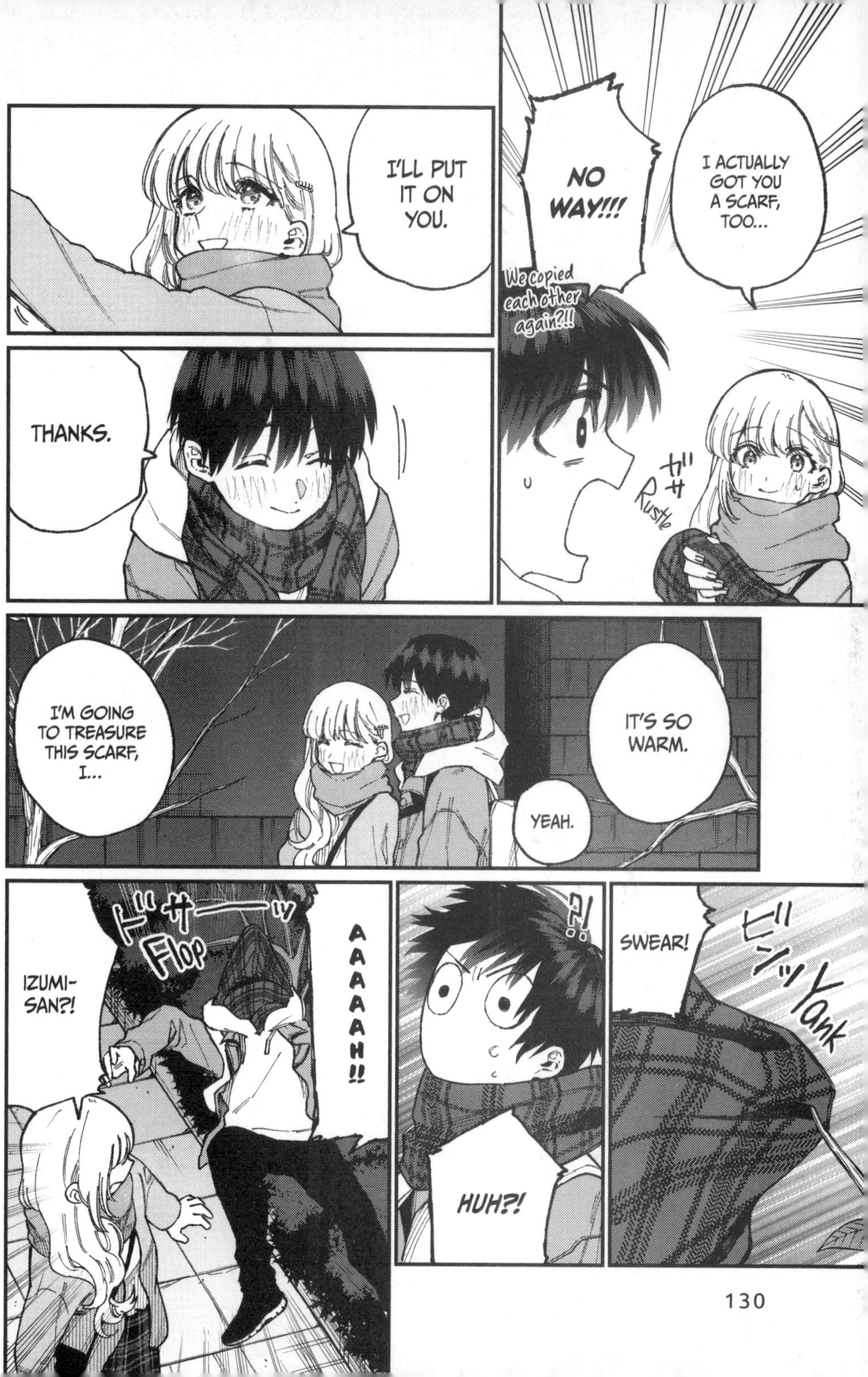
I ACTUALLY GOT YOU A SCARF, TOO...
NO WAY!!!
We copied each other again?!!
ガサ
Rustle
I'LL PUT IT ON YOU.
THANKS.
IT'S SO WARM.
YEAH.
I'M GOING TO TREASURE THIS SCARF, I...
ビンッ
Yank
SWEAR!
?!
HUH?!
ドサーーッ
Flop
AAAAAAH!!
IZUMI-SAN?!

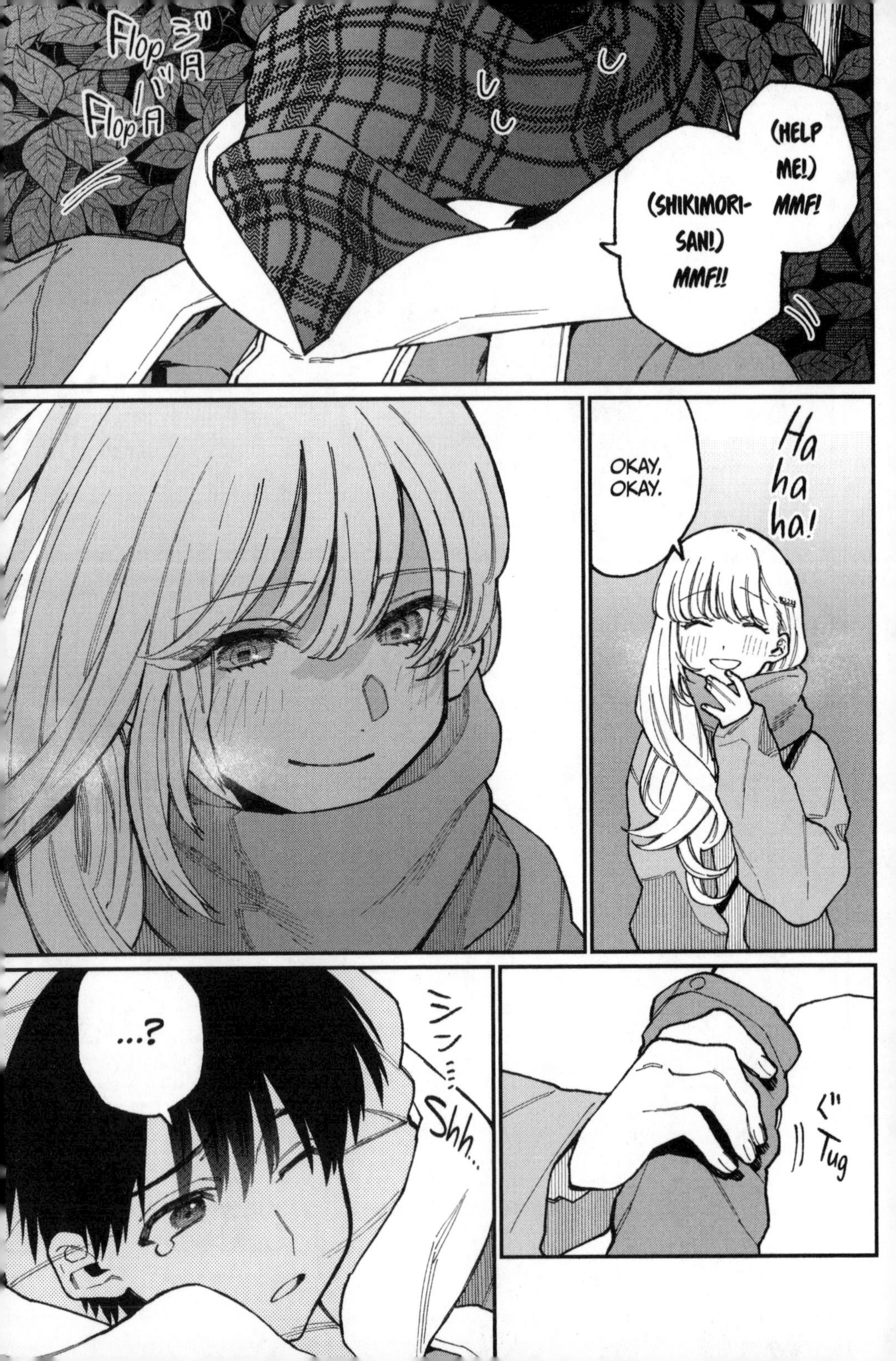
(HELP ME!) MMF! (SHIKIMORI-SAN!) MMF!!
Flop
Flop
Ha ha ha!
OKAY, OKAY.
Tug
Shh...
...?

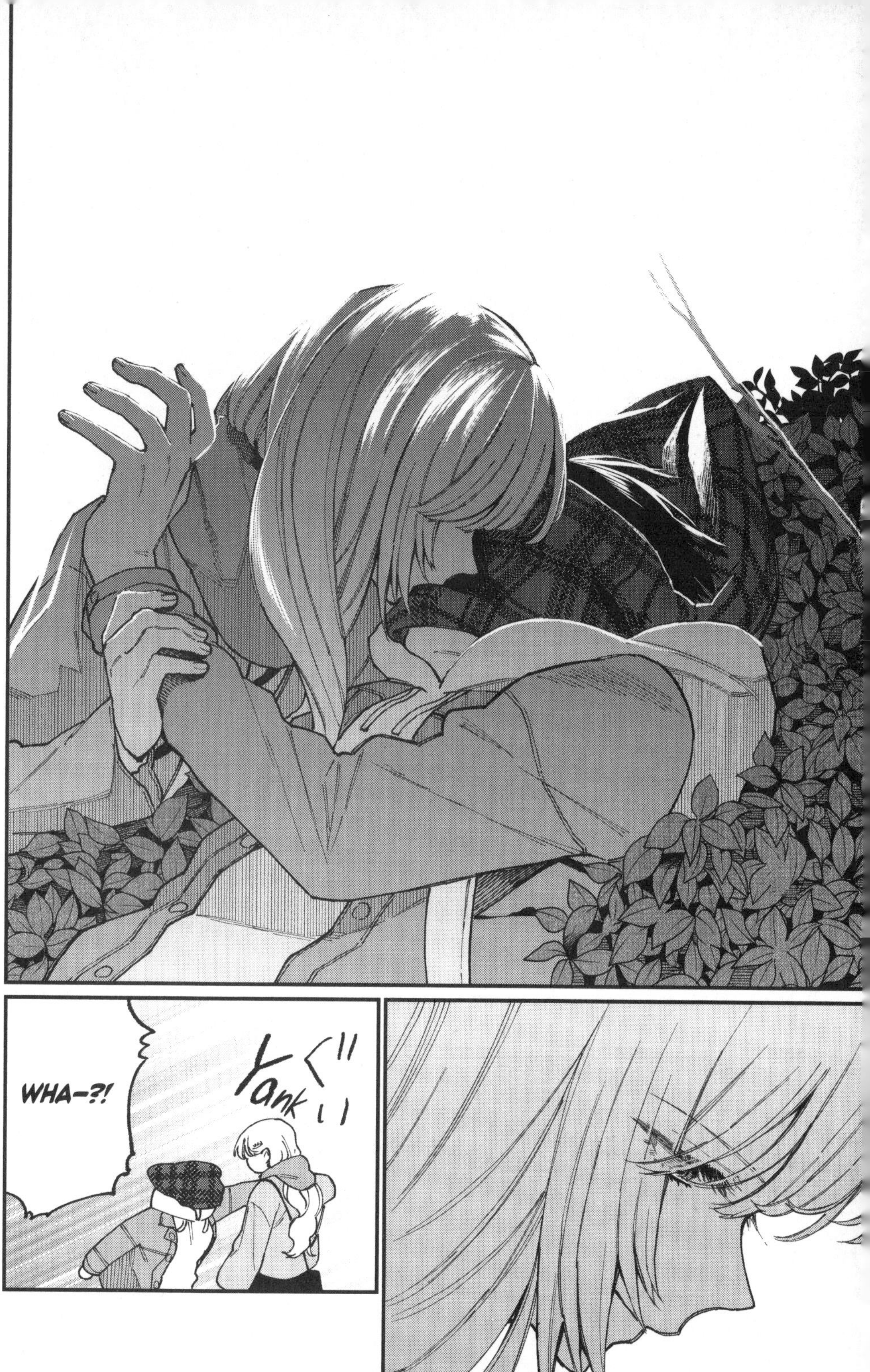
Yank
ぐい
WHA–?!

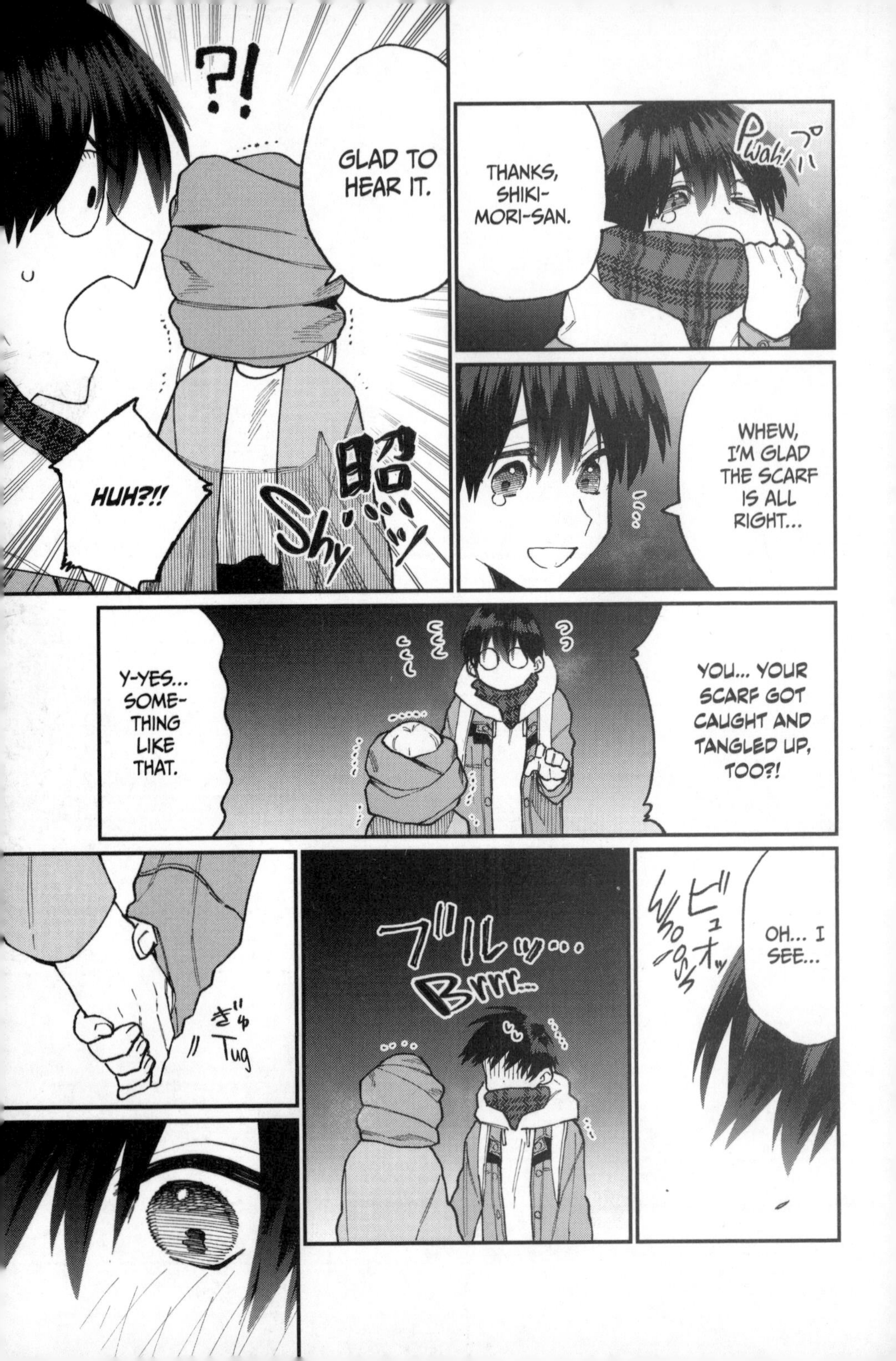
THANKS, SHIKI-MORI-SAN.
Pwah! プハ
WHEW, I'M GLAD THE SCARF IS ALL RIGHT...
GLAD TO HEAR IT.
?!
照 Shy
HUH?!!
YOU... YOUR SCARF GOT CAUGHT AND TANGLED UP, TOO?!
Y-YES... SOMETHING LIKE THAT.
OH... I SEE...
ビュオッ Whoosh
ブルッ... Brrr...
ぎゅ Tug

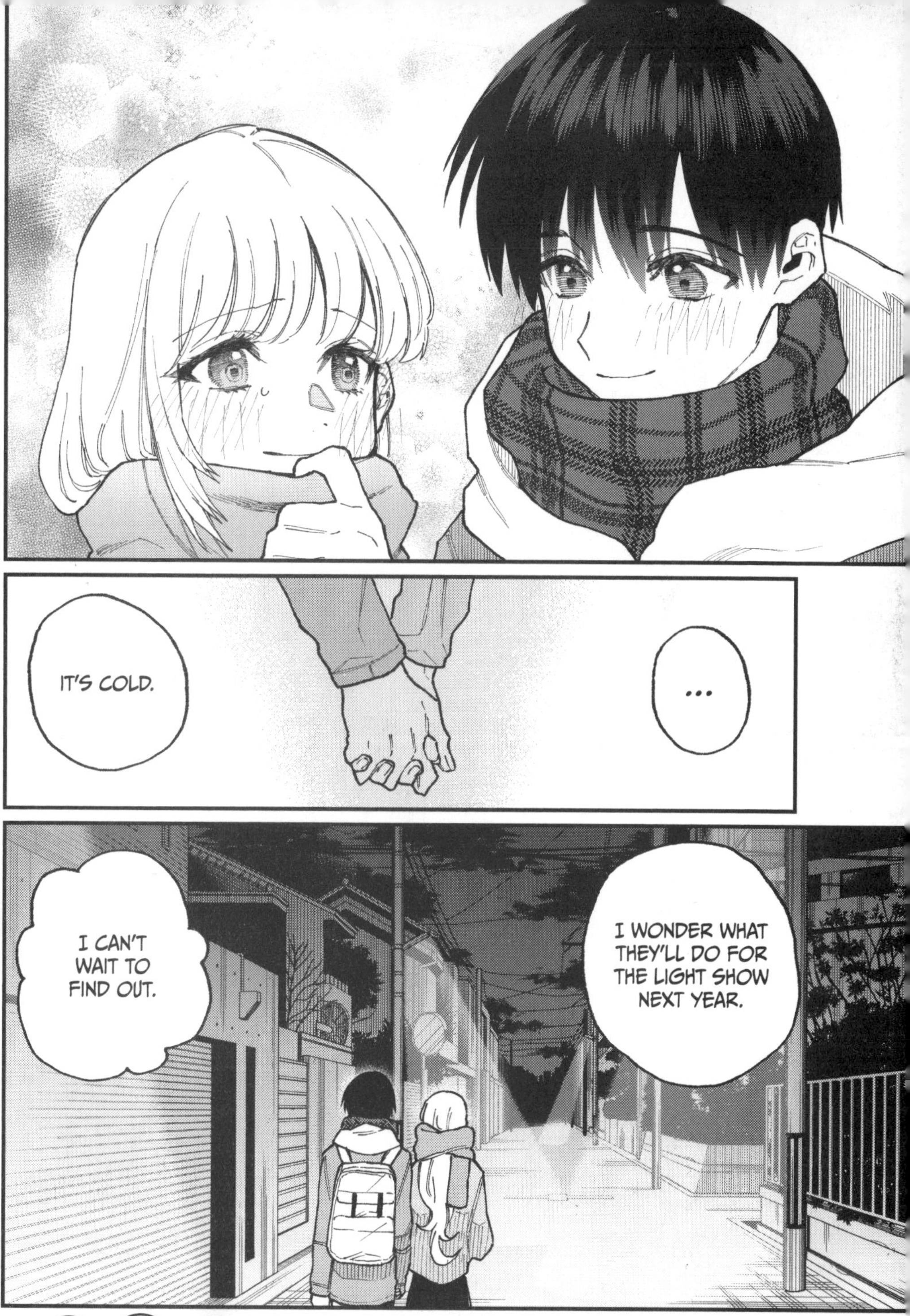
...
IT'S COLD.
I WONDER WHAT THEY'LL DO FOR THE LIGHT SHOW NEXT YEAR.
I CAN'T WAIT TO FIND OUT.

Chapter 74 END

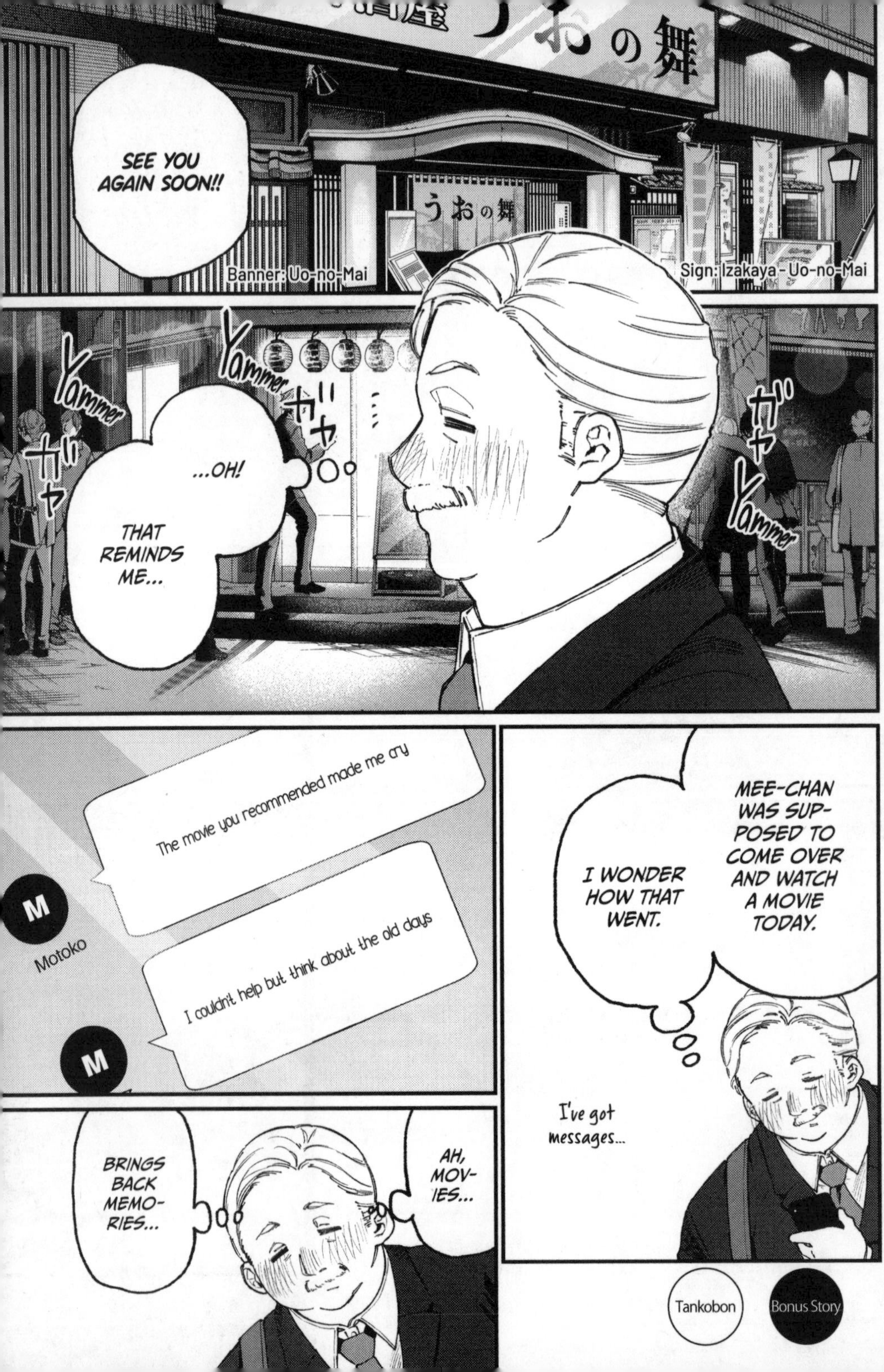
SEE YOU AGAIN SOON!!
うおの舞
Sign: Izakaya - Uo-no-Mai
Banner: Uo-no-Mai
ガヤ
Yammer
ガヤ
Yammer
...OH!
THAT REMINDS ME...
ガヤ
Yammer
MEE-CHAN WAS SUPPOSED TO COME OVER AND WATCH A MOVIE TODAY.
I WONDER HOW THAT WENT.
I've got messages...
M
Motoko
The movie you recommended made me cry
M
I couldn't help but think about the old days
AH, MOVIES...
BRINGS BACK MEMORIES...
Tankobon
Bonus Story

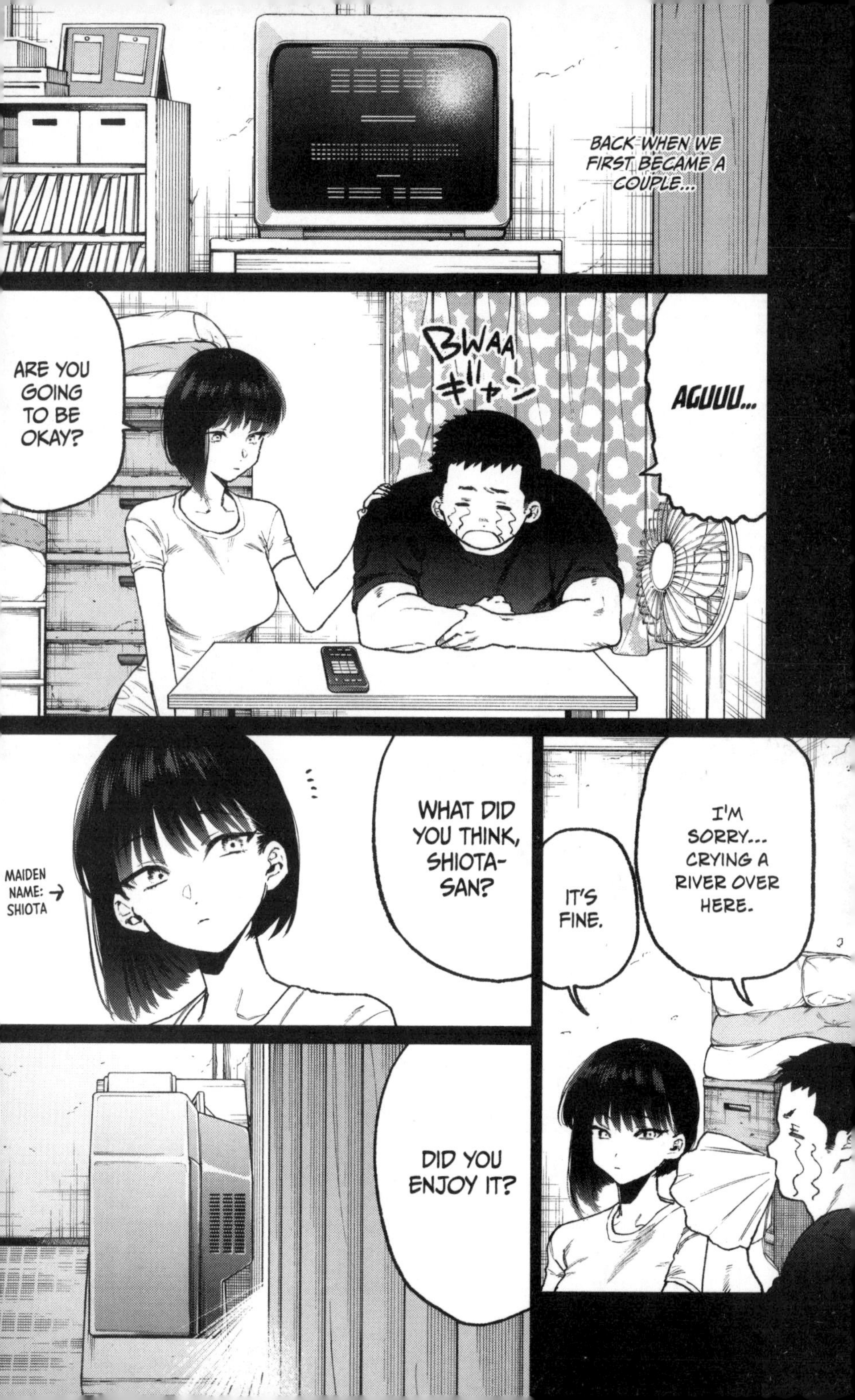
BACK WHEN WE FIRST BECAME A COUPLE...
BWAA ギャン
AGUUU...
ARE YOU GOING TO BE OKAY?
I'M SORRY... CRYING A RIVER OVER HERE.
IT'S FINE.
...
WHAT DID YOU THINK, SHIOTA-SAN?
MAIDEN NAME: → SHIOTA
DID YOU ENJOY IT?

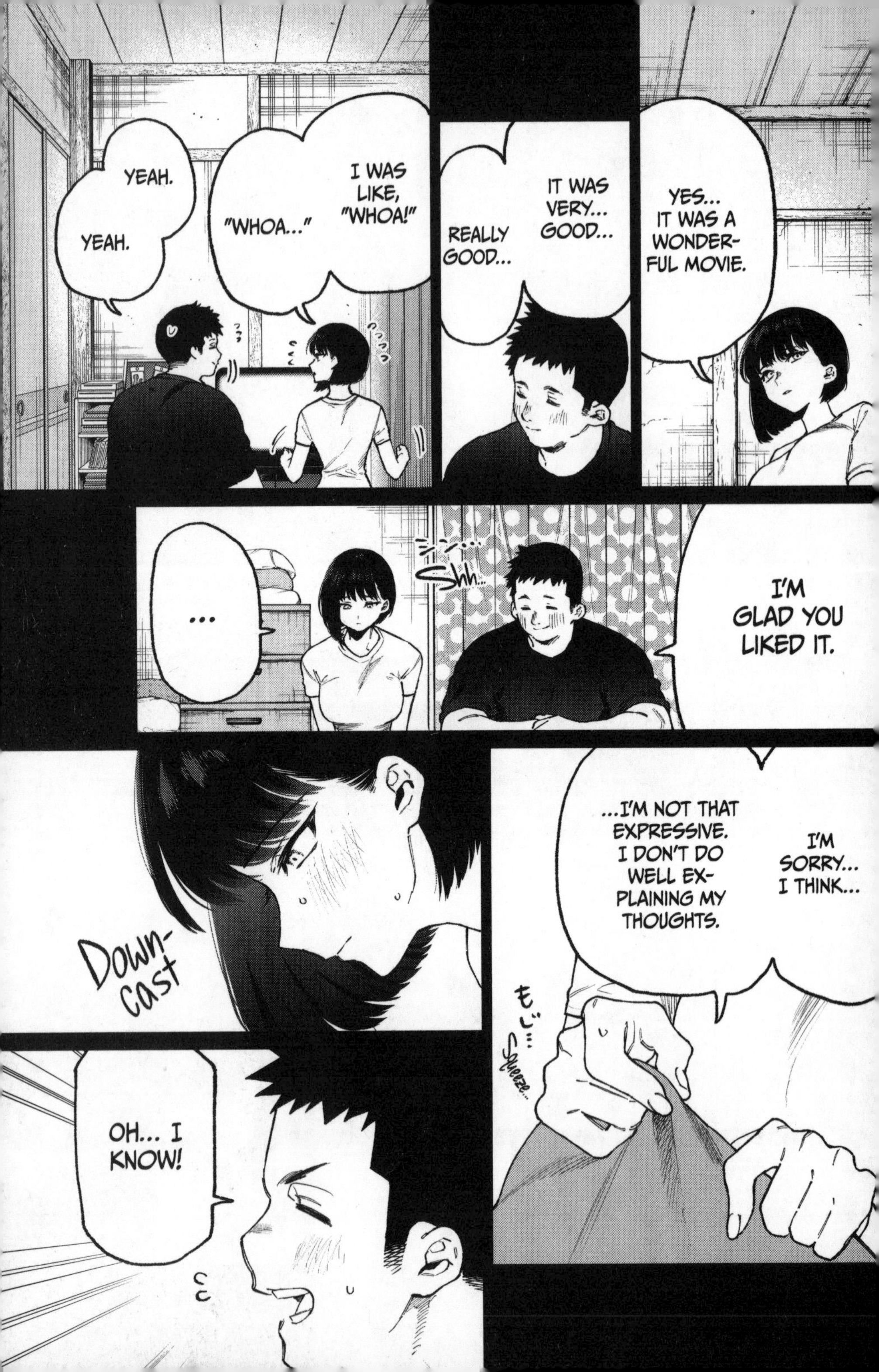
YES... IT WAS A WONDER-FUL MOVIE.
IT WAS VERY... GOOD...
REALLY GOOD...
I WAS LIKE, "WHOA!"
"WHOA..."
YEAH.
YEAH.
I'M GLAD YOU LIKED IT.
Shh...
...
I'M SORRY... I THINK...
...I'M NOT THAT EXPRESSIVE. I DON'T DO WELL EX-PLAINING MY THOUGHTS.
もじ…
Squeeze...
Down-cast
OH... I KNOW!

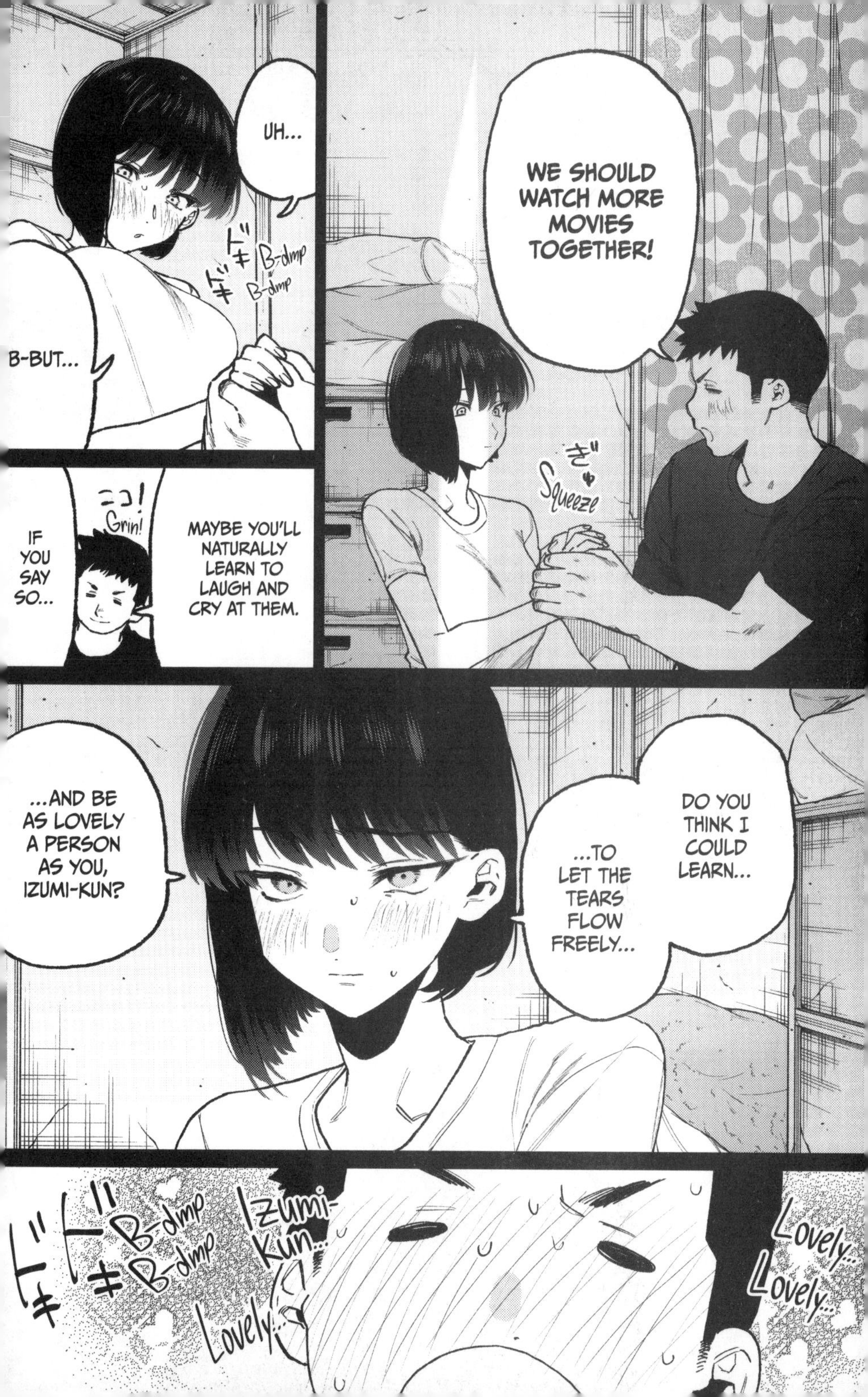
WE SHOULD WATCH MORE MOVIES TOGETHER!
ぎ Squeeze
UH...
ドキドキ B-dmp B-dmp
B-BUT...
MAYBE YOU'LL NATURALLY LEARN TO LAUGH AND CRY AT THEM.
ニコ! Grin!
IF YOU SAY SO...
DO YOU THINK I COULD LEARN...
...TO LET THE TEARS FLOW FREELY...
...AND BE AS LOVELY A PERSON AS YOU, IZUMI-KUN?
Lovely... Lovely...
Izumi-kun...
ドキドキ B-dmp B-dmp
Lovely...

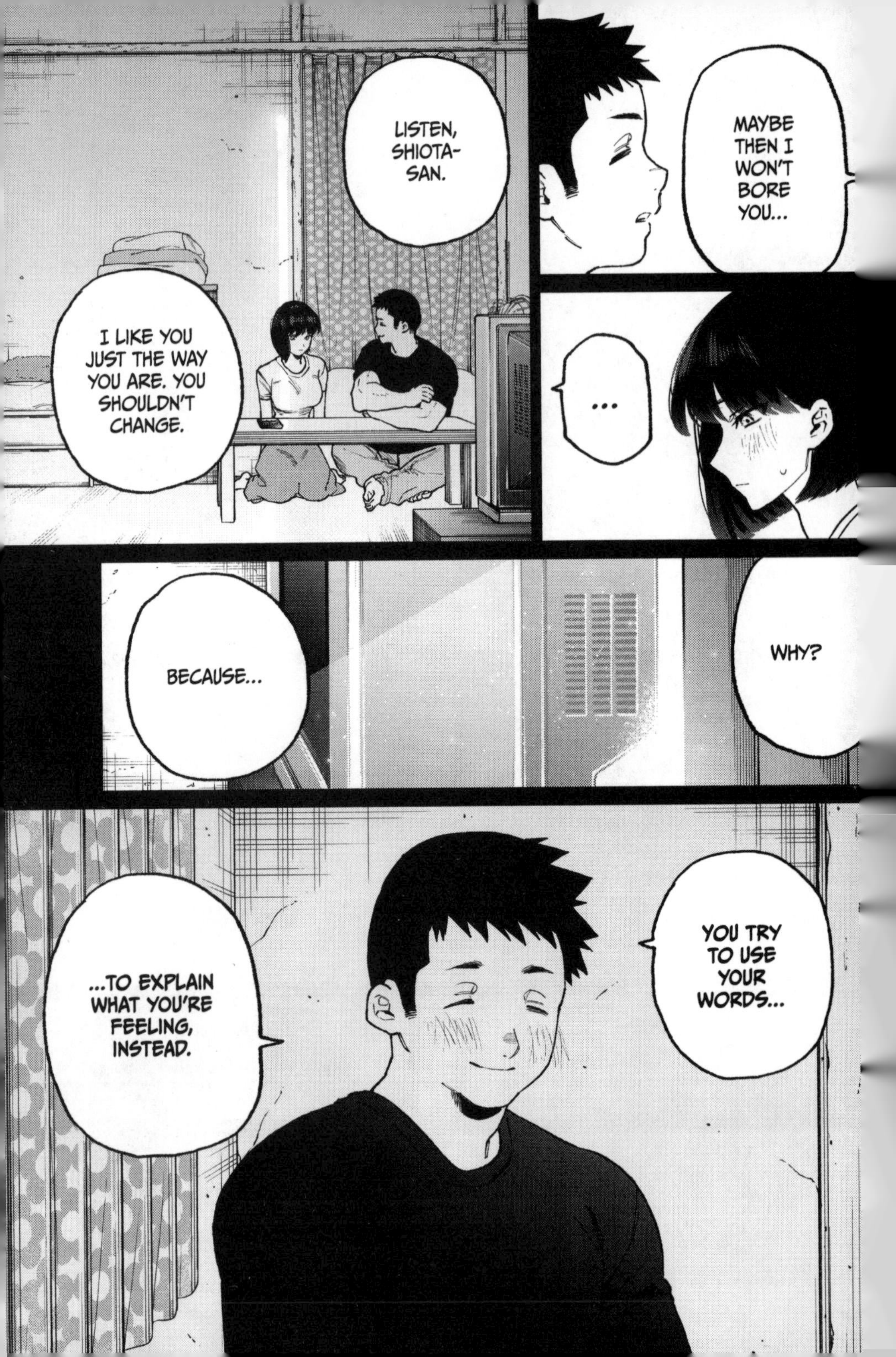
MAYBE THEN I WON'T BORE YOU...
...
LISTEN, SHIOTA-SAN.
I LIKE YOU JUST THE WAY YOU ARE. YOU SHOULDN'T CHANGE.
WHY?
BECAUSE...
YOU TRY TO USE YOUR WORDS...
...TO EXPLAIN WHAT YOU'RE FEELING, INSTEAD.

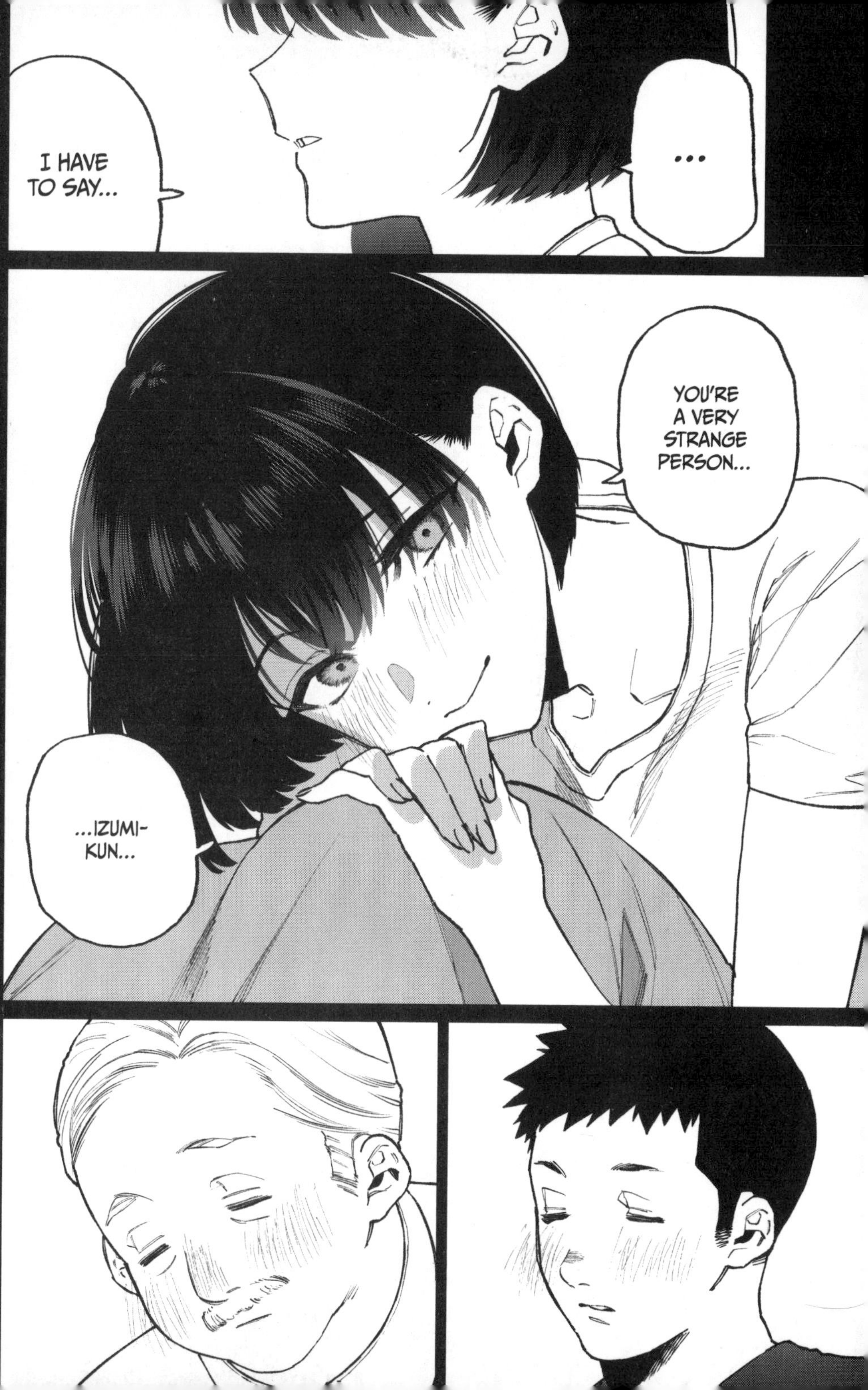
...
I HAVE TO SAY...
YOU'RE A VERY STRANGE PERSON...
...IZUMI-KUN...

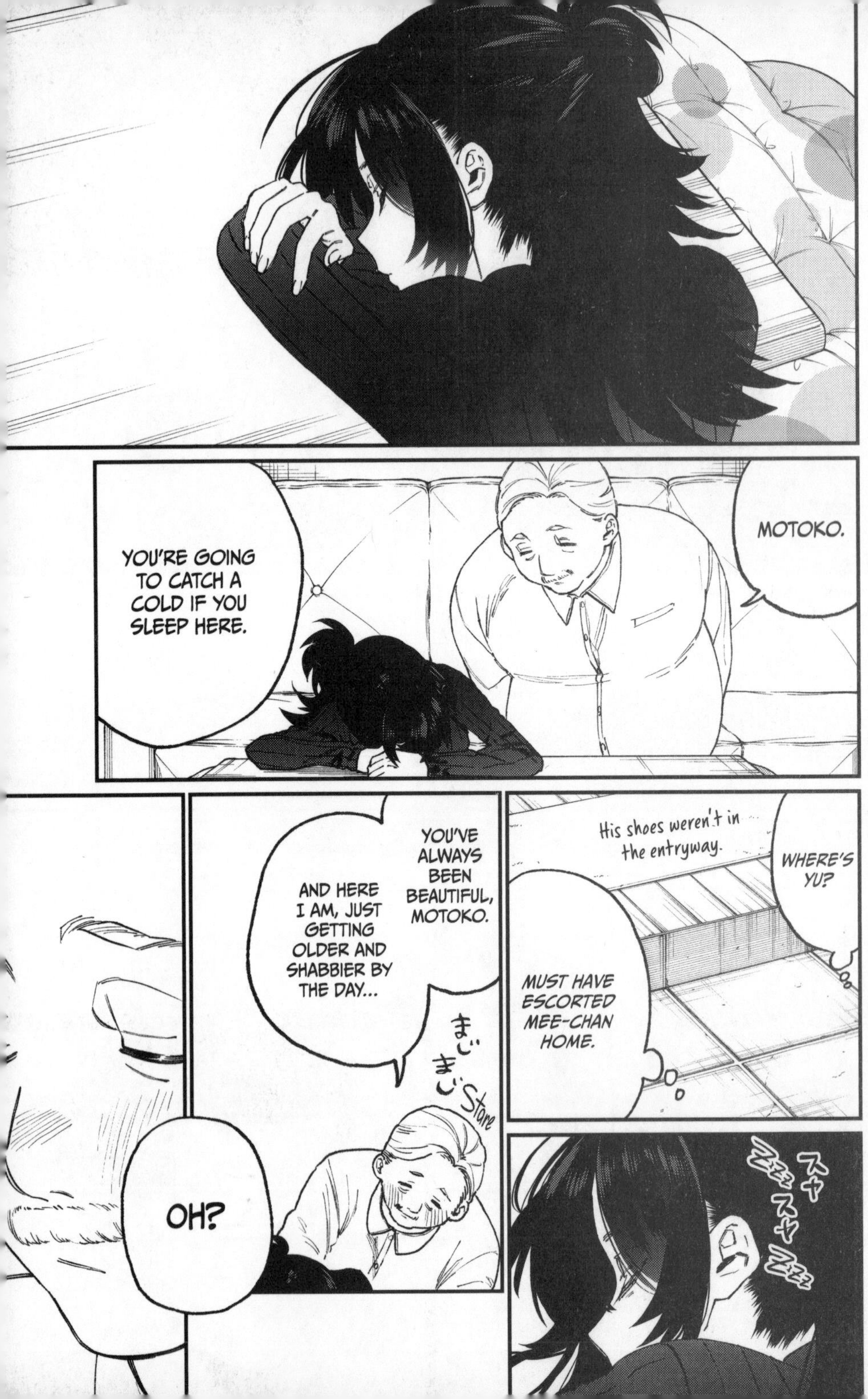
MOTOKO.
YOU'RE GOING TO CATCH A COLD IF YOU SLEEP HERE.
WHERE'S YU?
His shoes weren't in the entryway.
MUST HAVE ESCORTED MEE-CHAN HOME.
スヤスヤ
Zzz Zzz
YOU'VE ALWAYS BEEN BEAUTIFUL, MOTOKO.
AND HERE I AM, JUST GETTING OLDER AND SHABBIER BY THE DAY...
まじまじ
Stare
OH?

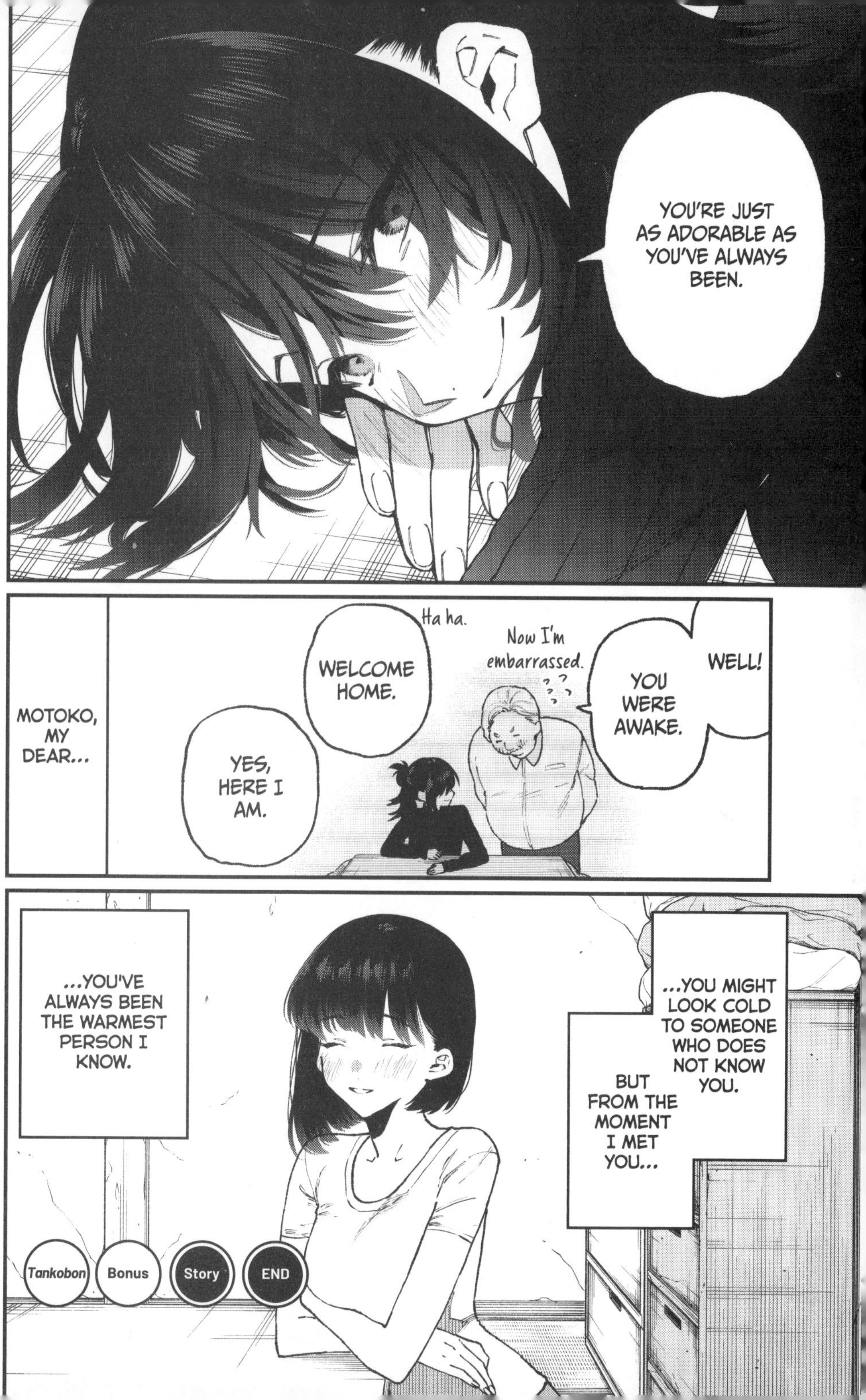
YOU'RE JUST AS ADORABLE AS YOU'VE ALWAYS BEEN.
WELL!
YOU WERE AWAKE.
Now I'm embarrassed.
Ha ha.
WELCOME HOME.
YES, HERE I AM.
MOTOKO, MY DEAR...
...YOU MIGHT LOOK COLD TO SOMEONE WHO DOES NOT KNOW YOU.
BUT FROM THE MOMENT I MET YOU...
...YOU'VE ALWAYS BEEN THE WARMEST PERSON I KNOW.
Tankobon
Bonus
Story
END

To be continued!

Thank you so much for
picking up Volume 7!

Editors: Hiraoka-san,
Toki-san

Staff: Na-san, Santo-san, Tsuchida-san

Design: Kuraji-san

TRANSLATOR'S NOTES

Demon Kakka, page 35

Demon Kakka ("His Excellency Demon"), formerly known as Demon Kogure, is a beloved heavy metal musician, entertainer, and voice actor, known for always being in full face paint and hair spikes (or headwear with a similar effect) and never breaking character. His persona was born "98,038 years before the Western calender began." Interestingly enough, he is also a highly regarded sumo commentator, and can often be seen on TV broadcasts of sumo competitions.

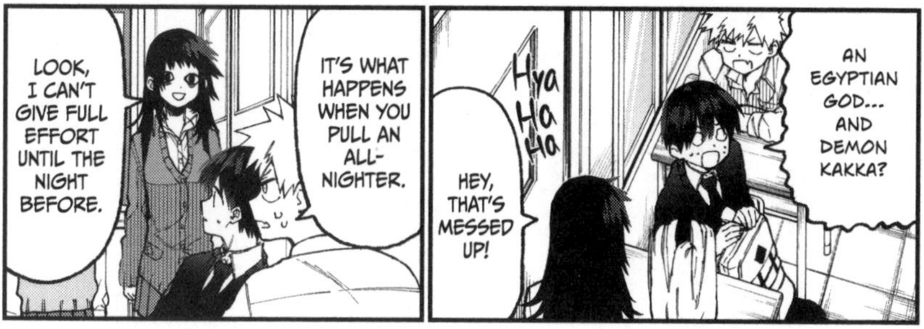
AN EGYPTIAN GOD... AND DEMON KAKKA?
Hya Ha Ha
HEY, THAT'S MESSED UP!
IT'S WHAT HAPPENS WHEN YOU PULL AN ALL-NIGHTER.
LOOK, I CAN'T GIVE FULL EFFORT UNTIL THE NIGHT BEFORE.

PERFECT WORLD

Rie Aruga

A TOUCHING
NEW SERIES
ABOUT LOVE AND
COPING WITH
DISABILITY

An office party reunites Tsugumi with her high school crush Itsuki. He's realized his dream of becoming an architect, but along the way, he experienced a spinal injury that put him in a wheelchair. Now Tsugumi's rekindled feelings will butt up against prejudices she never considered — and Itsuki will have to decide if he's ready to let someone into his heart...

"Depicts with great delicacy and courage the difficulties some with disabilities experience getting involved in romantic relationships... Rie Aruga refuses to romanticize, pushing her heroine to face the reality of disability. She invites her readers to the same tasks of empathy, knowledge and recognition."
—Slate.fr

"An important entry [in manga romance]... The emotional core of both plot and characters indicates thoughtfulness... [Aruga's] research is readily apparent in the text and artwork, making this feel like a real story."
—Anime News Network

The adorable new odd-couple cat comedy manga from the creator of the beloved *Chi's Sweet Home,* in full color!

Praise for Chi's Sweet Home

"Nearly impossible to turn away... a true all-ages title that anyone, young or old, cat lover or not, will enjoy. The stories will bring a smile to your face and warm your heart."

—School Library Journal

Sue & Tai-chan

Konami Kanata

Sue is an aging housecat who's looking forward to living out her life in peace... but her plans change when the mischievous black tomcat Tai-chan enters the picture! Hey! Sue never signed up to be a catsitter! *Sue & Tai-chan* is the latest from the reigning meow-narch of cute kitty comics, Konami Kanata.

KC
KODANSHA
COMICS

A SMART, NEW ROMANTIC COMEDY FOR FANS OF *SHORTCAKE CAKE* AND *TERRACE HOUSE*!

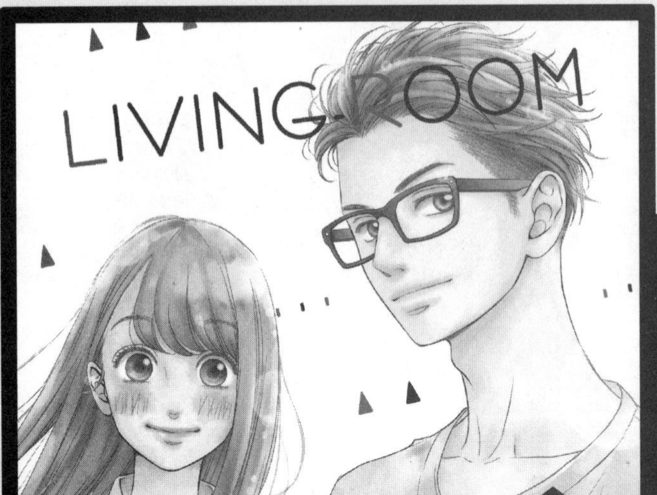
LIVING-ROOM
1
Keiko Iwashita
MATSUNAGA-SAN

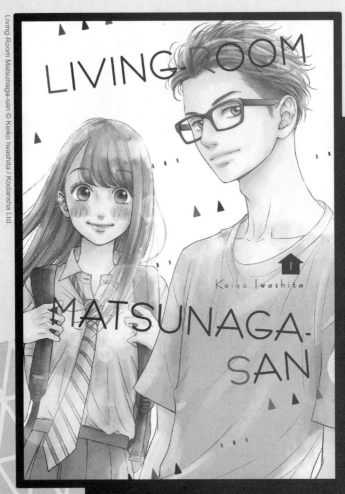

A romance manga starring high school girl Meeko, who learns to live on her own in a boarding house whose living room is home to the odd (but handsome) Matsunaga-san. She begins to adjust to her new life away from her parents, but Meeko soon learns that no matter how far away from home she is, she's still a young girl at heart — especially when she finds herself falling for Matsunaga-san.

KC KODANSHA COMICS

THE SWEET SCENT OF LOVE IS IN THE AIR! FOR FANS OF OFFBEAT ROMANCES LIKE *WOTAKOI*

Sweat and Soap © Kintetsu Yamada / Kodansha Ltd.

In an office romance, there's a fine line between sexy and awkward... and that line is where Asako — a woman who sweats copiously — meets Koutarou — a perfume developer who can't get enough of Asako's, er, scent. Don't miss a romcom manga like no other!